ART OF COOKERY

MADE

PLAIN AND EASY;

Excelling any Thing of the Kind ever yet published.

By Mrs. GLASSE.

A new EDITION, with modern Improvements.

Alexandria:

PRINTED BY COTTOM AND STEWART, 1805

IN FACSIMILE, WITH HISTORICAL NOTES BY

KAREN HESS

APPLEWOOD BOOKS

BEDFORD, MASSACHUSETTS

The Art of Cookery was first published in England in 1747. The first American edition was published in Alexandria, Virginia by Cottom & Stewart in 1805.

ISBN 1-55709-462-4

Thank you for purchasing an Applewood Book. Applewood reprints America's lively classics—books from the past that are of interest to modern readers. For a free copy of our current catalog, write to Applewood Books, P.O. Box 365, Bedford, MA 01730.

10 9 8 7 6 5 4 3 2 1

Library of Congress Cataloging-in-Publication Data
Glasse, Hannah, 1708–1770
The art of cookery made plain and easy; excelling any thing of the kind ever yet published / by Hannah Glasse; with an introduction by Karen Hess.
p. cm.
Originally published: 1st American ed. Alexandria, Va.: Cottom & Stewart, 1805.
ISBN 1-55709-462-4
1. Cookery, English—Early works to 1800.
I. Title.
TX705.G54 1997
641.5942–dc21 97-96
CIP

CONTENTS

Acknowledgements

I am reminded of my debt to the late Eleanor Lowenstein, bibliographer, antiquarian bookseller, and friend, who found me my precious copy of the Alexandria 1805 edition of *The Art of Cookery Made Plain and Easy* by Hannah Glasse, as well as that of 1755 and all the others. And, of course, so meticulously catalogued early American cookbooks.

As always, I want to honor my friend and mentor, the late Elizabeth David. It was she who first taught us that it was possible to write about cookery with erudition, wit, and honesty. Now, all we have to do is to try to emulate her.

And I thank Applewood Books for making it possible to bring this very important work in its original format to the attention of American readers.

Other books by Karen Hess

The Taste of America. Co-author with John L. Hess. Viking Press, 1977; University of South Carolina Press, 1989.

English Bread and Yeast Cookery by Elizabeth David. Editor of American edition. Viking Press, 1980.

Martha Washington's Book of Cookery. Columbia University Press, 1981, 1995.

The Carolina Rice Kitchen: The African Connection. University of South Carolina Press, 1992.

What Mrs. Fisher Knows About Old Southern Cooking by Abby Fisher. Afterword for facsimile edition, Applewood Books, 1995.

American Cookery by Amelia Simmons, Albany, 1796. Historical notes for bicentennial facsimile edition, Applewood Books, 1996.

Historical Notes

BY

KAREN HESS

Directions concerning Garden Things.

Most people spoil garden things by over-boiling them. All things green should have a little crispness, for if they are over-boiled, they neither have any sweetness or beauty.
—*The Art of Cookery* by Hannah Glasse, all editions, including that of Alexandria 1805 (page 35).

It was the most English of cookbooks. It was the most American of cookbooks. It first appeared in London in 1747, and reigned supreme in England and the Colonies through countless editions for more than half a century. The American Revolution may have put a crimp in sales here, but we hear of no copies having been thrown into Boston harbor, or the Potomac, or any other American waters. George Washington owned a copy, as did Thomas Jefferson; indeed, recipes attributed to Mrs. Glasse are included in cookery manuscripts kept by Jefferson's granddaughters, for example. And, for all his patriotic fire back in 1766 proclaiming the superiority of *American* cookery, Benjamin Franklin translated, or had translated, many of that estimable English-woman's recipes into French, this presumably in connection with one of his trips to Paris (1767 and again in 1776), including one for "Puff-paste," now grandly entitled "Pâte feuilletée," awkwardly translated and giving errors in equivalencies. If Dr. Franklin made so bold as to present those recipes to his French cook, history has not recorded the cook's reaction. (I might note that in spite of his very public views on the superiority of

American cooking and his equally public vows of vegetarianism and abstemiousness, he eschewed neither meat nor drink in Paris; he dined well, and on one occasion at least, October 1, 1778, "drank a good deal of champagne." His inventories for 1782 show a tidy cellar of over 1200 bottles of wine. French wine. The great man was human, after all.*)

The first cookbook known to have been published in the Colonies was *The Compleat Housewife* by E[liza?] Smith, this in Williamsburg in 1742, taken from the fifth edition of a London work first published in 1727. Other naturalized works were to follow, but until after the appearance of what seems to be the first published cookbook written by an American, *American Cookery* by Amelia Simmons (Hartford, 1796), English publishers had not deemed it necessary to so much as nod in the direction of catering to American taste or custom. Their books sold very well as it was; the publishers of Hannah Glasse had not even found it necessary to issue an American edition. The first note of concern over the unruly "Colonials" in this regard showed up in the 1803 New York edition of *The Frugal Housewife* by Susannah Carter. "To which is added an appendix, containing several new receipts adapted to the American mode of cooking." This English work had previously appeared in a 1772 Boston edition with the only American note being handsome plates by our own Paul Revere. The new appendix consisted of twenty-nine recipes, of which perhaps eighteen could be said to be American, but the others were for sturdy English classics on the order of "To make a Bath Pudding" or "To make a raised Pork pie." In addition, there is a truncated recipe of but three lines entitled, *The following curious Method of rearing Turkeys to advantage, translated from a Swedish book, entitled Rural Oeconomy*. This

*I have drawn on the work of Gilbert Chinard in *Benjamin Franklin on the Art of Eating*, printed for the American Philosophical Society by Princeton University Press, 1958. Eight of the recipes given by him in Franklin's French translation I have found in their original English in all editions of *The Art of Cookery* available to me, beginning with 1747, including the Alexandria edition of 1805.

is pertinent, because the identical appendix was to appear in the Alexandria 1805 edition of *The Art of Cookery* by Hannah Glasse (pages 137–144), identical down to the point of truncation. I have not identified the source of those recipes, but suspect that they came from some American publication such as an almanac, a highly popular form of publishing in the Colonies. (The entire recipe appears on pages 272–73.)

I should note that while eighteenth-century English works offered little or nothing in the way of American recipes, a number of American ingredients had long since entered the English repertory, such as turkey and what they persisted in calling "French beans," so long since that it never occurred to them that they were in fact American products; even the more exotic ones, such as tomatoes, chocolate, and vanilla, were beginning to show up in English works by mid-eighteenth century, that of Hannah Glasse, for example.

It is ironic that an American edition of Hannah Glasse appeared precisely on the eve of the decline of its preeminence, a lead taken over by A *New System of Domestic Cookery* by Maria Eliza Rundell, in 1807, in London and Boston. It is not that Mrs. Glasse toppled from favor altogether, particularly in our south, where she had always been exceptionally strong. Mary Randolph, the writer of *The Virginia House-wife* (1824) had been influenced by her, for example. Certainly she took to heart Mrs. Glasse's dictum on cooking garden vegetables. Also, recipes for "Transparent Pudding" and its prototypes, for example, seem to have first been given by Mrs. Glasse, later picked up by Mrs. Randolph. This is important, because it is the genre represented by any number of southern recipes for syrupy custardy puddings baked in crust that bake up surprisingly translucent, such as the generic orange and lemon puddings, but also "Chess Pie," and even "Pecan Pie." There is no recipe for "Transparent Pudding" in this 1805 edition, but there is one, "To make an Orange-Pudding," an archtypical generic example.

This brings up the question of the content of the Alexandria edition as compared to previous editions of Hannah Glasse. It is beyond the scope of this work to do a survey of the publishing history of *The Art of Cookery*, a tangled one, but I think it safe to say that the recipes in the work date from no later than mid-eighteenth century. That is, a number of her most famous recipes have been omitted in the American edition, but no new ones were included, except for the American appendix—and they were by no means new in terms of being recent in concept or method. Mrs. Glasse had long since gone to her reward by then, and while that did not stop others from messing around with her work, the essential dating of the material remains.

We often think of Hannah Glasse as being old-hat, but in fact she was something of a pioneer in giving recipes for ice cream, chocolate, vanilla, even tomatoes—that is, among English cookbook writers, who trailed the French in this regard. And not one of those items is so much as mentioned by Amelia Simmons in 1796, for example. Among those pioneering recipes there is one "To dress Haddock after the Spanish way," a recipe calling for "love apples," that is tomatoes, which dates from the 1750s (page 239). I note a misprint that crept in somewhere along the way: one is to *broil* the haddock, rather than boil it, as the directions say. She also gave an early recipe for ice cream; the one included in this work (page 231) calls for apricots, a very nice recipe, by the way; the earlier one called for raspberries.

She gives two recipes for chocolate (pages 261-62), one very archaic, hardly changed from those found in early Spanish sources, calling for cayenne pepper, achiote, ambergrease, etc.; the other is somewhat more modern, calling for "three good vanelas, or more or less as you please," to six pounds of cocoa beans, still not very useful. There is also a recipe for "Sham Chocolate," whose sole claim to being chocolate is that the mixture be made in a *chocolate-pot* and served in *chocolate-cups* (page 244); it does show, however, that the use of chocolate had reached home use among fairly ordinary people in England.

There are also interesting recipes attributed to Jewish cookery: "Marmalade of Eggs the Jews Way" (page 245), "To dress Haddocks the Jews Way" (page 239), and "The Jews way of preserving Salmon, and all Sorts of Fish" (page 286), which is finally what we know as *escabeche*, a dish that comes from Persia by way of the Arabs, but very likely came to England by way of Jews fleeing the Spanish inquisition.

We may find some of her recipes old-fashioned, even archaic, but there is a lot of most excellent cooking embodied in them. I note particularly her fine roasting techniques: "To roast a piece of beef about ten pounds will take an hour and a half at a good fire" (page 28). No gray sodden roasts for Mrs. Glasse, who knew the difference between roasted and baked meats, a difference lost on Americans brought up on Fannie Farmer and Irma Rombauer. I also want to comment on the blessed lack of alkali in her baking, that noisome substance that came to dominate American baking just about that time. And take to heart her instruction on cooking greens, given at the top of this little essay, all, all lost on the likes of Farmer and Rombauer.

Shall we return to the American appendix? Perhaps it is simplest just to list the indubitably American ones, that is, those made with American products: "To make a baked Indian Pudding," "An Indian Pudding boiled," "To make Mush," "To make Cranberry Tarts," "A receipt to make Maple Sugar," "To make Maple Molasses," "To make Maple Beer," and "To pickle Peppers." As I have so often written, even such recipes, with the exception of those involving maple syrup, are from English tradition, the only innovation being using an American product in place of a more familiar one in their old recipes—maize, for example, which the Colonists called *indian*, in place of oats. They learned about the taking of maple sap from the Native Americans, but the making of various syrups—including that of sugar cane and sorghum—had long been part of Old World tradition. There is nothing specifically American about buckwheat cakes, or even about pumpkin pie, or gingberbread, or doughnuts, or waffles, or crullers, although they all became highly popular in American cookery, so much so that Americans have come to assume that they were uniquely American. Spruce beer, often claimed to be American, is from Prussia, and has been in the literature as such, that is, made from the needles of the spruce fir, since 1500, a little early for *Americana* in that sense. One of the sturdiest myths is our misconception about pumpkin pie; not only were various pumpkin-like gourds documented in Europe since early Classical times, but the method is purely English, with recipes going back to at least the seventeenth century. As already noted, other recipes are solidly English, centuries old. In short, as I discussed in my notes to the facsimile of the 1796 Albany edition of *American Cookery* by Amelia Simmons, this is what early American cookery was about, the continuation of traditional cookery on foreign shores, making do with native ingredients when they fit their purpose. And I do want to repeat what I said concerning the Simmons work: this appendix came from a demonstrably northern source; it did not reflect in any way the cookery of the South, where slave women had long been "stirring the pots," transmuting the various cuisines brought from Europe, wafting the fragrances of Africa abroad the land. But those recipes had to wait for *The Virginia House-wife* (1824), and later works, to be recorded. I remind the reader that historically print lags behind practice, sometimes by centuries.

I must deal with her recipes "To make Carolina Snow-balls," and "A Carolina Rice Pudding" (pages 291-92). In fact, these recipes come into the English kitchen from Norman and Breton sources; apparently the term *Carolina* simply referred to the rice, a premium rice which had, after all, been grown in an English Colony.

There was to be but one more American edition of *The Art of Cookery*, that of Alexandria, 1812, so that this little book was in the nature of a swan song.

THE

ART OF COOKERY

MADE

PLAIN AND EASY;

Excelling any Thing of the Kind ever yet published.

CONTAINING

Directions how to Market; the Season of the Year for Butchers' Meat, Poultry, Fish, &c.
How to roast and boil to Perfection every Thing necessary to be sent up to Table.
Vegetables.
Broiling.
Frying.
To dress Fish.
Made Dishes.
Poultry.
Soups and Broths.
Puddings.
Pies.
Variety of Dishes for Lent, which may be made Use of any other Time.
Gravies.
Sauces.
Hashes.
Fricassees.
Ragouts.
To cure Hams, Bacon, &c.
Pickling.
Making Cakes.
Jellies.
Preserving.
&c. &c. &c. &c.

Also, the ORDER of a BILL of FARE for each MONTH, in the Manner the Dishes are to be placed upon the Table, in the present Taste.

By Mrs. GLASSE.

A new EDITION, with modern Improvements.

Alexandria:

PRINTED BY COTTOM AND STEWART,
and sold at their Book-Stores, in Alexandria and Fredericksburg. 1805.

THE

ART OF COOKERY

MADE

PLAIN *and* EASY.

I Believe I have attempted a branch of Cookery which nobody has yet thought worth their while to write upon: but as I have both seen, and found by experience, that the generality of Servants are greatly wanting in that point, I therefore have taken upon me to instruct them in the best manner I am capable; and, I dare say, that every Servant who can but read, will be capable of making a tolerable good Cook; and those who have the least notion of Cookery, cannot miss of being very good ones.

I do not pretend to teach professed Cooks, my design being to instruct the ignorant and unlearned, (which will likewise be of use in all private families.) and that in so full and plain a manner, that the most ignorant Person, who can but read, will know how to do Cookery well. As Marketing must be the first branch of Cookery, I shall begin with that Table first.

HOW TO MARKET,

And the Seasons of the Year for Butchers' Meat, Poultry, Fish &c.

BUTCHERS' MEAT.

To chuse Lamb.

if it be an azure blue, it is new and good; but if greenish or yellowish, it is near tainting, if not tainted, already. In the hinder-quarter, smell under the kidney, and try the knuckle: if you meet with a faint scent, and the knuckle be limber, it is stale killed. For a lamb's head, mind the eyes; if they be sunk or wrinkled, it is stale; if plump and lively, it is new and sweet. Lamb comes in in April, and holds good till the end of August.

Veal.

If the bloody vein in the shoulder looks blue, or of a bright red, it is new killed; but if blackish, greenish, or yellowish, it is flabby and stale: if wrapped in wet cloths, smell whether it be musty or not. The loin first taints under the kidney; and the flesh, if stale killed, will be soft and slimy.

The breast and neck taints first at the end, and you will perceive some dusky, yellowish, or greenish appearance; the sweet-bread on the breast will be clammy, otherwise it is fresh and good. The leg is known to be new by the stiffness of the joint; if limber, and the flesh seems clammy; and has green or yellowish specks, it is stale. The head is known as the lamb's. The flesh of a bull-calf is more red and firm than that of a cow-calf, and the fat more hard and curdled.

Mutton.

If the mutton be young, the flesh will pinch tender; if old, it will wrinkle, and remain so; if young, the fat will easily part from the lean; if old, it will stick by strings and skins; if ram-mutton, the fat feels spungy, the flesh close-grained and tough, not rising again when dented with your finger; if ewe mutton the flesh is paler than wether-mutton, a closer grain, and easily parting.

If there be a rot, the flesh will be palish, and the fat a faint whitish, inclining to yellow, and the flesh will be loose at the bone. If you squeeze it hard, some drops of water will stand up like sweat. As to the newness and staleness, the same is to be observed as by lamb.

Beef.

If it be right ox-beef, it will have an open grain; if young, a tender and oily smoothness: if rough and spungy, it is old, or inclining to be so, except the neck, brisket and such parts as are very fibrous, which in young meat will be more rough than in other parts. A carnation, pleasant colour betokens good spending meat; the suet a curious white; yellowish is not so good.

Cow-beef is less bound and closer grained than the ox, the fat whiter, but the lean somewhat paler; if young, the dent you make with your finger will rise again in a little time.

Bull-beef is of a close grain, deep dusky red, tough in pinching, the fat skinny, hard, and has a rammish rank smell; and for newness and staleness, this flesh bought fresh has but few signs, the more material is its clamminess, and the rest your smell will inform you. If it be bruised, these places will look more dusky or blackish than the rest.

Pork.

If it be young, the lean will break in pinching between your fingers; and if you nip the skin with your nails, it will make a dent; also if the fat be soft and pulpy, in a manner like lard; if the lean be tough, and the fat flabby and spungy, feeling rough, it is old, especially if the rind be stubborn, and you cannot nip it with your nails.

If of a boar, though young, or of a hog gelded at full growth, the flesh will be hard, tough, reddish, and rammish of smell; the fat skinny and hard; the skin very thick and tough, and, pinched up, will immediately fall again.

As for old and new killed, try the legs, hands, and springs, by putting your finger under the bone that comes out: for if it be tainted, you will there find it by smelling your finger; besides the skin will be sweaty and clammy when stale, but cool and smooth when new.

If you find little kernels in the fat of the pork, like hail-shot, if many, it is measly, and dangerous to be eaten. Pork comes in in the middle of August, and holds good till Lady-day.

How to chuse Brawn, Venison, Westphalia Hams, &c.

Brawn is known to be old or young by the extraordinary or moderate thickness of the rind; the thick is old, the moderate is young. If the rind and fat be very tender, it is not boar-brawn, but barrow or sow.

Venison.

Try the haunches or shoulders under the bones that come out, with your finger or knife, and as the scent is sweet or rank, it is new or stale, and the like of the sides in the most fleshy parts: if tainted, they will look greenish in some places, or more than ordinary black. Look on the hoofs, and if the clefts are very wide and rough, it is old; if close and smooth, it is young.

The buck venison begins in May, and is in high season till All-hallows-day: the doe is in season from Michaelmas to the end of December, or sometimes to the end of January.

Westphalia Hams, and English Bacon.

Put a knife under the bone that sticks out of the

ham, and if it comes ont in a manner clean, and has a curious flavour, it is sweet and good; if much smeared and dulled, it is tainted or rusty.

English gammons are tried the same way; and for the other parts, try the fat: if it be white, oily in feeling, does not break or crumble, good; but if the contrary, and the lean has some little streaks of yellow, it is rusty, or will soon be so.

To chuse Butter, Cheese, and Eggs.

When you buy butter, trust not to that which will be given you to take, but try in the middle, and if your smell and taste be good, you cannot be deceived.

Cheese is to be chosen by its moist and smooth coat: if old cheese be rough-coated, rugged, or dry at top, beware of little worms or mites: if it be over full of holes, moist, or spungy, it is subject to maggots: if any soft or perished place appear on the outside, try how deep it goes, for the greater part may be hid within.

Eggs hold the great end to your tongue; if it feels warm, be sure it is new, if cold, it is bad, and so in proportion to the heat and cold, is the goodness of the egg. Another way to know a good egg, is to put the egg into a pan of cold water; the fresher the egg the sooner it will fall to the bottom; if rotten, it will swim at the top. This is also a sure way not to be deceived. As to the keeping of them, pitch them all with the small end downwards in fine wood ashes, turning them once a week end-ways, and they will keep some months.

POULTRY IN SEASON.

January.—Hen-turkeys, capons, pullets with eggs, fowls, chickens, hares, all sorts of wild-fowl, tame-rabbits, and tame-pigeons.

February.—Turkeys, and pullets with eggs,

capons, fowls, small chickens, hares, all sorts of wild-fowl, (which in this month begin to decline,) tame and wild-pigeons, tame-rabbits, green-geese, young ducklings, and turkey-poults.

March.—This month the same as the preceding months; and in this month wild-fowl goes quite out.

April.—Pullets, spring fowls, chickens, pigeons, young wild-rabbits, leverets, young geese, ducklings, and turkey-poults.

May and *June.*—The same.

July.—The same; with young partridges, pheasants, and wild-ducks, called slappers or moulters.

August.—The same.

September, *October*, *November*, and *December*.—In these months all sorts of fowl, both wild and tame, are in season; and in the three last is the full season for all manner of wild-fowl.

How to chuse poultry,

To know whether a Capon is a true one, young or old, new or stale.

If he be young, his spurs are short, and his legs smooth: if a true capon, a fat vein on the side of his breast, the comb pale, and a thick belly and rump: if new, he will have a hard close vent; if stale, a loose open vent.

A Cock or Hen Turkey, Turkey-poults.

If the cock be young, his legs will be black and smooth and his spurs short: if stale, his eyes will be sunk in his head, and the feet dry; if new, the eyes lively, and feet limber. Observe the like by the hen; and moreover, if she be with egg she will have a soft open vent; if not, a hard close vent. Turkey-poults are known the same way, and their age cannot deceive you.

A Cock, or Hen, &c.

If young, his spurs are short and dubbed, but take particular notice they are not pared or scraped: if old, he will have an open vent; but if new, a close hard vent. And so of a hen for newness or staleness: if old, her legs and comb are rough; if young, smooth.

A Tame Goose, Wild Goose, and Bran Goose.

If the bill be yellowish, and she has but few hairs, she is young; but if full of hairs, and the bill and foot red, she is old: if new, limber-footted; if stale, dry-footed. And so of a wild goose bran goose.

Wild and Tame Ducks.

The ducks, when fat, is hard and thick on the belly; but if not, thin and lean: if new, limber-footed; if stale, dry-footed. A true wild duck has a reddish foot, smaller than the tame one.

Pheasant, Cock and Hen.

The cock, when young, has dubbed spurs; when old, sharp small spurs: if new, a fat vent; and if stale, an open flabby one. The hen if young, has smooth legs, and her flesh of a curious grain: if with egg, she will have a soft open vent; and if not, a close one. For newness or staleness, as the cock.

Partridge, Cock and Hen.

The bill white, and the legs bluish, shew age; for if young, the bill is black, and legs yellowish if new, a fast vent; if stale, a green and open one. If their crops be full, and they have fed on green wheat, they may taint there; and for this smell in their mouth.

Woodcock and Snipe.

The woodcock, if fat, is thick and hard; if new, limber-footed; when stale, dry-footed; or if their noses are snotty, and their throats muddy and moorish, they are not good. A snipe, if fat, has a fat vein in the side under the wing, and in the vent feels thick. For the rest, like the woodcock.

Doves and Pigeons.

To know the turtle-dove, look for a blueish ring round his neck, and the rest mostly white. The stock-dove is bigger; and the ring-dove is less than the stock dove. The dove-house pigeons, when old, are red-legged; if new and fat, they will feel full and fat in the vent, and are limber-footed; but if stale, a flabby and green vent.

And so green or grey plover, fieldfare, blackbird thrush, larks, &c.

Of Hare, Leveret, or Rabbit.

Hare will be whitish and stiff, if new and clean killed: if stale, the flesh blackish in most parts, and the body limber: if the cleft in her lips spread very much, and her claws wide and ragged, she is old; and the contrary, young: if the hare be young, the ears will tear like a piece of brown paper; if old, dry and tough. To know a true levere, feel on the fore-leg near the foot, and if there be a small bone or knob, it is right; if not, it is a hare. A rabbit, if stale, will be limber and slimy; if new, white and stiff: if old, her claws are very long and rough, the wool mottled with grey hairs; if young, the claws and wool smooth.

FISH IN SEASON.

Candlemas Quarter.

Lobsters, crabs, craw-fish, guard-fish, mackrel,

bream, barbel, roach, shad or alloc, lamprey or lamper-eels, dace, bleak, prawns, and horse mackrel.

The eels that are taken in running water are better than pond eels : of these the silver ones are most esteemed.

Midsummer Quarter.

Turbots and trouts, soals, grigs,, and shaffings and glout, tenes, salmon, dolphin flying-fish, sheep-head, tollis both land and sea, sturgeon, scale, chub, lobsters, and crabs.

Sturgeon is a fish commonly ſound in the northern seas ; but now and then we find them in our great rivers, the Thames, the Severn, and the Tyne. This fish is of a very large size and will sometimes measure eighteen feet in length. They are much esteemed when fresh, cut in pieces, roasted, baked, or pickled for cold treats. The cavier is esteemed a dainty, which is the spawn of this fish. The latter end of this quarter come smelts.

Michaelmas Quarter.

Cod and haddock, coal-fish, white and pouting hake, lyng, tuske and mullet (red and grey,) weaver, gurnet, rocket, herrings, sprats, soals, and flounders, plaise, dabs and smeare dabs, eels, chars, scate, thornback and homlyn, kinson, oysters and scollops, salmon, sea perch and carp, pike, tench, and sea tench.

Scate-maids are black, and thornback-maids white. Gray bass comes with the mullet.

In this quarter are fine smelts, and hold till after Christmas.

There are two sorts of mullets, the sea mullet and river mullet ; both equally good.

Christmas Quarter.

Dorey, brile, gudgeons, gollin, smelts crouch, perch, anchovy and loach, scollop and wilks, periwinkles, cockles, mussels, geare, bearbet, and holiebet.

How to chuse Fish.

To chuse Salmon, Pike, Trout, Carp, Tench, Grailing, Barbel, Chub, Ruff, Eel, Whiting, Smelt, Shad, &c.

All these are known to be new or stale by the colour of their gills, their easiness or hardness to open, the hanging or keeping up their fins, the standing out or sinking of eyes, &c. and by smelling their gills.

Turbot.

He is chosen by his thicknes and plumpness: and if his belly be of a cream color, he must spend well; but if thin, and his belly of a bluish white, he will eat very loose

Cod and Codling.

Chuse him by his thickness towards his head, and the whitness of his flesh when it is cut; and so of a codling.

Lyng.

For dried lyng, chuse that which is thickest in the poll, and the flesh of the brightest yellow.

Scate ond Thornback.

These are chosen by their thickness; and the she-scate is the sweetest, especially if large.

Soals.

These are chosen by their thicknes and stiffness. When their bellies are of a cream colour, they spend the firmer.

Sturgeon.

If it cuts without crumbling, and the veins and gristles give a true blue where they appear, and the flesh a perfect white, then conclude it to be good.

Fresh Herrings and Mackrel.

If their gills are of a lively shining redness, their eyes stand full, and the fish is stiff, then they are new; but if dusky and faded, or sinking and wrinkled, and tails limber, they are stale.

Lobsters.

Chuse them by their weight; the heaviest are best, if no water be in them: if new, the tail will pull smart, like a spring; if full, the middle of the tail will be full of hard, or reddish-skinned meat. Cock lobster is known by the narrow back part of the tail, and the two uppermost fins within his tail are stiff and hard; but the hen is soft, and the back of her tail broader.

Prawns, Shrimps, and Crakfish.

The two first, if stale, will be limber, and cast a kind of slimy smell, their colour fading and they slimy: the latter will be limber in their claws and joints, their red colour blackish and dusky, and will have an ill smell under their throats; otherwise all of them are good.

Plaise and Flounders.

If they are stiff, and their eyes be not sunk or look dull, they are new; the contrary when stale. The best sort of plaise look bluish on the belly.

Pickled Salmon.

If the flesh feels oily, and the scales are stiff and shining, and it comes in flakes and parts without crumbling, then it is new and good, and not otherwise.

Pickled and Red Herrings.

For the first, open the back to the bone, and if the flesh be w hite, flaky, and oily, and the bone white, or a bright red, they are good. If red herrings carry a good gloss, part well from the bone, and smell well, then conclude them to be good.

Of ROASTING, BOILING, *&c.*

I shall first begin with roast and boiled of all sorts, and must desire the cook to order her fire according to what she is to dress; if any thing very little or thin, then a pretty little brisk fire that it may be done quick and nice; if a very large joint, then be sure a good fire be laid to cake. Let it be clear at the bottom; and when your meat is half done, move the dripping-pan and spit a little from the fire, and stir up a good brisk fire; for according to the goodness of your fire, your meat will be done sooner or later.

B E E F.

IF beef, be sure to paper the top, and baste it well all the time it is roasting, and throw a handful of salt on it. When you see the smoak draw to the fire, it is near enough; then take off the paper, baste it well and druge it with a little flour to make a fine froth. Never salt your roast meet before you lay it to the fire, for that draws out all the gravy. If you would keep it a few days before you dress it, dry it very well with a clean cloth, then flour it all over, and hang it where the air will come to it; but be sure always to mind that there is no damp place about it, if there is, you must dry it well with a cloth. Take up your meat, and garnish your dish with nothing but horse-raddish.

MUTTON and LAMB.

AS to roasting of mutton, the loin, the chine of mutton, (which is the two loins,) and the saddle, (which is the two necks and part of the shoulders cut together,) must have the skin raised and skewered on, and, when near done, to take off the skin, baste, and flour it to froth it up. All other sorts of mutton and lamb must be roasted with a quick, clear fire, without the skin being raised, or paper put on, and, when near done, drudge it with a little flour to froth it up. Garnish mutton with horse-raddish; lamb, with cresses or small sallading.

VEAL.

AS to veal, you must be careful to roast it to a fine brown; if a large joint, a very good fire; if a small joint, a pretty little brisk fire; if a fillet or loin, be sure to paper the fat, that you lose as little of that as possible. Lay it some distance from the fire till it is soaked, then lay it near the fire. When you lay it down, baste it well with good butter; and when it is near enough, baste it again, and drudge it with a little flour. The breast you must roast with the caul on till it is enough; but skewer the sweetbread on the backside of the breast. When it is nigh enough, take off the caul, baste it and drudge it with a little flour.

PORK.

PORK must be well done, or it is apt to surfeit. When you roast a loin, take a sharp pen-knife and cut the skin across, to make the crackling eat the better. The chine must be cut, and so must all pork that has the rind on. Roast a leg of pork thus: take a knife, as above, and score it: stuff the knuckle part with sage and onion, chopped fine with pepper and salt: or cut a hole under the twist, and put the sage, &c. there and skewer it up with a skewer. Roast it crisp, because most people like the rind crisp, which they call crackling. Make some good apple-sauce, and send it up in a boat; then have a little drawn gravy to put in the dish. This they call a mock goose. The spring or hand of pork, if very young, roasted like a pig, eats very well; or take the spring, and cut off the shank or knuckle, and sprinkle sage and onion, over it, and roll it round, and tye it with a string and roast it two hours, otherwise it is better boiled. The spare rib should be basted with a little bit of butter a very little dust of flour, and some sage shred small; but we never make any sauce to it but apple-sauce. The best way to dress pork griskins is to roast them, baste them with a little butter and sage, and a little pepper and salt. Few eat any thing with these but mustard.

To roast a Pig.

SPIT your pig and lay it to the fire, which must be a very good one at each end, or hang a flat iron in the middle of the grate. Before you lay your pig down, take a little sage shred small, a piece of butter as big as a walnut, and a little pepper and salt: put them into the pig, and sew it up with coarse thread, then flour it all over very well, and keep flouring it till the eyes drop out, or you find the crackling hard. Be sure to save all the gravy that comes out of it, which you must do by setting basons or pans under the pig in the dripping-pan, as soon as you find the gravy begins to run. When the pig is enough, stir the fire up brisk; take a coarse cloth, with about a quarter of a pound of butter in it, and rub the pig all over till the chrackling is quite crisp, and then take it up.

Lay it in your dish, and with a sharp knife cut off the head, and then cut the pig in two before you draw out the spit. Cut the ears off the head and lay at each end, and cut the under jaw in two and lay on each side: melt some good butter, take the gravy you saved and put into it, boil it, and pour it into the dish with the brains bruised fine, and the sage mixed all together, and then send it to table.

Another way to roast a pig.

CHOP some sage and onion very fine, a few crumbs of bread, a little butter, pepper and salt rolled up together, put it into the belly, and sew it up before you lay down the pig; rub it all over with sweet oil; when it is done, take a dry cloth take it into a dish, cut it up, and wipe it, then send it to table with the sauce as above.

Different sorts of sauce for a Pig

NOW you are to observe there are several ways of making sauce for a pig. Some do not love any sage in the pig, only a crust of bread; but then you should have a little dryed sage rubbed and mixed with the gravy and butter. Some love bread-sauce in a bason, made thus: take a pint of water, put in a good piece of crumb of bread, a blade of mace, and a little whole pepper; boil it for about five or six minutes, and then pour all the water off: take out the spice, and beat up the bread with a good piece of butter, and a little milk or cream. Some love a few currants boiled in it, a glass of wine, and a little sugar, but that you must do just as you like it. Others take half a pint of good beef gravy, and the gravy which comes out of the pig, with a piece of butter rolled in flour, two spoonfuls of catchup, and boil them all together, then take the brains of the pig and bruise them fine; put all these together, with the sage in the pig, and pour it into your dish.

It is a very good sauce. When you have not gravy enough comes out of your pig with the butter for sauce, take about half a pint of veal gravy and add to it; or stew the petty-toes, and take as much of that liquor as will do for sauce, mixed with the other.—N. B. Some like the sauce sent in a boat or bason.

To roast the hind quarter of a Pig, lamb-fashion.

At the time of the year when house-lamb is very dear, take the hind-quarter of a large roasting pig, take off the skin and roast it, and it will eat like lamb with mint sauce, or with a sallad, or Seville orange. Half an hour will roast it.

To bake a Pig.

IF you should be in a place where you cannot roast a pig, lay it in a dish, flour it all over well, and rub it over with butter; butter the dish you lay it in, and put it into the oven. When it is enough, draw it out of the oven's mouth, and rub it over with a buttery cloth; then put it into the oven again till it is dry; take it out and lay it in a dish; cut it up, take a little veal gravy and take oft the fat in the dish it was baked in, and there well be some good gravy at the bottom; put that to it, with a little piece of butter rolled in flour; boil it up, and put it into the dish, with the brains and sage in the belly. Some love a pig brought whole to table; then you are only to put what sauce you like in to the dish.

To melt Butter.

IN melting of butter you must be very careful; let your saucepan be well tinned; sake a spoonful of cold water, a little dust of flour, and half a pound of butter cut to pieces: be sure to keep shaking your pan one way, for fear it should oil; when it is all melted, let it boil, and it will be smooth and fine. A silver pan is best, if you have one.

To roast Geese, Turkeys, &c.

WHEN you roast a goose, turkey or fowls of any sort, take care to singe them with a piece of white paper, and baste them with a piece of butter; drudge them with a little flour, and sprinkle a little salt on; and when the smoke begins to draw to the fire, and they look plump, baste them again, and drudge them with a little flour, and take them up.

Sauce for a Goose.

FOR a goose make a little good gravy, and put it into a bason by itself, and some apple-sauce into another.

Sauce for a Turkey.

FOR a turkey good gravy in the dish, and either bread or onion sauce in a bason, or both.

Sauce for Fowls.

TO fowls you should put good gravy in the dish and either bread, parsley, or egg sauce in a bason.

Sauce for Ducks.

FOR ducks, a little gravy in the dish, and onion-sauce in a cup, if liked.

Sauce for Pheasants and Partridges.

PHEASANTS and partridges should have gravy in the dish, and bread-sauce in a cup, and poverroy-sace.

To roast Larks.

PUT a small bird-spit through them, and tie them on another; roast them and all the time they are roasting keep basting them very gently with butter, and sprinkle crumbs of bread on them till they are almost done; then let them brown before you take them up.

The best way of making crumbs of bread is to rub them through a fine cullender, and put into a little butter in a stew-pan; melt it, put in your crumbs of bread, and keep them stirring till they are of a light brown; put them on a sieve to drain a few minutes; lay your larks in a dish, and the crumbs all around almost as high as the larks, with plain butter in a cup, and some gravy in another.

To roast Woodcocks and Snipes.

PUT them on a litttle bird spit, and tie them on another, and put them down to roast; take a round of a threepenny loaf, and toast it brown and butter it; then lay it in a dish under the birds; baste them with a little butter; take the trail out before you spit them, and put into a small stew-pan, with a little gravy; simmer it gently over the fire for five or six minutes; add a little melted butter to it, put it over your toast in the dish, and when your woodcocks are roasted put them on the toast, and set it over the lamp or chaffing-dish for three minutes, and send them to table.

To roast a Pigeon

TAKE some parsley shred fine, a piece of butter as big as a walnut, a little pepper and salt; tie the neck end tight; tie a string round the legs and rump, and fasten the other end to the top of the chimney-piece. Baste them with butter, and when they are enough lay them in the dish, and they will swim with gravy. You may put them on a little spit, and then tie both ends close.

To broil a Pigeon.

WHEN you broil them, do them in the same

manner, and take care your fire is very clear, and set your gridiron high, that they may not burn, and have a little parsley and butter in a cup. You may split them, and broil them with a little pepper and salt; and you may roast them only with a little parsley and butter in a dish.

Directions for Geese and Ducks.

AS to the geese and ducks, you should have sage and onions shred fine, with pepper and salt put into the belly.

PUT only pepper and salt into wild-ducks, easterling, wigeon, teal, and all other sorts of wild-fowl, with gravey in the dish, or some like sage and onion in one.

To roast a Hare.

TAKE your hare when it is cased; truss it in this manner, bring the two hind legs up to its sides, pull the fore legs back, your skewer first into the hind-leg, then into the fore leg, and thrust it through the body; put the fore-leg on, and then the hind-leg, and a skewer through the top of the shoulders and back part of the head, which will hold the head up. Make a pudding thus; take a quarter of a pound of beef-suet, as much crumb of bread, a handful of parsley chopped fine, some sweet herbs of all sorts, such as basil, marjoram, winter-savory, and a little thyme, chopped very fine, a littler nutmeg grated, some lemon-peel cut fine, pepper and salt, chop the liver fine, and put in with two eggs, mix it up and put it into the belly, and sew or shewer it up; then spit it and lay it to the fire, which must be a good one, A good sized hare takes one hour, and so on in proportion.

Different sorts of sauce for a Hare.

TAKE for sauce, a pint of cream, and half a pound of fresh butter; put them in a sauce-pan, and keep stirring it with a spoon till the butter is melted, and the sauce is thick; then take up the hare, and pour the sauce into the dish. Another way to make sauce for a hare is, to make good gravy, thickened with a little piece of butter rolled in flour, and pour it into your dish. You may leave the butter out, if you do not like it, and have some currant jelly warmed in a cup, or red wine and sugar boiled to a syrup, done thus: take a pint of red wine, a quarter of a pound of sugar, and set over a slow fire to simmer for about a qurter of an hour. You may do half the quantity, and put it into your sauce-boat or bason.

To broil Steaks.

FIRST have a very clear brisk fire: let your grid-iron be very clean; put it on the fire, and take a chaffing dish with a few hot coals out of the fire, put the dish on it which is to lay your steaks on, then take fine rump steaks about half an inch thick; put a little pepper and salt on them lay them on the gridiron, and (if you like it) take a shalot or two, or a fine onion, and cut it fine; put it into your dish. Keep turning your steaks quick till they are done, for that keeps the gravy in them.—When the steaks are enough, take them carefully off into your dish, that none of the gravy be lost; then have ready a hot dish and cover, and carry them hot to table with the cover on. You may send shalots in a plate, chopt fine.

Directions concerning the Sauce for Steaks.

IF you love pickles or horse-raddish with steaks never garnish your dish, because both the garnishing will be dry, and the steaks will be cold, but lay those things on little plates, and carry to table. The great nicety is to have them hot and full of gravy.

General Directions concerning Broiling.

As to mutton and pork steaks, you must keep them turning quick on the gridiron, and have your dish ready over a chaffing-dish of hot coals, and carry them to table covered hot. When you broil fowls or pigeons, always take care your fire is clear, and never baste any thing on the gridiron, for it only makes it smoked and burnt.

General Directions concerning Boiling.

As to all sorts of boiled meats, allow a quarter of an hour to every pound, be sure the pot is very clean, and skim it well, for every thing will have a scum rise, and if that boils down, it makes the meat black. All sorts of fresh meat you are to put in when the water boils, but salt meat when the water is warm.

To boil a Ham.

WHEN you boil a ham, put it into your copper when the water is pretty warm, for cold water draws the colour out: when it boils, be careful it boils very slowly. A ham of twenty pounds takes four hours and an half, larger and smaller in proportion. Keep the copper well skimmed. A Green ham wants no soaking, but an old ham must be soaked sixteen hours in a large tub of soft water.

To boil a Tongue.

A Tongue, if salt, soak it in soft water all night boil it three hours ; if fresh out of the pickle, two hours and an half, and put it in when the water boils, take it out and pull it, trim it, garnish with greens and carrots.

To boil Fowls and House-lamb.

FOWLS and house-lamb boiled in a pot by themselves, in a good deal of water, and if any scum arises take it off. They will be both sweeter and whiter than boiled in a cloth. A little chicken will be done in fifteen minutes, a large chicken in twenty minutes, a good fowl in half an hour, a little turkey or goose in an hour, and a large turkey in an hour and a half.

Sauce for a boiled Turkey.

THE best sauce for a boiled turkey is a good oyster and celery sauce. Make oyster-sauce thus: take a pint of oysters and set them off, strain the liquor from them, put them in cold water, and wash and beard them, put them into your liquor in a stew pan, with a blade of mace, and some butter rolled in flour, and a quarter of a lemon; boil them up, then put in half a pint of cream, and boil it all together gently; take the lemon and mace out, squeeze the juice of the lemon into the sauce, then serve it in your boats or basons. Make celery-sauce thus: take the white part of the celery, cut it about one inch long; boil it in some water till it is tender, then take half a pint of veal broth, a blade of mace, and thicken it with a little flour and butter, put in half a pint of cream, boil them up gently together, put in your celery and boil it up, then pour it into your boats.

Sauce for a boiled Goose.

SAUCE for a boiled goose must be either onions or cabbage, first boiled and then stewed in butter for five minutes.

Sauce for boiled Ducks or Rabbits.

TO boiled ducks or rabbits, you must pour boiled onions over them, which do thus; take the onions, peel them, and boil them in a great deal of water; shift your water, then let them boil about two hours, take them up, and throw them into a cullender to drain, then with a knife chop them on a board, and rub them through a cullender; put them into a sauce-pan, just shake a little flour over them, put in a little milk or cream, with a good piece of butter, and a little salt; set them over the fire, and when the butter is melted they are enough. But if you would have onion-sauce in half an hour take your onions peel them and cut them in thin slices, put them into milk and water, and when the water boils they will be done in twenty minutes, then throw them into a cullender to drain, and chop them and put them into a sauce-pan; shake in a little flour, with a little cream if you have it, and a good piece of butter; stir all together over the fire till the butter is melted, and they will be very fine. The sauce is very good with roast mutton, and it is the best way of boiling onions.

To roast Venison.

TAKE a haunch of venison and spit it; rub some butter all over your haunch; take four sheets of paper well buttered, put two on the haunch; then make a paste with some flour, a little butter and water; roll it out half as big as your haunch, and put it over the fat part, then put the other two sheets of paper on, and tie them with some pack-thread; lay it to a brisk fire, and baste it well all the time of roasting; if a large haunch of twenty-four pounds it will take three hours and an half, except it is a very large fire, then three hours will do: smaller in proportion.

To dress a Haunch of Mutton.

HANG it up for a fortnight, and dress it as directed for haunch of venison.

Different sorts of Sauce for Venison.

You may take either of these sauces for venison. Currant-jelly warmed; or a pint of red wine, with a quarter of a pound of sugar, simmered over a clear fire for five or six minutes; or a pint of vinegar, and a quarter of a pound of sugar, simmered till it is a syrup.

To roast Mutton Venison-fashion.

TAKE a hind quarter of fat mutton, and cut the leg like an haunch; lay it in a pan with the backside of it down, pour a bottle of red wine over it and let it lie twenty-four hours then spit it and baste it with the same liquor and butter all the time it is roasting at a good quick fire, two hours will do it. Have a little good gravy in a cup and sweet sauce in another. A good fat neck of mutton eats finely thus.

To keep Venison or Hares sweet; or to make them fresh when they stink.

IF your venison be very sweet, only dry it with a cloth, and hang it where the air comes. If you would keep it any time, dry it very well with clean cloths, rub it all over with ground pepper and hang it in an airy place, and it will keep a great while. If it stinks, or is musty, take some lukewarm water and wash it clean; then take fresh milk and water lukewarm and wash it again; then dry it in clean cloths very well, and rub it all over with ground pepper, and hang it in an airy place. When you roast it, you need only wipe it with a clean cloth, and paper it as before mentioned. Never do any thing else to Venison, for all other things spoil your venison, and take away the fine flavour, and this preserves it better than any thing you can do. A hare you may manage just the same way.

To roast a Tongue and Udder.

PARBOIL them first for two hours, then roast

it, stick eight or ten cloves about it; baste it with butter, and have some gravy and gallintine-sauce, made thus; take a few bread crumbs and boil in a little water, beat it up, then put in a gill of red wine, some sugar to sweeten it; put it in a bason or boat.

To roast Rabbits.

BASTE them with good butter, and drudge them with a little flour. Half an hour will do them, at a very quck, clear fire; and if they are very small, twenty minutes will do them. Take the liver with a little bunch of parsley and boil them, and then chop them very fine together. Melt some good butter, and put half the liver and parsly into the butter; pour it into the dish, and garnish the dish with the other half—Let your rabbits be done of a fine light brown; or put the sauce in a boat.

To roast a Rabbit Hare-fashion.

LARD a rabbit with bacon; roast it as you do a hare, with the stuffing in the belly, and it eats very well. But then you must make gravy sauce; but if you do not laid it, white sauce made thus: take a little veal broth, boil it up with a little flour and butter, to thicken it, then add a gill of cream; keep it stirring one way till it is smooth, then put it in a boat or in the dish.

Turkies, Pheasants, &c. may be larded.

YOU may lard a turkey or pheasant, or any thing, just as you lik it.

To roast a Fowl Pheasant-fashion.

IF you should have but one pheasant, and want two in a dish, take a large full grown fowl, keep the head on, and truss it just as you do a pheasant; lard it with bacon, but do not lard the pheasant, and nobody will know it.

Rules to be observed in Roasting.

IN the first place, take great care that the spit be very clean ; and be sure to clean it with nothing but sand and water. Wash it clean, and wipe it with a dry cloth, ; for oil, brick-dust, and such things, will spoil your meat.

BEEF.

TO roast a piece of beef about ten pounds will take an hour and an half, at a good fire. Twenty pounds weight will take three house, if it be a thick piece ; but if it be a thin piece of twenty pounds weight, two hours and a half will do it ; and so on according to the weight of your meat, more or less.—Observe, in frosty weather beef will take half an hour longer.

MUTTON.

A Leg of Mutton of six pounds will take an hour at a quick fire ; if frosty weather an hour and a quarter ; nine pounds, an hour an a half ; twelve pounds will take two hours ; if frosty, two hours and a half ; a large saddle of mutton will take three hours, because of papering it ; a small saddle will take an hour and a half, and so on according to the size ; a breast will take half an hour at a quick fire ; a neck, if large, an hour ; if very small, little better than half an hour ; a shoulder much about the same as a leg ; a chine of twelve pounds an hour and an half, and so on.

PORK.

PORK must be well done. To every pound allow a quarter of an hour : for example, a joint of twelve pounds weight, three hours, and so on ; if it be a thin piece of that weight, two hours will roast it.

Directions concerning Beef, Mutton, and Pork.

THESE three you may baste with fine nice dripping. Be sure your dripping be very good and brisk; but do not lay your meat too near the fire, for fear of burning or scorching.

VEAL.

VEAL takes much the same time roasting as pork; but be sure to paper the fat of a loin or fillet and baste your veal with good butter.

HOUSE-LAMB.

IF a large fore-quarter, an hour and an half; if a small one, an hour. The outside must be papered, basted with good butter, and you must have a very quick fire. If a leg, about three quarters of an hour: if very small, half an hour will do.

A PIG.

IF just killed an hour; if killed the day before an hour and a quarter; if a very large one, an hour and a half. But the best way to judge, is when the eyes drop out, and the skin is grown very hard; then you must rub it with a coarse cloth, with a good piece of butter rolled in it, till the crackling is crisp, and of a fine light brown.

A HARE.

YOU must have a quick fire. If it be a small hare, put three pints of milk and half a pound of fresh butter in the dripping-pan, which must be very clean and nice; if a large one, two quarts of milk and half a pound of fresh butter. You mush baste your hare well with this all the time it is roasting; and, when the hare has soaked up all the butter and milk, it will be enough. Put your gravy, and hot currant-jelly, in boats.

A TURKEY.

A middling turkey will take an hour; a very large one, an hour and a quarter; a small one three quarters of an hour. You must paper the breast till it is near done enough, then take the paper off and froth it up. Your fire must be very good.

A GOOSE.

Observe the same rules.

FOWLS.

A large fowl, three quarters of an hour; a middling one, half an hour; very small chickens twenty minutes. Your fire must be quck and clear when you lay them down.

TAME DUCKS.

Observe the same rules.

WILD DUCKS.

Twenty minuts; if you love them well done, twenty-five minutes.

TEAL, WIGEON, &c.

Wigeon a quarter of an hour. Teal eleven or twelve minutes.

WOODCOCKS.

Twenty-five minutes.

PATRIDGES and SNIPES.

Twenty minutes.

PIGEONS and LARKS.

Twenty minutes.

Directions concerning Poultry.

IF your fire is not very quck and clear when you lay your poultry down to roast, it will not eat near so sweet, or look so beautiful to the eye.

To keep Meat hot.

THE best way to keep meat hot, if it be done before your company is ready, is to set the dish over a pan of boiling water; cover the dish with a deep cover, so as to not touch the meat and throw a cloth over all. Thus you may keep your meat hot a long time, and it is better than over roasting and spoiling the meat. The steam of the water keeps the meat hot, and does not draw the gravy out, or draw it up; whereas, if you set a dish of meat any time over a chaffing dish of coals, it will dry up all the gravy, and spoil the meat.

To dress Greens, Roots, &c.

ALWAYS be very careful that your greens be nicely picked and washed. You should lay them in a clean pan, for fear of sand or dust which is apt to hang round wooden vessels. Boil all your greens in a copper or sauce-pan by themselves, with a great quantity of water. Boil no meat with them, for that discolours them. Use no iron pans, &c. for they are not proper, but let them be copper, brass or silver.

To dress Spinach.

PICK it very clean, and wash it in five or six waters; put it in a sauce-pan that will just hold it, throw a little salt over it, and cover the pan close. Do not put any water in, but shake the pan often. You must put your sauce-pan on a clear quick fire, As soon as you find the greens are shrunk and fallen on the bottom, and that the liquor which comes out of them boils up, they are enough.

Throw them into a clean sieve to drain, and squeeze it well between two plates, and cut it in any form you like, Lay it in a plate, or small dish, and never put any butter on it, but put it in a cup.

To dress Cabbages, &c.

CABBAGE, and all sorts of young sprouts, must be boiled in a great deal of water. When all the stalks are tender, or fall to the bottom, they are enough; then take them off, before they lose their colour. Always throw salt in your water before you put your greens in. Young sprouts you send to table just as they are, but cabbage is best chopped and put into a sauce-pan with a good piece of butter, stirring it for about five or six minutes, till the butter is all melted, and then send it to table.

To dress Carrots.

LET them be scraped very clean, when they are enough, rub them in a clean cloth then slice them into a plate, and pour some melted butter over them. If they are young spring carrots, half an hour will boil them; if large, an hour; but old Sandwich carrots will take two hours.

To dress Turnips.

THEY eat best boiled in the pot, and when enough take them out and put them in a pan, and mash them with butter, a little cream, and a little salt, and send them to table. But you may do them thus: pare your turnips, and cut them into dices, as big as the top of one's finger, put them into a clean sauce-pan, and just cover them with water. When enough, throw them into a sieve to drain, and put them in to a sauce-pan with a good piece of butter and a little cream; stir them over the fire for five or six minutes, and send them to table.

To dress Parsnips.

THEY should be boiled in a great deal of water, and when you find they are soft (which you will know by running a fork into them,) take them up, and carefully scrape all the dirt off them, and then with a knife scrape them all fine, throwing away all the sticky parts, and send them up plain in a dish with melted butter.

To dress Broccoli.

STRIP all the little branches off till you come to the top one, then with a knife peel off all the hard outside skin, which is on the stalks and little branches, and throw them into water. Have a stew-pan of water with some water in it: when it boils put in the broccoli, and when the stalks are tender it is enough, then send it to table with a piece of toasted bread soaked in the water the broccoli is boiled in under it, the same way as asparagus, with butter in a cup. The French eat oil and vinegar with it.

To dress Potatoes.

YOU must boil them in as little water as you can, without burning the sauce-pan. Cover the sauce-pan close, and when the skin begins to crack they are enough. Drain the water out, and let them stand covered for a minute or two; then peel them, lay them in your plate, and pour some melted butter over them. The best way to do them is, when they are peeled to lay them on a gridiron till they are of a fine brown, and send them to table. Another way is to put them into a sauce-pan with some good beef dripping, cover them close, and shake the sauce-pan often for fear of burning to the bottom. When they are of a fine brown, and crisp, take them up in a plate, then put them into another for fear of the fat, and put butter in a cup.

To dress Cauliflowers.

TAKE your flowers, cut off all the green parts and then cut the flowers into four, and lay them into water for an hour: then have some milk and water boiling, put in the cauliflowers, and be sure to skim the sauce-pan well. When the stalks are tender, take them carefully up, and put them into a cullender to drain: then put a spoonful of water into a clean stew-pan with a little dust of flour, about a quarter of a pound of butter, and shake it round till it is all finely melted, with a little pepper and salt; then take half the cauliflower and cut it as you would for pickling, lay it into the stew-pan, turn it, and shake the pan round. Ten minutes will do it. Lay the stewed in the middle of your plate, and the boiled round it. Pour the butter you did it in over it, and send it to table.

Another way.

CUT the cauliflower stalks off, leave a little green on and boil them in spring water and salt: about fifteen minutes will do them. Take them out and drain them; send them whole in a dish, with some melted butter in a cup.

To dress French Beans.

FIRST string them, and cut them in two, and afterwards across; but if you would do them nice, cut the bean into four, and then across, which is eight pieces. Lay them into water and salt, and when your pan boils put in some salt and the beans, when they are tender they are enough; they will be soon done. Take care they do not lose their fine green. Lay them in a plate and have butter in a cup.

To dress Artichokes.

WRING off the stalks, and put them into cold

water, and wash them well, then put them in, when the water boils, with the tops downwards, that all the dust and sand may boil out. An hour and half will do them.

To dress Asparagus.

SCRAPE all the stalks very carefully till they look white, then cut all the stalks even alike, throw them into water, and have ready a stew-pan boiling. Put in some salt, and tie the asparagus in little bundles. Let the water keep boiling, and when they are a little tender take them up. If you boil them too much you lose both colour and taste. Cut the round of a small loaf, about half an inch thick, toast it brown on both sides, dip it in the asparagus liquor, and lay it in your dish: pour a little butter over the toast, then lay your asparagus on the toast all round the dish, with the white tops outward. Do not pour butter over the asparagus, for that makes them greasy to the fingers, but have your butter in a bason, and send it to table.

Directions concerning Garden Things.

MOST people spoil garden things by over-boiling them. All things that are green should have a little crispness, for if they are over-boiled, they neither have any sweetness or beauty.

To dress Beans and Bacon.

WHEN you dress beans and bacon, boil the bacon by itself, and the beans by themselves, for the bacon will spoil the colour of the beans. Always throw some salt into the water, and some parsley, nicely picked. When the beans are enough (which you will know by their being tender,) throw them into a cullender to drain. Take up the bacon and skin it; throw some raspings of bread over the top, and if you have an iron, make it red hot and hold over it, to brown the top of the bacon; if you have not one, hold it to the fire to brown, put the bacon in the middle of the dish, and the beans all round, close up to the bacon, and send them to table, with parsley and butter in a bason.

To make Gravy for a Turkey or any sort of Fowls.

TAKE a pound of the lean part of the beef, hack it with a knife, flour it well, have ready a stew-pan with a piece of fresh butter. When the butter is melted, put in the beef, fry it till it is brown, and then pour in a little boiling water; shake it round, and then fill up with a tea-kettle of boiling water. Stir it altogether, and put in two or thee blades of mace, four or five cloves, some whole pepper, an onion, a bundle of sweet herbs, a little crust of bread baked brown, and a little piece of carrot. Cover it close, and let it stew till it is as good as you would have it. This will make a pint of rich gravy.

To make Veal, Mutton, or Beef Gravy.

TAKE a rasher or two of bacon or ham, lay it at the bottom of your stew-pan; put your meat, cut in thin slices over it, and cut some onions, turnips, carrots, and cellery, a little thyme, and put over the meat, with a little all-spice; put a little water at the bottom, then set it on the fire which must be a gentle one, and draw it till it is brown at the bottom (which you may know by the pan's hissing,) then pour boiling water over it, and stew it gently for one hour and a half: if a small quantity, less time will do it. Season it with salt.

Brown colouring for Made-dishes.

TAKE four ounces of sugar, beat fine; put into an iron-frying-pan, or earthen pipkin; set it over a clear fire and when the sugar is melted it will be frosty ; put it higher from the fire till it is a fine brown ; keep it stirring all the time, fill the pan up with red wine, take care it don't boil over, add a little salt and lemon ; put a little cloves and mace, a shallot or two, boil it gently for ten minutes ; pour it in a bason till it is cold then bottle it for use.

To bake a Leg of Beef.

Do it just in the same manner as before directed in the making gravy for soups, &c. and when it is baked, strain it through a coarse sieve. Pick out all the sinews and fat, put them into a saucepan with a few spoonfuls of the gravy, a little red wine, a little piece of butter rolled in flour, and some mustard : shake your sauce-pan often ; and when the sauce is hot and thick, dish it up, and send it to table. It is a pretty dish.

To bake an Ox's Head.

Do it just in the same manner as the leg of beef is directed to be done in making the gravy for soups, &c. and it does full as well for the same uses. If it should be too strong for any thing you want it for, it is only putting some hot water to it. Cold water will spoil it.

To boil Pickled Pork.

Be sure you put it in when the water boils. If a middling piece, an hour will boil it ; if a very large piece, an hour and a half, or two hours. If you boil pickled pork too long, it will go to a jelly.

To Dress Fish.

Observe always in the frying of any sort of fish : first, that you dry your fish very well in a clean cloth, then do your fish in this manner :

beat up the yolks of two or three eggs, according to your quantity of fish; take a small pastry-brush, and put the egg on, shake some crumbs of bread and flour mixt over the fish, and then fry it. Let the stew-pan you fry them in be very nice and clean, and put in as much beef dripping, or hog's-lard, as will almost cover your fish: and be sure it boils before you put in your fish. Let it fry quick, and let it be of a fine light brown, but not too dark a colour. Have your fish-slice ready, and if there is occasion turn it: when it is enough, take it up, and lay a coarse cloth on a dish, on which lay your fish, to drain all the grease from it. If you fry parsley, do it quick, and take great care to whip it out of the pan as soon as it is crisp, or it will lose its fine colour. Take great care that your dripping be very nice and clean. You have directions in another place how to make it fit for use, and have it always in readiness.

Some love fish in batter; then you must beat an egg fine, and dip your fish in just as you are going to put it in the pan; or as good a batter as any, is a little ale and and flour beat up, just as you are ready for it, and dip the fish, to fry it.

Lobster Sauce.

Take a fine hen lobster, take out all the spawn, and bruise it in a mortar very fine, with a little butter; then take all the meat out of the claws and tail, and cut it in small square pieces; put the spawn and meat in a stew-pan with a spoonful of anchovy liquor, and one spoonful of catchup, a blade of mace, a piece of a stick of horse-radish, half a lemon, a gill of gravy, a little butter rolled in flour, just enough to thicken it; put in half a pound of butter nicely melted, boil it gently up for six or seven minutes; take out the horse-radish, mace, and lemon, and squeeze the juice of the lemon into the sauce; just simmer it up, and then put it in your boats.

Shrimp Sauce.

Take half a pint of shrimps, wash them very clean, put them in a stew-pan with a spoonful of fish-lear, or anchovy-liquor, a pound of butter melted thick, boil it up for five minutes, and squeeze in half a lemon; toss it up, and then put it in your cups or boats.

To make Anchovy Sauce.

Take a pint of gravy, put in an anchovy, take a quarter of a pound of butter rolled in a litttle flour, and stir all together till it boils. You may add a little juice of a lemon, catchup, red wine, and walnut liquor, just as you please.

Plain butter melted thick, with a spoonful of walnut pickle, or catchup, is good sauce, or anchovy. In short, you may put as many things as you fancy into sauce.

To dress a Brace of Carp.

Take a piece of butter, and put into a stew-pan, melt it, and put in a large spoonful of flour, keep it stirring till it is smooth; then put in a pint of gravy, and a pint of red-port or claret, a little horse-radish scraped, eight cloves, four blades of mace, and a dozen corns of all-spice, tie them in a little linen rag, a bundle of sweet herbs, half a lemon, three anchovies, a little onion chopped very fine; season with pepper, salt and Cayanne pepper, to your liking; stew it for half an hour, then strain it through a sieve into the pan you intend to put your fish in. Let your carp be well cleaned and scaled, then put the fish in with the sauce, and stew them very gently for half an hour; then turn them, and stew them fifteen minutes longer; put in along with your fish some truffles and morels scalded, some pickled mushrooms, a artichoke-bottom, and about a dozen large oysters, squeeze the juice of half a lemon in, stew it five minutes; then put your carp in your dish, and pour all the sauce over. Garnish with fried sippets, and the roe of the fish, done thus: beat the roe up well with the yolks of two eggs, a little flour, a little lemon-peel chopped fine some pepper, salt, and a little anchovy-liquor; have ready a pan of beef-dripping boiling, drop the roe in, to be about as big as a crown piece, fry it of a light brown, and put it round the dish, with some oysters fried in batter, and some scraped horse-radish.

N. B. Stick your fried sippets in the fish.

You may fry the carp first, if you please, but the above is the most modern way. Or, if you are in a great hurry, while the sauce is making, you may boil the fish with spring water, half a pint of vinegar, a little horse-radish, and bay-leaf; put your fish in the dish, and pour the sauce over.

To stew a Brace of Carp.

Scrape them very clean, then gut them, wash them and the roes in a pint of good stale beer, to preserve all the blood, and boil the carp, with a little salt in the water.

In the mean time strain the beer, and put it into a sauce pan, with a pint of red-wine, two or three blades of mace, some whole pepper, black and white, an onion stuck with cloves, half a nutmeg bruised, a bundle of sweet herbs, a piece of lemon-peel as big as a six-pence, an anchovy, and a little piece of horse-radish. Let these boil together softly for a quarter of an hour, covered close then strain it, and add to it half the hard roe beat to pieces, two or three spoonfuls of catchup, a quarter of a pound of fresh butter, and a spoonful of mushroom pickle; let it, boil and keep stirring it till the sauce is thick and enough. If it wants any salt, you, must put some in: then take the rest of the roe, and beat it up with the yolk of an egg, some nutmeg, and a little lemon-peel cut small; fry them in fresh butter in little cakes, and some pieces of bread cut three-corner-ways, and fried brown. When the carp are enough take them up, pour your sauce over them, lay the cakes round the dish, with horse-radish scraped fine and fried parsley. The rest lay on the carp, and stick the bread about them, and lay round them, then sliced lemon notched, and lay round the dish, and two or three pieces on the carp. Send them to table hot.

The boiling of carp at all times is the best way, they eat fatter and finer. The stewing of them is no addition to the sauce, and only hardens the fish, and spoils it. If you would have your sauce white, put in good fish-broth instead of beer, and white-wine in the room of red-wine. Make your broth with any sort of fresh fish you have, and season it as you do gravy.

To fry Carp.

First scale and gut them, wash them clean, lay them in a cloth to dry, then flour them, and fry them of a fine light brown. Fry some toast cut three corner-ways, and the roes; when your fish is done, lay them on a coarse cloth to drain. Let your sauce be butter and anchovy, with the juice of lemon. Lay your carp in the dish, the roes on each side, and garnish with fried toast and lemon.

To bake Carp.

Scale, wash, and clean a brace of carp very well; take an earthen pan deep enough for them to lie in, butter it a little, and lay in your carp; season with mace, cloves, nutmegs, and black and white pepper, a bundle of sweet herbs, an onion, and anchovy; pour in a bottle of white-wine, cover it close, and let them bake an hour in a hot oven, if large; if small, a less time will do them. When they are enough, carefully take them up, and lay them in a dish: set it over hot water to keep it hot, and cover it close; then put all the liquor they were baked in into a sauce-pan, let it boil a minute or two, then strain it, and add half a pound of butter rolled in flour. Let it boil, keep stirring it, squeeze in the juice of half a lemon, and put in what salt you want; pour the sauce over the fish, lay the roes round, and garnish with lemon. Observe to skim all the fat off the liquor.

To fry Tench.

Slime your tenches, slit the skin along the backs, and with the point of your knife raise it up from the bone, then cut the skin across at the head and tail, strip it off, and take out the bone; then take another tench, or a carp, and mince the flesh small with mushrooms, cives, and parsley. Season them with salt, pepper, beaten mace, nutmeg, and a few savory herbs minced small. Mingle all these well together, then pound them in a mortar with crumbs of bread, as much as two eggs soaked in cream, the yolks of three or four eggs, and a piece of butter. When these have been well pounded, stuff the tenches with this sauce; take clarified butter, put it into a pan, set it over the fire, and when it is hot flour your tenches, and put them into the pan one by one, and fry them brown; then take them up, and lay them in a coarse cloth before the fire to keep hot. In the mean time pour all the grease and fat out of the pan, put in a quarter of a pound of butter, shake some flour all over the pan, keep stirring with a spoon till the butter is a little brown; then pour in half a pint of white wine, stir it together, pour in half a pint of boiling water, an onion stuck with cloves, a bundle of sweet herbs, and two blades of mace. Cover them close, and let them stew as softly as you can for a quarter of an hour; then strain off the liquor; put it into the pan again, add two spoonfuls of catchup, have ready an ounce of truffles or morels boiled in half a pint of water tender, pour in truffles, water and all, into the pan, a few mushrooms, and either half a pint of oysters clean washed in their own liquor, and the liquor and all put into the pan, or some crawfish; but then you must put in the tails, and, after clean picking them, boil them in half a pint of water, then strain the liquor, and put into the sauce; or take some fish-melts, and toss up in your sauce. All this as you fancy.

When you find your sauce is very good, put your tench into the pan, make them quite hot, then lay them in your dish, and pour the sauce over them. Garnish with lemon. Or you may, for change, put in half a pint of stale beer instead of water. You may dress tench just as you do carp.

To boil a Cod's Head.

Set a fish-kettle on the fire, with water enough to boil it, a good handful of salt, a pint of vinegar, a bundle of sweet herbs, and a piece of horse-radish: let it boil a quarter of an hour, then put in the head, and when you are sure it is enough, lift up the fish-plate with the fish on it, set it across the kettle to drain, then lay it in your dish, and lay the liver on one side. Garnish with lemon and horse-radish scraped; melt some butter, with a little of the fish-liquor, an anchovy, oysters, or shrimps, or just what you fancy.

To stew Cod.

Cut your cod into slices an inch thick, lay them in the bottom of a large stew-pan ; season them with nutmeg, beaten pepper and salt, a bundle of sweet herbs, and an onion, half a pint of white-wine, and a quarter of a pint of water ; cover it close, and let it simmer softly for five or six minutes, then squeeze in the juice of a lemon, put in a few oysters and the liquor strained, a piece of butter as big as an egg rolled in flour, and a blade or two of mace ; cover it close, and let it stew softly, shaking the pan often. When it is enough, take out the sweet herbs and onion, and dish it up ; pour the sauce over it, and garnish with lemon.

To bake a Cod's Head.

Butter the pan you intend to bake it in, make your head very clean, lay it in the pan, put a bundle of sweet herbs, an onion stuck with cloves, three or four blades of mace, half a large spoonful of black and white pepper a nutmeg bruised, a quart of water, a little piece of lemon-peel, and a little piece of horse-radish. Flour your head, grate a little nutmeg over it stick pieces of butter all over it, and throw raspings all over that. Send it to the oven to bake ; when it is enough, take it out of that dish, and lay it carefully into the dish you intend to serve it up in. Set the dish over boiling water, and cover it up to keep it hot. In the mean time be quick, pour all the liquor out of the dish it was baked in into a sauce-pan, set it on the fire to boil three or four minutes, then strain it, and put to it a gill of red wine, two spoonfuls of catchup, a pint of shrimps, half a pint of oysters, or mussels, liquor and all, but first strain it ; a spoonful of mushroom pickle, a quarter of a pound of butter rolled in flour, ; stir it all together till it is thick and boils ; then pour it into the dish, have ready some toast cut three-corner-ways, and fried crisp. Stick pieces about the head and mouth, and lay the rest round the head. Garnish with lemon notched, scraped horse-radish, and parsley crisped in a plate before the fire. Lay one slice of lemon on the head, and serve it up hot.

To broil Crimp, Cod, Salmon, Whiting or Haddock.

Flour it, and have a quick clear fire, set your gridiron high, broil it of a fine brown, lay it in your dish, and, for sauce have good melted butter. Take a lobster bruise the spawn in the butter, cut the meat small, put all together into the melted butter, make it hot, and pour it into your dish, or into basons. Garnish with horse-radish and lemon.

Oyster Sauce is made thus.

Take half a pint of oysters, and simmer them till they are plump, strain the liquor from them through a sieve, wash the oysters very clean, and beard them ; put them in a stew-pan, and pour the liquor over them, but mind you do not pour the sediment with the liquor ; then add a blade of mace, a quarter of a lemon, a spoonful of anchovy liquor, and a little bit of horse-radish, a little butter rolled in flour, half a pound of butter nicely melted, boil it up gently for ten minutes ; then take out the horse-radish, the mace, and lemon, squeeze the juice of the lemon into the sauce, toss it up a little, then put it into your boats or basons.

To dress little Fish.

As to all sorts of little fish, such as smelts, roach, &c. they should be fried dry and of a fine brown and nothing but plain butter. Garnish with lemon.

And to boil salmon the same, only garnish with lemon and horse-radish.

And with all boiled fish, you should put a good deal of salt and horse-radish in the water, except mackerel, with which put salt and mint, parsley and fennel, which you must chop to put into the butter; and some love scalded gooseberries with them. And be sure to boil your fish well; but take great care they do not break.

To broil Mackerel.

Clean them, split them down the back, season them with pepper and salt, some mint, parsley, and fennel, chopped very fine, and flour them; broil them of a fine light brown, put them on a dish and strainer. Garnish with parsley; let your sauce be fennel and butter in a boat.

To boil a Turbot.

Lay it in a good deal of salt and water an hour or two, and if it is not quite sweet, shift your water five or six times; first put a good deal of salt in the mouth and belly.

In the mean time set on your fish-kettle with clean spring water and salt, a little vinegar, and a piece of horse-radish. When the water boils, lay the turbot on a fish plate, put it into the kettle, let it be well boiled, but take great care it is not too much done; when enough, take off the fish-kettle, set it before the fire, then carefully lift up the fish-plate, and set it across the kettle to drain: in the mean time melt a good deal of fresh butter, and bruise in either the spawn of one or two lobsters, and the meat cut small, with a spoonful of anchovy-liquor; then give it a boil, and pour it into basons. This is the best sauce; but you may make what you please. Lay the fish in the dish. Garnish with scraped horse-radish and lemon

To bake a Turbot.

Take a dish the size of your turbot, rub butter all over it thick, throw a little salt, a little beaten pepper, and half a large nutmeg, some parsley minced fine, and throw all over, pour in a pint of white-wine; cut off the head and tail lay the turbot in the dish, pour another pint of white-wine all over, grate the other half of the nutmeg over it, and a little pepper, some salt and chopped parsley. Lay a piece of butter here and there all over, and throw a little flour all over, and then a good many crumbs of bread. Bake it, and be sure that it is of a fine brown; then lay it in your dish, stir the sauce in your dish all together, pour it into a sauce-pan, shake in a little flour, let it boil, then stir in a piece of butter and two spoonfuls of catchup, let it boil, and pour it into basons. Garnish your dish with lemon; and you may add what you fancy to the sauce, as shrimps, anchovies, mushrooms, &c. If a small turbout, half the wine will do. It eats finely thus. Lay it in a dish, skim off all the fat, and pour the rest over it. Let it stand till cold, and it is good with vinegar, and a fine dish to set out a cold table.

To broil Salmon.

Cut fresh salmon into thick pieces, flour them and broil them, lay them in your dish, and have plain melted butter in a cup.

Baked Samon.

Take a little piece cut into slices about an inch thich, butter the dish that you would serve it to table on, lay the slices in the dish, take off the skin, make a force-meat thus: take the flesh of an eel, the flesh of a salmon an equal quantity, beat in a mortar, season it with beaten pepper, salt, nutmeg, two or three cloves, some parsley, a few mushrooms, a piece of butter, and ten or a dozen coriander-seeds, beat fine. Beat all together; boil the crumbs of a penny-roll in milk, beat up four eggs, stir it together till is thick, let it cool, and mix it well together with the rest; then mix all together with four raw eggs; on every slice lay this force-meat all over, pour a very little melted butter over them, and a few crumbs of bread, lay a crust round the edge of the dish, and stick oysters round upon it. Bake it in an oven, and when it is of a very fine brown serve it up; pour a little plain butter (with a little red-wine in it) into the dish, and the juice of a lemon; or you may bake it in any dish, and when it is enough lay the slices into another dish. Pour the butter and wine into the dish it was baked in, give it a boil, and pour it into the dish. Garnish with lemon. This is a fine dish. Squeeze the juice of a lemon in.

To broil Mackerel whole.

Cut off their heads, gut them, wash them clean pull out the roe at the neck-end, boil it in a little water then bruse it with a spoon, beat up the yolk of an egg, with a little nutmeg, a little lemon-peel cut fine, a little thyme, some parsley boiled and chopped fine, a little pepper and salt, a few crumbs of bread: mix all well together, and fill the mackerel; flour it well, and broil it nicely. Let your sauce be plain butter, with a little catchup or walnut pickle.

To broil Herrings

Scale them, gut them, cut off their heads, wash them clean, dry them in a cloth, flour them and broil them; take the heads and mash them, broil them in small-beer or ale, with a little whole pepper and an onion. Let it boil a quarter of an hour, then strain it; thicken it with butter and flour, and a good deal of mustard. Lay the fish in the dish, and pour the sauce into a bason, or plain melted butter and mustard.

To fry Herrings.

Clean them as above, fry them in butter; have ready a good many onions peeled and cut thin; fry them of a light brown with the herrings; lay the herrings in your dish, and the onions round, butter and mustard in a cup. You must do them with a quick fire.

To stew Eels with broth.

Clean your eels, put them into a sauce-pan with a blade or two of mace and a crust of bread. Put just water enough to cover them close, and let them stew very softly; when they are enough, dish them up with the broth, and have a little plain melted butter and parsley in a cup to eat with them. The broth will be very good, and it is fit for weakly and consumptive constitutions.

To dress a Pike.

Gut it, clean it, and make it very clean, then turn it round with the tail in the mouth, lay it in a little dish, cut toast three-corner-ways, fill the middle with them, flour it, and stick pieces of butter all over; then throw a little more flour, and send it to the oven to bake: or it will do better in a tin oven before the fire, as you can then baste it as you will. When it is done lay it in your dish, and have ready melted butter, with an anchovy dissolved in it, and a few oysters or shrimps; and if there is any liquor in the dish it was baked in, add it to the sauce, and put in just what you fancy. Pour your sauce into the dish. Garnish it with toast about the fish, and lemon about the dish. You should have a pudding in the belly, made thus : take grated bread, two hard eggs chopped fine, half a nutmeg grated, a little lemon-peel cut fine, and either the roe or liver, or both, if any, chopped fine ; and if you have none, get either a piece of the liver of a cod, or the roe of any fish, mix them all together with a raw egg and a good piece of butter ; roll it up, and put it into the fish's belly before you bake it. A haddock done this way eats very well.

To broil Haddocks, when they are in high Season.

Scale them, gut and wash them clean ; do not rip open their bellies, but take the guts out with the gills ; dry them in a clean cloth very well : if there be any roe or liver, take it out, but put it in again ; flour them well, and have a clear good fire. Let your gridiron be hot and clean, lay them on, turn them quick two or three times for fear of sticking ; then let one side be enough, and turn the other side. When that is done, lay them in a dish, and have plain butter in a cup, or anchovy and butter.

They eat finely salted a day or two before you dress them, and hung up to dry, or boiled with egg-sauce. Newcastle is a famous place for salted haddocks. They come in barrels, and keep a great while.

To broil Cods-Sounds.

You may first lay them in hot water a few minutes ; take them out, and rub them well with salt, to take off the skin and black dirt, then they will look white, then put them in water, and give them a boil. Take them out, and flour them well, pepper and salt them, and broil them. When they are enough, lay them in your dish, and pour melted butter and mustard into the dish. Broil them whole.

To dress Salmon au Court-Bouillon.

After having washed and made your salmon very clean, score the side pretty deep, that it may take the seasoning: take a quarter of an ounce of mace, a quarter of an ounce of cloves, a nutmeg, dry them and beat them fine, a quarter of an ounce of black pepper beat fine, and an ounce of salt. Lay the salmon in a napkin, season it well with this spice, cut some lemon peel fine, and parsly, throw all over, and in the notches put about a pound of fresh butter rolled in flour, roll it up tight in the napkin, and bind it about with pack-thread. Put it in a fish-kettle, just big enough to hold it, pour in a quart of white-wine, a quart of vinegar, and as much water as will just boil it.

Set it over a quick fire, cover it close; when it is enough, which you must judge by the bigness of your salmon, set it over a stove to stew till you are ready. Then have a clean napkin folded in the dish it is to lay it in, out of the napkin it was boiled in on the other napkin. Garnish the dish with a good deal of parsley crisped before the fire.

For sauce have nothing but plain butter in a cup, or horse-radish and vinegar. Serve it up for a first course.

To dress Flat Fish.

In dressing all sorts of flat-fish, take great care in the boiling of them, be sure to have them enough, but do not let them be broke; mind to put a good deal of salt in, and horse-radish in the water: let your fish be well drained, and mind to cut the fins off. When you fry them, let them be well drained in a cloth, and floured, and fry them of a fine light brown, either in oil or butter. If there be any water in your dish with the boiled fish, take it out with a spunge. As to your fried fish, a coarse cloth is the best thing to drain it on.

To dress Salt Fish.

Old ling, which is the best sort of salt-fish, lay in water twelve hours, then lay it twelve hours on a board, and then twelve more in water. When you boil it, put it into the water cold; if it is good, it will take about fifteen minutes boiling softly. Boil parsnips very tender, scrape them, and put them into a sauce-pan, put to them some milk, stir them till thick, then stir in a good piece of butter, and a little salt; when they are enough, lay them in a plate, the fish by itself dry, and butter, and hard eggs chopped in a bason.

As to water-cod, that need only be boiled and well skimmed.

Scotch haddocks you must lay in water all night. You may boil or broil them. If you broil, you must split them in two.

You may garnish your dishes with hard eggs and parsnips.

To fry Lampreys.

Bleed them and save the blood, then wash them in hot water to take off the slime, and cut them to pieces. Fry them in a little fresh butter not quite enough, pour out the fat, put in a little white-wine, give the pan a shake round, season it with whole pepper, nutmeg, salt, sweet herbs and a bay-leaf, put in a few capers, a good piece of butter rolled up in flour, and the blood, give the pan a shake round often, and cover them close. When you think they are enough take them out, strain the sauce, then give them a boil quick, squeeze in a little lemon, and pour over the fish. Garnish with lemon, and dress them just what way you fancy.

To fry Eels.

Make them very clean, cut them into pieces,

season them with pepper and salt, flour them, and fry them in butter. Let your sauce be plain butter melted, with the juice of lemon. Be sure they be well drained from the fat before you lay them in the dish.

To broil Eels.

Take a large eel, skin it and make it clean. Open the belly, cut it in four pieces; take the tail end, strip off the flesh, beat it in a morter season it with a little beaten mace, a little grated nutmeg, pepper, and salt, a little parsley and thyme, a little lemon-peel, an equal quantity of crumbs of bread, roll it in a little piece of butter; then mix it again with the yolk of an egg, roll it up again, and fill the three pieces of belly with it. Cut the skin of the ell, wrap the pieces in, and sew up the skin. Broil them well, have butter and an anchovy for sauce, with the juice of lemon.

To roast a Piece of fresh Sturgeon.

Get a piece of fresh sturgeon of about eight or ten pounds, let it lay in water and salt six or eight hours, with its scales on; then fasten it on the spit, and baste it well with butter for a quarter of an hour, then with a little, flour grate a nutmeg all over it, a little mace and pepper beaten fine, and salt thrown over it, and a few sweet herbs dried and powdered fine, and then crumbs of bread; then keep; basting a little, and drudging with crumbs of bread, and with what falls from it till it is enough. In the mean time prepare this sauce: take a pint of water, an anchovy, a little piece of lemon-peel, an onion, a bundle of sweet herbs, mace, cloves, whole pepper, black and white, a little piece of horse-radish; cover it close, let it boil a quarter of an hour, then strain it, put it into the sauce-pan again, pour in a pint of white-wine, about a dozen oysters and the liquor, two spoonfuls of catchup, two of walnut-pickle, the inside of a crab bruised fine, or lobster, shrimps or prawns, a good piece of butter rolled in flour, a spoonful of mushroom-pickle, or juice of lemon. Boil it all together; when your fish is enough, lay it in your dish, pour the sauce over it. Garnish with fried toasts and lemons.

To boil Sturgeon.

Clean your sturgeon, and prepare as much liquor as will just boil it. To two quarts of water, a pint of vinegar, a stick of horse-radish, two or three bits of lemon-peel, some whole pepper, and a bay-leaf, add a small handful of salt. Boil your fish in this, and serve it with the following sauce: melt a pound of butter, dissolve an anchovy in it, put in a blade or two of mace, bruise the body of a crab in the butter, a few shrimps or craw fish, a little catchup, a little lemon-juice; give it a boil, drain your fish well, and lay it in your dish. Garnish with fried oysters, sliced lemon, and scraped horse-radish; pour your sauce into boats or basons. So you may fry it, ragoo it, or bake it.

To crimp Cod the Dutch Way.

Take a gallon of pump-water and a pound of salt, mix them well together: take your cod whilst alive, and cut it in slices of one inch and a half thick, throw it into the salt and water for half an hour; then take it out, and dry it well with a clean cloth, flour it and broil it; or have a stew-pan with some pump water and salt boiling, put in your fish, and boil it quick for five minutes; send oyster-sauce, anchovy-sauce, shrimp-sauce, or what sauce you please. Garnish with horse-radish and green parsley.

To crimp Scate.

Cut it into long slips cross-ways, about an inch broad, and put it into spring-water and salt, as above; then have spring-water and salt boiling, put it in, and boil it fifteen minutes. Shrimp-sauce, or what sauce you like.

To boil Soals.

Take three quarts of spring-water, and a handful of salt, let it boil; then put in your soals, boil them gently for ten minutes; then dish them up in a clean napkin, with anchovy-sauce, or shrimp-sauce, in boats.

To roast Lobsters.

Boil your lobsters, then lay them before the fire, and baste them with butter till they have a fine froth. Dish them up with plain melted butter in a cup. This is as good a way to the full as roasting them, and not half the trouble.

To make a fine Dish of Lobsters.

Take three lobsters, boil the largest as above, and froth it before the fire. Take the other two boiled, and butter them as in the foregoing receipt. Take the two body shells, heat them hot, and fill them with the buttered meat. Lay the large lobster in the middle, and the two shells on each side; and the two great claws of the middle lobster at each end; and the four pieces of chines of the two lobsters broiled, and laid on each end. This, if nicely done makes a pretty dish.

To dress a Crab.

Having taken out the meat, and cleansed it from the skin, put it into a stew-pan, with half a pint of white-wine, a little nutmeg, pepper, and salt, over a slow fire. Throw in a few crumbs of bread, beat up one yolk of an egg with one spoonful of vinegar, throw it in, then shake the sauce pan round a minute, and serve it up on a plate.

To stew Prawns, Shrimps, or Craw-Fish.

Pick out the tail, lay them by, about two quarts; take the bodies, give them a bruise, and put them into a pint of white-wine, with a blade of mace; let them stew a quarter of an hour, stir them together, and strain them; then wash out the sauce-pan, put to it the strained liquor and tails: grate a small nutmeg in, add a little salt, and a quarter of a pound of butter rolled in flour: shake it all together; cut a pretty thin toast round a quartern-loaf toast it brown on both sides, cut into six pieces, lay it close together in the bottom of your dish, and pour your fish and sauce over it. Send it to table hot. If it be craw-fish or prawns, garnish your dish with some of the biggest claws laid thick round. Water will do in the room of wine, only add a spoonful of vinegar.

To make Scollops of Oysters.

Put your osters into scollop-shells for that purpose, set them on your gridiron over a good clear fire, let them stew till you think your oysters are enough, then have ready some crumbs of bread rubbed in a clean napkin, fill your shells, and set them before a good fire, and baste them well with butter. Let them be of a fine brown, keeping them turning, to be brown all over alike: but a tin oven does them best before the fire. They eat much the best done this way, though most people stew the oysters first in a sauce-pan, with a blade of mace, thickened with a piece of butter, and fill the shells, and then cover them with crumbs, and brown them with a hot iron: but the bread has not the fine taste of the former.

To stew Mussels.

Wash them very clean from the sand in two or three waters, put them into a stew-pan, cover them close, and let them stew till all the shells are opened; then take them out one by one, pick them out of the shells, and look under the tongue to see if there be a crab; if there is, you must throw away the mussel; some will only pick out the crab and eat the mussel. When you have picked them all clean, put them into a sauce-pan: to a quart of mussles put half a pint of the liquor strained through a sive, put in a blade or two of mace, a piece of butter as big as a large walnut rolled in flour; let them stew: toast some bread brown, and lay them round the dish, cut three-cornerways; pour in the mussels, and send them to table hot.

To stew scollops.

Boil them very well in salt and water, take them out and stew them in a little of the liquor, a little white-wine, a little vinegar, two or three blades of mace, two or three cloves, a piece of butter rol'ed in flour, and the juice of a Seville orange. Stew them well, and dish them up.

MADE DISHES.

To dress Scotch Collops.

Take a piece of fillet of veal, cut it in thin pieces, about as big as a crown piece, but very thin; shake a little flour over it, then put a little butter in a frying-pan, and melt it; put in your collops, and fry them quick till they are brown, then lay them in a dish. have ready a good ragoo made thus: take a little butter in your stew-pan, and melt it, then add a large spoonful of flour; stir it about till it is smooth, then put in a pint of good brown gravy; season it with pepper and salt, pour in a small glass of white-wine, some veal sweet-breads, force meat balls, truffles and morels, ox pa ates, and mushrooms; stew them gently for half an hour, add the juice of half a lemon to it, put it over the collops, and garnish with rashers of bacon. Some like Scotch collops made thus: put the collops into the ragoo, and stew them for five minutes.

To dress White Scotch Collops

Cut the veal the same as for Scotch collops; throw them into a stew-pan; put some boiling water over them, and stir them about, then strain them off, take a pint of good veal broth, and thicken it; add a bundle of sweet herbs, with some mace; put sweet-bread, force-meat balls, and fresh mushrooms; if no fresh to be had, use pickled ones washed in warm water; stew them about fifteen minutes; add the yolk of one egg and half, and a pint of cream: beat them well together with some nutmeg grated, and keep stirring till it boils up; add the juice of a quarter of a lemon, then put it in your dish. Garnish with lemon.

To dress a Fillet of Veal with Collops.

For an alteration, take a small fillet of veal, cut what collops you want, then take the udder and fill it with force-meat, roll it round, tie it with a packthread across, and roast it; lay your collops in the dish, and lay your udder in the middle. Garnish you dishes with lemon.

To make Force-meat Balls.

Now you are to observe, that force-meat balls are a great addition to all made dishes; made thus: take half a pound of veal, and half a pound of suet, cut fine, and beat in a marble mortar or wooden bowl; have a few sweet herbs shred fine, a little mace dried and beat fine a small nutmeg grated, or half a large one, a little lemon-peel cut very fine, a little pepper and salt, and the yolks of two eggs; mix all these well together, then roll them in little round balls, and some in little long balls; roll them in flour, and fry them brown. If they are for any thing of white sauce, put a little water in a sauce-pan, and when the water boils put them in, and let them boil for a few minutes, but never fry them for white sauce.

Truffles and Morels good in Sauces and Soups.

Take half an ounce of truffles and morels, let them be well washed in warm water to get the sand and dirt out, then simmer them in two or three spoonfuls of water for a few minutes, and put them with the liquor into the sauce. They thicken both sauce and soup, and give it a fine flavour.

To stew Ox Palates.

Stew them very tender; which must be done by putting them into cold water, and let them stew very softly over a slow fire till they are tender, then take off the two skins, cut them in pieces, and put them either into your made-dish or soup; and cock's-combs and artichoke-bottoms, cut small, and put into the made dish. Garnish your dishes with lemon, sweet-breads stewed, or white dishes, and fried for brown ones, and cut in little pieces.

To ragoo a Leg of Mutton.

Take all the skin and fat off, cut it very thin the right way of the grain, butter your stew-pan, and shake some flour into it: slice half a lemon and half an onion, cut them very small, with a little bundle of sweet herbs, and a blade of mace.

Put all together with your meat into the pan, stir it a minute or two, and then put in six spoonfuls of gravy, and have ready an anchovy minced small; mix it with some butter and flour, stir it all together for six minutes, and then dish it up.

To make a Brown Fricasey.

You must take your rabbits or chickens and skin them, then cut them into small pieces, and rub them over with yolks of eggs. Have ready some grated bread, a little beaten mace, and a little grated nutmeg mixed together, and then roll them in it: put a little butter into a stew-pan, and when it is melted put in your meat. Fry it of a fine brown, take care they do not stick to the bottom of the pan, then pour the butter from them, and pour in half a pint of brown gravy, a glass of white-wine, a few mushrooms, or two spoonfuls of the pickle, a little salt, (if wanted), and a piece of butter rolled in flour. When it is of a fine thickness dish it up, and send it to table.

To make a White Fricasey.

Take two chickens, and cut them in small pieces, put them in warm water to draw out the blood, then put them into some good veal broth, if no veal broth, a little boiling water, and stew them gently with a bundle of sweet herbs, and a blade of mace, till they are tender; then take out the sweet herbs, add a little flour and butter boiled togeter, to thicken it a little, then add half a pint of cream, and the yolk of an egg beat very fine; some pickled mushrooms: the best way is to put some fresh mushrooms in at first; if no fresh, then pickled: keep stirring it till it boils up, then add the juice of half a lemon, stir it well to keep it from curdling, then put it in your dish, Garnish with lemon.

To fricasey Rabbits, Lamb, Veal, or Tripe.

Observe the directions given in the preceeding article.

To ragoo Hogs Feet and Ears.

Take your ears out of the pickle they are soused in, or boil them till they are tender, then cut them into little long thin bits, about two inches long and about a quarter of an inch thick; put them into your stew-pan with half a pint of good gravy, a glass of white wine, a good deal of mustard, a good piece of butter rolled in flour, and a little pepper and salt: stir all together till it is of a fine thickness, and then dish it up. The hogs feet must not be stewed but boiled tender, then slit them in two, and put the yolk of an egg over and crumbs of bread, and boil or fry them; put the ragoo of ears in the middle, and the feet round it.

Note, they make a very pretty dish fried with butter and mustard, and a little good gravy, if you like it. Then only cut the feet and ears in two. You may add halt an onion, cut small.

To fry Tripe.

Cut your tripe in long pieces of about three inches wide, and all the breadth of the double; put it in some small beer batter, or yolks of eggs: have a large pan of good fat, and fry it brown, then take it out, and put it to drain: dish it up with plain butter in a cup.

To stew Tripe,

Cut it just as you do for frying, and set on some water in a sauce-pan, with two or three onions cut in slices, and some salt. When it boils, put in your tripe. Ten minuets will boil it Send it to table with the liquor in the dish and the onions.

Have butter and mustard in a cup, and dish it up. You may put in as many onions as you like, to mix with your sauce, or leave them out, just as you please.

A Fricasey of Pigeons.

Take eight pigeons, new killed, cut them in small pieces, and put them in a stew-pan with a pint of claret and a pint of water. Season your pigeons with salt and pepper, a blade or two of mace, an onion, a bundle of sweet herbs, a good piece of butter just rolled in a very little flour; cover it close, and let them stew till there is just enough for sauce, and then take out the onion and sweet herbs, beat up the yolks of three eggs, grate half a nutmeg in, and with your spoon push the meat all to one side of the pan and the gravy to the other side, and stir in the eggs; keep them stirring for fear of turning to curds, and when the sauce is fine and thick shake all together, and then put the meat into the dish, pour the sauce over it, and have ready some slices of bacon toasted, and fried oysters; throw the oysters all over, and lay the bacon round. Garnish with lemon.

A Fricasey of Lamb Stones and Sweetbreads.

Have ready some lamb-stones blanched, par-boiled and sliced, and flour two or three sweet-breads; if very thick, cut them in two; they yolks of six hard eggs whole; a few pistachio-nut kernels, and a few large oysters: fry these all of a fine-brown, then pour out all the butter, and add a pint of drawn-gravy, the lamb-stnoes, some asparagus tops about an inch long, some grated nutmeg, a little pepper and salt, two shalots shred small, and a glass of white wine. Stew all these together for ten minutes, then add the yolks of three eggs beat very fine, with a little white wine, and a little beaten mace; stir all together till it is a fine thickness, and then dish it up. Garnish with lemon.

To hash a Calf's Head.

Boil the head almost enough, then take the best half, and with a sharp knife take it nicely from the bone, with the two eyes. Lay it in a little deep dish before a good fire, and take great care no ashes fall into it, and then hack it with a knife cross and cross: grate some nutmeg all over, the yolks of two eggs, a very little pepper and salt, a few sweet herbs, some crumbs of bread, and a little lemon-peel, chopped very fine, baste it with a little butter, then baste it again; keep the dish turning that it may be all brown alike: cut the other half and tongue into little thin bits, and set on a pint of drawn-gravy in a sauce-pan, a little bundle of sweet herbs, an onion; a little pepper and salt, a glass of white wine, and two shalots; boil all these together a few minutes, then strain it through a sieve, and put it into a clean stew-pan with the hash. Flour the meat before you put it in, and put in a few mushrooms, a spoonful of the pickle, two spoonfuls of catchup, and a few truffles and morels: stir all these together for a few minutes, then beat up half the brains, and stir into the stew-pan, and a little piece of butter rolled in flour. Take the other half of the brains, and beat them up with a little lemon-peel cut fine, a little nutmeg grated, a little beaten mace, a little thyme shred small, a little parsley, the yolk of an egg, and have some good dripping boiling in a stew-pan: then fry the brains in little cakes, about as big as a crown-piece, Fry about twenty oysters, dripped in the yolk of an egg, toast some slices of bacon, fry a few force-meat balls, and have ready a hot dish; if pewter, over a few clear coals; if china, over a pan of hot water. Pour in your hash, then lay in your toasted head, throw the force-meat balls over the hash, and garnish the dish with fried oysters the fried brains, and lemon; throw the rest over the hash, lay the bacon round the dish, and send it to table.

To bake a Calf or Sheep's Head.

Take the head, pick it and wash it very clean; take an earthen dish large enough to lay the head in, rub a little piece of butter all over the dish, then lay some long iron skewers across the top of the dish, and put the head on them; skewer up the meat in the middle that it do not lie on the dish, then grate some nutmeg all over it, a few sweet herbs shred small, some crumbs of bread, a little lemon-pael cut fine, and then flour it all over: stick pieces of butter in the eyes and all over the head, and flour it again. Let it be well baked, and of a fine brown; you may throw a little pepper and salt over it, and put into the dish a piece of beef cut small, a bundle of sweet herbs, an onion, some whole pepper, a blade of mace, two cloves, a pint of water, and boil the brains with some sage. When the head is enough, lay it in a dish, and set it to the fire to keep warm, then stir all together in the dish, and boil it in a sauce-pan; strain it off, put it into the sauce-pan again, add a piece of butter rolled in flour, and the sage in the brains chopped fine, a spoonful of catchup, and two spoonfuls of red-wine; boil them together, take the brains, beat them well, and mix them with the sauce; pour it into the dish, and send it to table. You must bake the tongue with the head, and do not cut it out. It will lie the handsomer in the dish.

the liver be too much done. Take the head up, hack it cross and cross with a knife, grate some nutmeg over it, and lay it in a dish before a good fire; then grate some crumbs of bread, some sweet herbs rubbed, a little lemon-peel chopped fine, a very little pepper and salt, and baste with a little butter; then throw a little flour over it, and just as it is done do the same, baste it and drudge it. Take half the liver, the lights, the heart and tongue, chop them very small, with six or eight spoonfuls of gravy or water; first shake some flour over the meat, and stir it together, then put in the gravy or water, a good piece of butter rolled in a little flour, a little pepper and salt, and what runs from the head in the dish; simmer all together a few minutes, and add half a spoonful of vinegar, pour it into your dish, lay the head in the middle of the mince-meat, have ready the other half of the liver cut thin, with some slices of bacon broiled, and lay round the head. Garnish the dish with lemon and send it to table.

To ragoo a Neck of Veal.

Cut a neck of veal into steaks, flatten them with a rolling-pin, season them with salt, pepper, cloves, and mace, lard them with bacon, lemon-peel and thyme, dip them in the yolks of eggs, make a sheet of strong cap-paper up at the four corners, in the form of a dripping-pan; pin up the corners, butter the paper and also the gridiron, and set it over a fire of charcoal; put in your meat, let it do leisurely, keep it basting and turning to keep in the gravy; and when it is enough, have ready half a pint of strong gravy, season it high, put in mushrooms and pickles, force-meat balls dipped in the yolks of eggs, oysters stewed and fried, to lay round and at the top of your dish, and then serve it up. If for a brown ragoo, put in red-wine ; if for a white one, put in white-wine, with the yolks of eggs beat up with two or three spoonfuls of cream.

To force a Leg of Lamb.

With a sharp knife carefully take out all the meat, and leave the skin whole and the fat on it, make the lean you cut out into force-meat, thus : to two pounds of meat, add three pounds of beef-suet cut fine, and beat in a marble mortar till it is very fine, and take away all the skin of the meat and suet, then mix it with four spoonfuls of grated bread, eight or ten cloves, five or six large blades of mace dried and beat fine, half a large nutmeg grated, a little pepper and salt, a little lemon-peel cut fine, a very little thyme, some parsley, and four eggs ; mix all together, put it into the skin again just as it was, in the same shape, sew it up, roast it, baste it with butter, cut the loin into steaks and fry it nicely, lay the leg in the dish and the loin round it ; pour a pint of good gravy into the dish, and send it to table.

To boil a Leg of Lamb.

Let the leg be boiled very white. An hour will do it. Cut the loin into steaks, dip them in a few crumbs of bread and egg, fry them nice and brown, boil a good deal of spinach, and lay in the dish ; put the leg in the middle, lay the loin round it ; cut an orange in four and garnish the dish, and have butter in a cup. Some love the spinach boiled, then drained, put into a sauce-pan with a good piece of butter, and stewed.

To force a large Fowl.

Cut the skin down the back, and carefully slip it up so as to take out all the meat, mix it with one pound of beef-suet, cut it small, and beat them together in a marble mortar : take a pint of large oysters cut small, two anchovies cut small, one shalot cut fine, a few sweet herbs, a little pepper, a little nutmeg grated, and the yolks of four eggs; mix all together, and lay this on the bones, draw over the skin and sew up the back, put the fowl into a bladder, boil it an hour and a quarter, stew some oysters in good gravy thickened with a piece of butter rolled in flour, take the fowl out of the bladder, lay it in your dish, and pour the sauce over it. Garnish with lemon.

It eats much better roasted with the same sauce.

To roast a Turkey the genteel Way.

First cut it down the back, and with a sharp penknife bone it, then make your force-meat thus: take a large fowl, or a pound of veal, as much grated bread, half a pound of suet cut and beat very fine, a little beaten mace, two cloves, half a nutmeg grated, about a large tea-spoonful of lemon-peel, and the yolks of two eggs; mix all together, with a little pepper and salt, fill up the places where the bones came out, and fill the body, that it may look just as it did before, sew up the back, and roast it. You may have oyster-sauce, celery-sauce, just as you please; put good gravy in the dish, and garnish with lemon, which is as good as any thing. Be sure to leave the pinions on.

To stew a Turkey or Fowl.

First let your pot be very clean, lay four clean skewers at the bottom, and your turkey or fowl upon them, put in a quart of gravy; take a bunch of celery, cut it small, and wash it very clean, put it into your pot, with two or three blades of mace, let it stew softly till there is just enough for sauce, then add a good piece of butter rolled in flour, two spoonfuls of red-wine, two of catchup, and just as much pepper and salt as will season it;

lay your fowl or turkey in the dish, pour the sauce over it, and send it to table. If the fowl or turkey is enough before the sauce, take it up, and keep it up till the sauce is boiled enough, then put it in, let it boil a minute or two, and dish it up.

To stew a Knuckle of Veal.

Be sure let the pot or sauce-pan be very clean, lay at the bottom four clean wooden skewers, wash and clean the knuckle very well, then lay it in the pot with two or three blades of mace, a little whole pepper, a little piece of thyme, a small onion, a crust of bread, and two quarts of water. Cover it down close, make it boil, then only let it simmer for two hours, and when it is enough take it up, lay it in a dish, and strain the broth over it.

To force a Surloin of Beef.

When it is quite roasted, take it up, and lay it in the dish with the inside uppermost, with a sharp knife lift up the skin, hack and cut the inside very fine, shake a little pepper and salt over it, with two shalots, cover it with the skin, and send it to table. You may add red-wine or vinegar, just as you like.

To make Beef Alamode.

Take a small buttock of beef, or leg-of-mutton-piece, or a piece of buttock of beef; also a dozen cloves, eight blades of mace, and some alspice beat very fine; chop a large handful of parsley, and all sorts of herbs very fine; cut your bacon as for beef a-la-daub, and put them into the spice and herbs, with some pepper and salt, and thrust a large pin through the beef; put it into a pot, and cover it with water, chop four onions and four blades of garlic, very fine, six bay leaves, and a handful of champignons ; put all into the pot with a pint of porter or ale, and half a pint of red wine ; cover the pot very close, and stew it for six hours, according to the size of the piece ; if a large piece, eight hours ; then take the beef out, put it in a dish, cover it close, and keep it hot, take the gravy and skim all the fat off ; strain it through a sieve, pick out all the champignons, and put them into the gravy ; season it with Cayenne pepper and salt, and boil it up fifteen minutes ; then put the beef into a soup dish and the gravy over it, or cut it into slices and pour the liquor over it ; or put it into a deep dish, with all the gravy into another : when cold cut it in slices, and put some of the gravy round it, which will be of a strong jelly.

Beef Collops.

Take some rump steaks, or tender piece cut like Scotch collops, only larger, hack them a little with a knife, and flour them ; put a little butter in a stew-pan, and melt it, then put in your collops, and fry them quick for about two minutes : put in a pint of gravy, a little butter rolled in flour, season with pepper and salt : cut four pickled cucumbers in thin slices, half a walnut, and a few capers, a little onion shred very fine ; stew them five minutes, then put them into a hot dish, and send them to table. You may put half a glass of white wine into it.

To stew Beef-Steaks.

Take rump steaks, pepper and salt them, lay them in a stew-pan, pour in half a pint of water, a blade or two mace, two or three cloves, a little bundle of sweet herbs, an anchovy, a piece of butter rolled in flour, a glass of white wine, and an onion : cover them close, and let them stew softly till they are tender; then take out the steaks, flour them, fry them in fresh butter, and pour away all the fat, strain the sauce they were stewed in, and pour into the pan: toss it all up together till the sauce is quite hot and thick. If you add a quarter of a pint of oysters, it will make it the better. Lay the steaks in the dish, and pour the sauce over them. Garnish with any pickle you like.

To fry Beef-Steaks.

Take rump steaks, pepper and salt them, fry them in a little butter very quick and brown; take them out, and put them into a dish, pour the fat out of the frying-pan, and then take half a pint of hot gravy; if no gravy, half a pint of hot water, and put into the pan, and a little butter rolled in flour, a little pepper and salt, and two or three shalots chopped fine: boil them up in your pan for two minutes, then put it over the steaks, and send them to table.

To stew a Rump of Beef.

Having boiled it till it is little more then half enough, take it up, and peel off the skin: take salt, pepper, beaten mace, grated nutmeg, a handful of parsley, a little thyme, winter-savery, sweet-marjoram, all chopped fine and mixed, and stuff them in great holes in the fat and lean, the rest spread over it, with the yolks of two eggs; save the gravy that runs out, put to it a pint of claret, and put the meat in a deep pan, pour the liquor in, cover in close, and let it bake two hours, then put it into the dish, pour the liquor over it, and send it to table.

To fricasey Neats Tongues brown.

Take neats tongues, boil them tender, peel them, cut them into thin slices, and fry them in fresh butter; then pour out the butter, put in as much gravy as you shall want for sauce, a bundle of sweet herbs an onion, some pepper and salt, and a blade or two of mace, a glass of white wine, simmer all together half an hour: then take our your tongue, strain the gravy, put it with the tongue in the the stew-pan again, beat up the yolks of two eggs, a little grated nutmeg, a piece of butter as big as a walnut rolled in flour, shake all together for four or five minutes, dish it up, and send it to table.

To stew Neats Tongues whole.

Take two tongues, let them stew in water just to cover them for two hours, then peel them, put them in again with a pint of strong gravy, half a pint of white wine, a bundle of sweet herbs, a little pepper and salt, some mace, cloves, and whole pepper tied in a muslin rag, a spoonful of capers chopped, turnips and carrots sliced, and a piece of butter rolled in flour; let all stew together very softly over a slow fire for two hours, then take out the spice and sweet herbs, and send it to table. You may leave out the turnips and carrots, or boil them by themselves, and lay them in a dish, just as you like.

To roast a Leg of Mutton with Oysters or Cockles.

Take a leg about two or three days killed, stuff it all over with oysters, and roast it. Garnish with horse-radish.

To make a Mutton Hash.

Cut your mutton in little bits as thin as you can; strew a little flour over it, have ready some gravy (enough for sauce) wherein sweet herbs, onion, pepper and salt, have been boiled; strain it, put in your meat, with a little piece of butter rolled in flour, and a little salt a shalot cut fine, a few capers and gerkins chopped fine; toss all together for a minute or two; have ready some bread toasted and cut into thin sippets, lay them round the dish, and pour in your hash. Garnish your dish with pickles and horse-radish.

Note, Some love a glass of red wine, or walnut pickle. You may put just what you will into a hash. If the sippets are toasted it is better.

To dress Pigs Petty-toes.

Put your petty-toes into a sauce-pan with half a pint of water, a blade of mace, a little whole pepper, a bundle of sweet herbs, and an onion. Let them boil five minutes, then take out the liver, lights, and heart, mince them very fine, grate a little nutmeg over them, and shake a little flour on them; let the feet do till they are tender, then take them out and strain the liquor, put all together with a little, salt and a piece of butter as big as a walnut, shake the saucepan often, let it simmer five or six minutes, then cut some toasted sippets and lay round the dish, lay the mince-meat and sauce in the middle, and the petty-toes split round it. You may add the juice of half a lemon, or a very little vinegar.

To dress a Leg of Mutton to eat like Venison.

Take a hind quarter of mutton, and cut the leg in the shape of a haunch of venison; save the blood of the sheep, and steep it for five or six hours, then take it out, and roll it in three or four sheets of white paper well buttered on the inside, tie it with a packthread, and roast it, basting it with good beef dripping or butter. It will take two hours at a good fire, for your mutton must be fat and thick. About five or six minutes before you take it up, take off the paper, baste it with a piece of butter, and shake a little flour over it to make it have a fine froth, and then have a little good drawn gravy in a bason, and sweet sauce in another. Do not garnish with any thing.

Baked Mutton Chops.

Take a loin or neck of mutton, cut it into steaks, put some pepper and salt over it, butter your dish, and lay in your steaks; then take a quart of milk, six eggs beat up fine, and four spoonfuls of flour; beat your flour and eggs in a little milk first, and then put the rest to it; put in a little beaten ginger, and a little salt. Pour this over the steaks, and send it to the oven; an hour and an half will bake it.

To fry a Loin of Lamb.

Cut your lamb into chops, rub it over on both sides with the yolk of an egg, and sprinkle some bread crumbs, a little parsley, thyme, marjoram, and winter savory chopped very fine, and a little lemon peel chopped fine, fry it in butter of a nice light brown, send it up in a dish by itself. Garnish with a good deal of fried parsley.

To make a Ragoo of Lamb.

Take a fore-quarter of lamb, cut the knuckle-bone off, lard it with little thin bits of bacon, flour it, fry it of a fine brown and then put it into an earthen pot or stew-pan: put to it a quart of broth or good gravy, a bundle of herbs, a little mace, two or three cloves, and a little whole pepper; cover it close, and let it stew pretty fast for half an hour, pour the liquor all out, strain it, keep the lamb hot in the pot till the sauce is ready. Take half a pint of oysters, flour them fry them brown, drain out all the fat clean that you fried them in, skim all the fat of the gravy; then pour into it the oysters, put in an anchovy, and two spoonfuls of either red or white wine; boil all together till there is just enough for sauce, add some fresh mushrooms (if you can get them) and some pickled ones, with a spoonful of the pickle, or the juice of half a lemon. Lay your lamb in the dish, and pour the sauce over it. Garnish with lemon

To stew a Lamb's or Calf's Head.

First wash it, and pick it very clean, lay it in water for an hour, take out the brains, and with a sharp penknife carefully take out the bones and the tongue, but be careful you do not break the meat; then take out the two eyes; and take two pounds of veal and two pounds of beef suet, a very little thyme, a good piece of lemon-peel minced, a nutmeg grated, and two anchovies: chop all very well together; grate two stale rolls, and mix all together with the yolks of four eggs: save enough of this meat to make about twenty balls; take half a pint of fresh mushrooms, clean peeled and washed, the yolks of six eggs chopped, half a pint oysters clean washed; or pickled cockles; mix all these together but first stew your oysters, and put to it two quarts of gravy, with a blade or two of mace. It will be proper to tie the head with packthread, cover it close, and let it stew two hours: in the mean time beat up the brains with some lemon-peel cut fine, a little parsley chopped, half a nutmeg grated, and the yolk of an egg; have some dripping boiling, fry half the brains in little cakes, and fry the balls, keep them both hot by the fire; take half an ounce of truffles and morels, then strain the gravy the head was stewed in, put the truffles and morels to it with the liquor, and a few mushrooms ? boil all together, then put in the rest of the brains that are not fried, stew them together for a minute or two, pour it over the head, and lay the fried brains and balls round it. Garnish with lemon. You may fry about twelve oysters.

To dress Sweet breads.

Do not put any water or gravy into the stew-pan, but put the same veal and bacon over the sweetbreads, and season as under directed; cover them close, put fire over as well as under, and when they are enough, take out the sweetbreads; put in a ladleful of gravy, boil it, and strain it, skim off all the fat, let it boil till it jellies, then put in the sweetbreads to glaze: lay essence of ham in the dish, and lay the sweetbreads upon it; or make a very rich gravy with mushrooms, truffles and, morels, a glass of white wine, and two spoonfuls of catchup. Garnish with cocks-combs forced and stewed in the gravy.

Note, You may add to the first, truffles, morels, mushrooms, cocks-combs, palates, artichoke bottoms, two spoonfuls of white wine, two of catch-up, or just as you please.

N. B. There are many ways of dressing sweetbreads: you may lard them with thin slips of bacon, and roast them, with what sauce you please; or you may marinate them, cut them into thin slices, flour them and fry them. Serve them up with fried parsley, and either butter or gravy. Garnish with lemon.

To broil a Haunch or Neck of Venison.

Lay it in salt for a week, then boil it in a cloth well floured; for every pound of venison allow a quarter of an hour for the boiling. For sauce you must boil some cauliflowers, pulled into little sprigs, in milk and water, some fine white cabbage, some turnips cut into dice, with some beet-root cut into long narrow pieces, about an inch and a half long, and half an inch thick: lay a sprig of cauliflower, add some of the turnips mashed with some cream and a little butter; let your cabbage be boiled, and then beat in a saucepan with a piece of butter and salt, lay that next the cauliflower, then the turnips, then cabbage, and so on till the dish is full ; place the beet-root here and there, just as you fancy ; it looks very pretty, and is a fine dish. Have a little melted butter in a cup, if wanted.

Note, A leg of mutton cut venison fashion, and dressed the same way, is a pretty dish ; or a fine neck, with the scrag cut off. This eats well boiled, or hashed, with gravy and sweet sauce, the next day.

To roast Tripe.

Cut your tripe in two square pieces, somewhat long ; have a force meat made of crumbs of bread, pepper, salt nutmeg, sweet herbs, lemon peel, and the yolks of eggs, mixed all together ; spread in on the fat side of the tripe, and lay the other fat side next it ; then roll it as light as you can, and tie it with a packthread ; spit it, roast it, and baste it with butter ; when roasted, lay it in your dish, and for sauce melt some butter, and add what drops from the tripe. Boil it together, and garnish with raspings.

TO DRESS POULTRY.

To roast a Turkey.

The best way to roast a turkey is to loosen the skin on the breast of the turkey, and fill it with force-meat, made thus take a quarter of a pound of beef-suet, as many crumbs of bread, a little lemon peel, an anchovy, some nutmeg, pepper, parsley, and a little thyme. Chop and beat them all together, mix them with the yolk of an egg, and stuff up the breast ; when you have no suet, butter will do : or you may make your force-meat thus: spread bread and butter thin, and grate some nutmeg over it; when you have enough roll it up, and stuff the breast of the turkey; then roast it of a fine brown, but be sure to pin some white paper on the breast till it is near enough. You must have good gravy in the dish, and bread-sauce, made thus: take a good piece of crumb, put it into a pint of water, with a blade or two of mace, two or three cloves, and some whole pepper. Boil it up five or six times, then with a spoon take out the spice you had before put in, and then you must pour off the water, (you may boil an onion in it, if you please); then beat up the bread with a good piece of butter and a little salt. Or onion-sauce made thus: take some onions, peel them and cut them into thin slices, and boil them half an hour in milk and water; then drain the water from, and beat them up with a good piece of butter; shake a little flour in, and stir it all together with a little cream, if you have it, (or milk will do); put the sauce into boats, and garnish with lemon.

Another way to make sauce: take half a pint of oysters, strain the liquor, and put the oysters with the liquor into a sauce-pan, with a blade or two of mace, let them just lump, then pour in a glass of white-wine, let it boil once, and thicken it with a piece of butter rolled in flour. Serve this up in a bason by itself, with good gravy in the dish for every body does not love oyster-sauce. This makes a pretty side-dish for supper, or a corner-dish of a table for dinner. If you chafe it in a dish, add half a pint of gravy to it, and boil it up together. This sauce is good either with boiled or roasted turkies or fowls; but you may leave the gravy out, adding as much butter as will do for sauce, and garnishing with lemon.

Another bread-sauce. Take some crumbs of

bread, rubbed through a fine cullender, put to it a pint of milk, a little butter, and some salt, a few corns of white pepper, and an onion; boil them for fifteen minutes, take out the onion and beat it up well, then toss it up, and put it in your sauce-boats.

To make Mushroom-sauce for white Fowls of all Sorts.

Take a quart of fresh mushrooms, well cleaned and washed, cut them in two, put them in a stew-pan, with a little butter, a blade of mace, and a little salt; stew it gently for an hour; then add a pint of cream and the yolks of two eggs beat very well; and keep stirring it till it boils up; then squeeze half a lemon, put it over your fowls, or turkies, or in basons, or in a dish, with a piece of French bread first buttered, then toasted brown, and just dip it in boiling water; put it in the dish, and the mushrooms over.

Mushroom-sauce for white Fowls boiled.

Take half a pint of cream, and a quarter of a pound of butter, stir them together one way till it is thick; then add a spoonful of mushroom pickle, pickled mushrooms, or fresh, if you have them. Garnish only with lemon.

To make Celery-sauce, either for roasted or boiled Fowls, Turkies, Patridges, or any other Game.

Take a large bunch of celery, wash and pare it very clean, cut it into little thin bits, and boil it softly in a little water till it is tender; then add a little beaten mace, some nutmeg, pepper, and salt, thickened with a good piece of butter rolled in flour; then boil it up, and pour it into your dish.

You may make it with cream thus: boil your celery as above, and add some mace, nutmeg, a piece of butter as big as a walnut rolled in flour, and a half pint of cream; boil them all together.

To make Egg sauce proper for roasted Chickens.

Melt your butter thick and fine, chop two or three hard-boiled eggs fine, put them into a bason, pour the butter over them, and have good gravy in the dish.

To stew a Turkey Brown.

Take your turkey, after it is nicely picked and drawn, fill the skin of the breast with force-meat, and put an anchovy, a shalot, and a little thyme in the belly, lard the breast with bacon; then put a good piece of butter in the stew-pan, flour the turkey, and fry it just of a fine brown; then take it out, and put it into a deep stew-pan, or little pot, that will just hold it, and put in as much gravy as will barely cover it, a glass of white-wine, some whole pepper, mace, two or three cloves, and a little bundle of sweet herbs; cover it close, and stew it for an hour; then take up the turkey, and keep it hot covered by the fire, and boil the sauce to about a pint, strain it off, add the yolks of two eggs, and a piece of butter rolled in flour; stir it till it is thick, and then lay your turkey in the dish, and pour your sauce over it. You may have ready some little French loaves, about the bigness of an egg, cut off the tops, and take out the crumb, then fry them of a fine brown, fill them with stewed oysters, lay them round the dish and garnish with lemon.

To force a Fowl.

Take a good fowl, pick and draw it, slit the skin down the back, and take the flesh from the bones, mince it very small, and mix it with one pound of beef-suet shred, a pint of large oysters chopped, two anchovies, a shalot, a little grated bread, and some sweet herbs; shred all this very well, mix them together, and make it up with the yolks of eggs; then turn all these ingredients on the bones again, and draw the skin over again, then sew up the back. and either boil the fowl in a bladder an hour and a quarter, or roast it; then stew some more oysters in gravy, bruise in a little of your force-meat, mix it up with a little fresh butter, and a very little flour; then give it a boil, lay your fowl in the dish, and your the sauce over it. Garnish with lemon,

To roast a Fowl wih Chesnuts.

First take some chesnuts, roast them very carefully, so as not to burn them, take off the skin, and peel them, take about a dozen of them cut small, and bruise them in a mortar; par-boil the liver of the fowl, bruise it, cut about a quarter of a pound of ham or bacon, and pound it; them all together, with a good deal of parsley chopped small, a little sweet herbs, some mace, pepper, salt, and nutmeg; mix these together, and put into your fowl, and roast it. The best way of doing it is to tie the neck, and hang it up by the legs to roast with a string and baste it with butter. For sauce take the rest of the chesnuts peeled and skinned, put them into some good gravy, with a little white wine, and thicken it with a piece of butter rolled in flour; then take up your fowl, lay it in the dish, and pour in the sauce. Garnish with lemon.

Mutton Chops in disguise.

Take as many mutton chops as you want, rub them with pepper, salt, nutmeg, and a little parsley; roll each chop in half a sheet of white paper, well buttered on the inside, and rolled on each end close. Have some hog's lard or beef dripping boiling in a stew-pan, put in the steaks, fry them of a fine brown, lay them in your dish, and garnish with fried parsley; throw some all over; have a little good gravy in a cup; but take great care you do not break the paper, nor have any fat in the dish, but let them be well drained.

To broil Chickens.

Slit them down the back, and season them with pepper and salt, lay them on a very clear fire, and at a great distance. Let the inside lie next the fire till it is above half done; then turn them, and take great care the fleshy side does not burn, and let them be of a fine brown. Let your sauce be good gravy, with mushrooms, and garnish with lemon and the livers broiled, the gizzards cut, slashed, and broiled with pepper and salt.

Or this sauce; take a handful of sorrel, dipped in boiling water, drain it, and have ready half a pint of good gravy, a shalot shred small, and some parsley boiled very green; thicken it with a piece of butter rolled in flour, and add a glass of red-wine, then lay your sorrel in heaps round the fowls, and pour the sauce over them. Garnish with lemon.

Note, You may make just what sauce you fancy.

A pretty Way of stewing Chickens.

Take two fine chickens, half boil them, then take them up in a pewter or silver dish, if you have one, cut up your fowls, and separate all the joint bones one from another, and then take out the breast-bones. If there is not liquor enough from the fowls, add a few spoonfuls of the water they were boiled in, put in a blade of mace, and a little salt; cover it close with another dish, set it over a stove or chafing dish of coals, let it stew till the chickens are enough, and then send them hot to the table in the same dish they were stewed in.

Note, This is a very pretty dish for any sick person, or for a lying in lady. For change, it is better than butter, and the sauce is very agreeable and pretty.

N. B. You may do rabbits, patridges, or moor-game, this way.

Chickens with tongues. A good Dish for a great deal of Company.

Take six small chickens, boiled very white, six hogs tongues, boiled and peeled, a cauliflower boiled very white in milk and water whole, and a good deal of spinach boiled green ; then lay your cauliflower in the middle, then your chickens close all round, and the tongue round them with the roots outward, and the spinach in little heaps between the tongues. Garnish with little pieces of bacon toasted; and lay a little piece on each of the tongues.

To boil a Duck or a Rabbit with Onions.

Boil your duck or rabbit in a good deal of water ; be sure to skim your water, for there will always rise a scum, which, if it boils down, will discolour your fowls, &c. They will take about half an hour boiling. For sauce, your onions must be peeled, and throw them into water as you peel them, then cut them into thin slices, boil them in milk and water, and skim the liquor. Half an hour will boil them. Throw them into a clean sieve to drain, put them into a sauce-pan, and chop them small, shake in a little flour, put to them two or three spoonfuls of cream, a good piece of butter, stew all together over the fire till they are thick and fine, lay the duck or rabbit in the dish, and pour the sauce all over ; if a rabbit you must cut off the head, cut it in two, and lay it on each side of the dish.

Or you may make this sauce for change : take one large onion, cut it small, half a handful of parſley clean waſhed and picked, chop it ſmall, a lettuce cut ſmall, a quarter of a pint of good gravy, a good piece of butter rolled in a little flour; add a little juice of lemon, a little pepper and ſalt; let all ſtew together for half an hour, then add two ſpoonfuls of red wine. This ſauce is moſt proper for ducks; lay your duck in the diſh, and pour your ſauce over it.

To dreſs a Duck with green peas.

Put a deep ſtew-pan over the fire, with a piece of freſh butter; ſinge your duck and flour it, turn it in the pan two or three minutes, then pour out all the fat, but let the duck remain in the pan: put to it a pint of good gravy, a pint of peas, two lettuces cut ſmall, a ſmall bundle of ſweet herbs, a little pepper and ſalt, cover them cloſe, and let them ſtew for half an hour, now and then give the pan a ſhake; when they are juſt done, grate in a little nutmeg, and put in a very little beaten mace, and thicken it either with a piece of butter rolled in flour, or the yolk of an egg beat up with two or three ſpoonfuls of cream; ſhake it all together for three or four minutes, take out the ſweet herbs lay the duck in the diſh, and pour the ſauce over it. You may garniſh with boiled mint chopped, or let it alone.

Directions for roaſting a Gooſe.

Take ſome ſage, waſh and pick it clean, and an onion, chop them very fine, with ſome pepper and ſalt, and put them into the belly; let your gooſe be clean picked, and wiped dry with a dry cloth, inſide and out; put it down to the fire, and roaſt it brown: one hour will roaſt a large gooſe, three quarters of an hour a ſmall one. Serve it in your diſh with ſome brown gravy, apple ſauce in a boat, and ſome gravy in another.

To stew Giblets.

Let them be nicely scalded and picked, cut the pinions in two, cut the head and the neck and legs in two, and the gizzards in four; wash them very clean, put them into a stew pan or soup pot, with three pounds of scrag of veal, just cover them with water; let them boil up, take all the scum clean off; then put three onions, two turnips, one carrot, a little thyme and parsley stew them till they are tender, strain them through a sieve, wash the giblets clean with some warm water out of the herbs &c. then take a piece of butter as big as a large walnut, put it in a stew-pan, melt it, and put in a large spoonful of flour keep it stirring till it is smooth, then put in your broth and giblets, stew them for a quarter of an hour; season with salt: or you may add a gill of Lisbon, and just before you serve them up chop a handful of green parsley and put in; give them a boil up, and serve them in a tureen or soup-dish.

N. B. Three pair will make a handsome tureen full.

To boil Pigeons.

Boil them by themselves for fifteen minutes; then boil a handsome square piece of bacon, and lay in the middle, stew some spinach to lay round and lay the pigeons on the spinach. Garnish your dish with parsley, laid in a plate before the fire to crisp. Or you may lay one pigeon in the middle, and the rest round, and the spinach between each pigeon, and a slice of bacon on each pigeon. Garnish with slices of bacon and melted butter in a cup.

To jug Pigeons.

Pull, crop, and draw pigeons but do not wash them; save the livers and put them in scalding water and set them on the fire for a minute or two; then take them out and mince them small, and bruise them with the back of a spoon; mix them with a little pepper, salt, grated nutmeg, and lemon-peel shred very fine, chopped parsley, and two yolks of eggs very hard; bruise them as you do the liver, and put as much suet as liver, shaved exceedingly fine, and as much grated bread; work these together with raw eggs, and roll it in fresh butter; put a piece into the crops and bellies, and sew up the necks and vents; then dip your pigeons in water, and season them with pepper and salt as for a pie, put them in your jug, with a piece of celery, stop them close, and set them in a kettle of cold water; first cover them close, and lay a tile on the top of the jug and let it boil three hours; then take them out of the jug, and lay them in the dish, take out the celery, put in a piece of butter rolled in flour, shake it about till it is thick, and pour it on your pigeons. Garnish with lemon.

To stew Pigeons.

Season your pigeons with pepper and salt, a few cloves and mace, and some sweet herbs; wrap this seasoning up in a piece of butter, and put it in their bellies, then tie up the neck and vent, and half roast them; put them in a stew-pan, with a quart of good gravy, a little white-wine, a few pepper corns, three or four blades of mace, a bit of lemon, a bunch of sweet herbs, and a small onion; stew them gently till they are enough; then take the pigeons out, and strain the liquor through a sieve; skim it, and thicken it in your stew-pan, put in the pigeons, with some pickled mushrooms and oysters, stew it five minutes, and put the pigeons in a dish, and the sauce over.

To roast Partridges.

Let them be nicely roasted, but not too much;

baste them gently with a little butter, and drudge with flour, sprinkle a little salt on, and froth them nicely up; have good gravy in the dish, with bread sauce in a boat, made thus: take about a handful or two of crumbs of bread, put in a pint of milk or more, a small whole onion, a little whole white pepper, a little salt, and a bit of butter, boil it all well up; then take the onion out, and beat it well with a spoon: take poverroy-sauce in a boat, made thus; chop four shalots fine, a gill of good gravy, and a spoonful of vinegar, a little pepper and salt; boil them up one minute, then put it in a boat.

To roast Pheasants.

Pick and draw your pheasants, and singe them; lard one with bacon, but not the other; spit them, roast them fine and paper them all over the breast; when they are just done, flour and baste them with a little nice butter, and let them have a fine white froth: then take them up, and pour good gravy in the dish, and bread sauce in plates.

Or you may put water-cresses with gravy in the dish, and lay the cresses under the pheasants.

Or you may make celery-sauce, stewed tender, strained and mixed with cream, and poured into the dish.

If you have but one pheasant, take a large fowl about the bigness of a pheasant, pick it nicely with the head on, draw it, and truss it with the head turned as you do a pheasant's, lard the fowl all over the breast and legs with a large piece of bacon cut in little pieces: when roasted, put them both in a dish, and no body will know it. They will take an hour doing, as the fire must not be too brisk. A Frenchman would order fish sauce to them, but then you spoil your pheasants.

A stewed Pheasant.

Take your pheasant and stew it in veal gravy;

take artichoke-bottoms parboiled, some chesnuts roasted and blanched: when your pheasant is enough, (but it must stew till there is just enough for sauce, then skim it,) put in the chesnuts and artichoke-bottoms, a little beaten mace, pepper and salt enough to season it, and a glass of white-wine; if you do not think it thick enough, thicken it with a little piece of butter rolled in flour; squeeze in a lemon, pour the sauce over the pheasants, and have some force-meat balls fried and put into the dish.

Note, A good fowl will do full as well, trussed with the head on, like a pheasant. You may fry sausages instead of force-meat balls.

To boil a pheasant.

Take a fine pheasant, boil it in a good deal of water, keep your water boiling; half an hour will do a small one, and three quarters of an hour a large one. Let your sauce be celery stewed and thickened with cream, and a little piece of butter rolled in flour; take up the pheasant, and pour the sauce all over. Garnish with lemon. Observe to stew your celery so, that the liquor will not be all wasted away before you put your cream in; if it wants salt put in some to your palate.

To roast Snipes or Woodcocks.

Spit them on a small bird-spit, flour and baste them with a piece of butter, then have ready a slice of bread toasted brown, lay it in a dish, and set it under the snipes for the trail to drop on; when they are enough, take them up and lay them on a toast; have ready for two snipes, a quarter of a pint of good gravy and butter; pour it into the dish, and set it over a chafing dish two or three minutes. Garnish with lemon, and send them hot to table.

To dress Ruffs and Reiss.

They are Lincolnshire birds, and you may fatten them as you do chickens, with white bread, milk, and sugar: they feed fast, and will die in their fat, if not killed in time: truss them cross-legged, as you do a snipe, spit them the same way, but you must gut them; and must have good gravy in the dish thickened with butter and toast under them. Serve them up quick.

To dress Larks.

Spit them on a bird-spit, tie them on another, and roast them; baste them gently with butter, and strew crumbs of bread on them till they are almost done, then brown them; put them in a dish with fried crumbs of bread round them.

To dress Plovers.

To two plovers take two artichoke-bottoms, boiled, some chesnuts roasted and blanched, some skirrets boiled, cut all very small, mix with it some marrow or beef-suet, the yolks of two hard eggs, chop all together; season with pepper salt, nutmeg, and a little sweet herbs: fill the bodies of the plovers, lay them in a sauce-pan, put to them a pint of gravy, a glass of white-wine, a blade or two of mace, some roasted chesnuts blanched, and artichoke-bottoms cut into quarters, two or three yolks of eggs, and a little juice of lemon; cover them close, and let them stew very softly an hour. If you find the sauce is not thick enough, take a piece of butter rolled in flour, and put it into the sauce; shake it round, and when it is thick take up your plovers, and pour the sauce over them. Garnish with roasted chesnuts.

Ducks are very good done this way.

Or you may roast your plovers as you do any other fowl, and have gravy-sauce in the dish.

Or boil them in good celery-sauce, either white or brown just as you like.

The same way you may dress wigeons.

N. B. The best way to dress plovers, is to roast them the same as woodcocks, with a toast under them, and gravy and butter.

To dress a Jugged Hare.

Cut it into little pieces, lard them here and there with little slips of bacon, season them with a very little pepper and salt, put them into an earthen jug, with a blade or two of mace, an onion stuck with cloves, and a bundle of sweet herbs; cover the jug or jar you do it in so close that nothing can get in, then set it in a pot of boiling water, and three hours will do it; then turn it out into the dish, and take out the onion and sweet herbs, and send it to table hot. If you do not like it larded, leave it out.

To boil Rabbits.

Truss them for boiling, boil them quick and white, put them into a dish, with onion-sauce over them, made thus: take as many onions as you think will cover them; peel them, and boil them very tender, strain them off, squeeze them very dry, and chop them very fine; put them into a stew-pan, with a piece of butter, half a pint of cream, a little salt, and shake in a little flour; stir them well over a gentle fire till the butter is melted; then put them over your rabbits; or a sauce made thus: blanch the livers, and chop them very fine, with some parsley blanched and chopped; mix them with melted butter, and put it over; or with gravy and butter.

Cod Sounds broiled with Gravy.

Scald them in hot water, and rub them with salt well; blanch them; that is take off the black dirty skin, then set them on in cold water, and let them simmer till they begin to be tender; take them out and flour them, and broil them on the gridiron. In the mean time take a little good gravy, a little mustard, a little bit of butter rolled in flour, give it a boil, season it with pepper and salt. Lay the sounds in your dish and pour your sauce over them.

Fried Sausages.

Take half a pound of sausages, and six apples, slice four about as thick as a crown, cut the other two in quarters, fry them with the sausages of a fine light brown, lay the sausages in the middle of the dish, and the apples round. Garnish with the quartered apples.

Stewed cabbage and sausages fried is a good dish; then heat cold peas-pudding in the pan, lay it in the dish and the sausages round, heap the pudding in the middle, and lay the sausages all round thick up, edge-ways, and one in the middle at length.

Collops and Eggs.

Cut either bacon, pickled beef, or hung mutton, into thin slices, broil them nicely, lay them in a dish before the fire, have ready a stew-pan of water boiling, break as many eggs as you have collops, break them one by one in a cup, and pour them into the stew-pan. When the whites of the eggs begin to harden, and all look of a clear white, take them up one by one in an egg-slice, and lay them on the collops.

To dress cold Fowl or Pigeon.

Cut them in four quarters, beat up an egg or two according to what you dress, grate a little nutmeg in, a little salt, some parsley chopped, a few crumbs of bread; beat them well together, dip them in this batter, and have ready some dripping hot in a stew-pan, in which fry them of a fine light brown; have ready a little good gravy, thickened with a little flour, mixed with a spoonful of catchup: lay the fry in the dish, and pour the sauce over. Garnish with lemon, and a few mushrooms, if you have any. A cold rabbit eats well done thus.

To mince Veal.

Cut your veal as fine as possible, but do not chop it; grate a little nutmeg over it, shred a little lemon-peel very fine, throw a very little salt on it, dredge a little flour over it. To a large plate of veal take four or five spoonfuls of water, let it boil, then put in the veal, with a piece of butter as big as an egg, stir it well together; when it is all thorough hot, it is enough. Have ready a very thin piece of bread toasted brown, cut it into three corner sippets, lay it round the plate, and pour in the veal. Just before you pour it in, squeeze in half a lemon, or half a spoonful of vinegar. Garnish with lemon. You may put gravy in the room of water, if you love it strong; but it is better without.

To fry cold Veal.

Cut it in pieces about as thick as half a crown, and as long as you please, dip them in the yolk of an egg, and then in crumbs of bread, with a few sweet herbs and shred lemon-peel in it; grate a little nutmeg over them, and fry them in fresh butter. The butter must be hot, just enough to fry them in: in the mean time, make a little gravy of the bone of the veal. When the meat is fried, take it out with a fork, and lay it in a dish before the fire; then shake a little flour into the pan, and stir it round; then put in a little gravy, squeeze in a little lemon, and pour it over the veal. Garnish with lemon.

To toss up cold Veal White.

Cut the veal into little thin bits, put milk enough to it for sauce, grate in a little nutmeg, a very little salt, a little piece of butter rolled in flour : to half a pint of milk, the yolks of two eggs well beat, a spoonful of mushroom pickle ; stir all together till it is thick, then pour it into your dish, and Garnish with lemon.

Cold fowl skinned, and done this way, eats well ; or the best end of a cold breast of veal ; first fry it, drain it from the fat, then pour this sauce to it.

To hash cold Mutton.

Cut your mutton with a very sharp knife into very little bits, as thin as possible ; then boil the bones with an onion, a few sweet herbs, a blade of mace, a very little whole pepper, a little salt, a piece of crust toasted very crisp ; let it boil till there is just enough for sauce, strain it, and put it into a sauce-pan with a piece of butter rolled in flour ; put in the meat ; when it is very hot it is enough. Have ready some thin bread toasted brown, cut three-corner-ways, lay them round the dish, and pour in the hash. As to walnut pickle, and all sorts of pickles, you must put in according to your fancy. Garnish with pickles. Some love a small onion peeled, and cut very small, and done in the hash.

To hash Mutton like Venison.

Cut it very thin as above ; boil the bones as above ; strain the liquor, where there is just enough for the hash ; to a quarter of a pint of gravy put a large spoonful of red wine, an onion peeled and chopped fine, a very little lemon-peel shred fine, a piece of butter, as big as a small walnut, rolled in flour ; put it into a sauce pan with the meat, shake it all together, and when it is thoroughly hot, pour it into your dish. Hash beef the same way.

To make Collops of cold Beef.

If you have any cold inside of a sirloin of beef, take off all the fat, cut it very thin in little bits, cut an onion very small, boil as much water or gravy as you think will do for sauce; season it with a little pepper and salt, and a bundle of sweet herbs. Let the water boil, then put in the meat, with a good piece of butter rolled in flour, shake it round, and stir it. When the sauce is thick, and the meat done, take out the sweet herbs, and pour it into your dish. They do better than fresh meat.

To make Salmagundy.

Mince two chickens, either boiled or roasted, very fine, or veal, if you please: also mince the yolks of hard eggs very small, and mince the whites very small by themselves; shred the pulp of two or three lemons very small, then lay in your dish a layer of mince-meat, and a layer of yolks of eggs, a layer of whites, a layer of anchovies, a layer of your shred lemon pulp, a layer of pickles, a layer of sorrel, a layer of spinach, and shalots shred small. When you have filled a dish with the ingredients, set an orange or lemon on the top; then garnish with horse-radish scraped, barberries, and sliced lemon. Beat up some oil with the juice of lemon, salt, and mustard, thick, and serve it up for a second course, side dish, or middle-dish, for supper.

To make Essence of Ham.

Take a ham, and cut off all the fat, cut the lean in thin pieces, and lay them in the bottom of your stew-pan: put over them six onions sliced, two carrots, and one parsnip, two or three leeks, a few fresh mushrooms, a little parsley and sweet herbs, four or five shalots, and some cloves and mace; put a little water at the bottom, set it on a gentle stove till it begins to stick; then put in a gallon of veal broth to a ham of fourteen pounds, (more or less broth, according to the size of the ham;) let it stew very gently for one hour, then strain it off, and put it away for use.

Rules to be observed in all Made-Dishes.

First, that the stew-pans, or sauce-pans, and covers, be very clean, free from sand, and well tinned; and that all the white sauces have a little tartness and be very smooth, and of a fine thickness; and all the time any white sauce is over the fire, keep stirring it one way.

And as to drawn sauce, take great care no fat swims at the top, but that it be all smooth alike, and about as thick as good cream, and not to taste of one thing more then another. As to pepper and salt, season to your palate, but do not put too much of either, for that will take away the fine flavor of every thing. As to most made-dishes, you may put in what you think proper to enlarge it, or make it good; as mushrooms pickled, dried, fresh, or powdered, truffles, morels, cocks-combs stewed, ox-palates cut in small bits, artichoke bottoms, either pickled, fresh, boiled, or dried ones softened in warm water, each cut in four pieces, asparagus tops. the yolks of hard eggs, force-meat balls, &c. The best things to give a sauce tartness, are mushroom pickle, white walnut pickle, elder vinegar or lemon juice.

OF SOUPS AND BROTHS.

To make strong Broth for Soup and Gravy.

Take a shin of beef, a knuckle of veal, and a scrag of mutton, put them in five gallons of water ; then let it boil up, skim it clean, and season it with six large onions, four good leeks, four heads of celery, two carrots, two turnips, a bundle of sweet herbs, six cloves, a dozen corns of all-spice, and some salt ; skim it very clean, and let it stew gently for six hours ; then strain it off, and put it by for use.

When you want very strong gravy, take a slice of bacon, lay it in a stew-pan ; take a pound of beef, cut it thin, lay it on the bacon, slice a good peace of carrot in, an onion sliced, a good crust of bread, a few sweet herbs, a little mace, cloves, nutmeg, and whole pepper, an anchovy ; cover it, and set it on a slow fire five or six minutes, and pour in a quart of the above gravy ; cover it close and let it boil softly till half is wasted. This will be a rich, high brown sauce for fish, fowl, or ragoo.

Gravy for White Sauce.

Take a pound of any part of the veal, cut it into small pieces, boil it in a quart of water, with an onion, a blade of mace, two cloves, and a few whole pepper-corns. Boil it till it is as rich as you would have it.

Gravy for Turkey, Fowl, or Ragoo.

Take a pound of lean beef, cut and hack it well, then flour it well, put a piece of butter as big as a hen's egg in a stew-pan ; when it is melted, put in your beef, fry it on all sides a little brown, then pour in three pints of boiling water, and a bundle of sweet herbs two or three blades of mace, three or four cloves, twelve whole pepper-corns, a little bit of carrot, a little piece of crust of bread toasted brown ; cover it close, and let it boil till there is about a pint or less ; then season it with salt, and strain it off.

Gravy for a Fowl, when you have no Meat nor Gravy ready.

Take the neck, liver, and gizzard, boil them in half a pint of water, with a little piece of bread toasted brown, a little pepper and salt, and a little bit of thyme. Let them boil till there is about a quarter of a pint, then pour in half a glass of red-wine, boil it and strain it, then bruise the liver well in, and strain it again, thicken it with a little piece of butter rolled in flour, and it will be very good.

An ox's kidney makes good gravy, cut all to pieces, and boiled with spice, &c. as in the foregoing receipts.

You have a receipt in the beginning of the book, for gravies.

To make Mutton or Veal Gravy.

Cut and hack your veal well, set it on the fire with water, sweet herbs, mace, and pepper. Let it boil till it is as good as you would have it, then strain it off. Your fine cooks always, if they can, chop a partridge or two and put into gravies.

To make a strong Fish Gravy.

Take two or three eels, or any fish you have, skin or scale them, gut them and wash them from grit, cut them into little pieces, put them into a sauce-pan, cover them with water, a little crust of bread toasted brown, a blade or two of mace, and some whole pepper, a few sweet herbs and a very little bit of lemon-peel. Let it boil till it is rich and good, then have ready a piece of butter, according to your gravy; if a pint, as big as a walnut. Melt it in the sauce-pan, then shake in a little flour, and toss it about till it is brown, and then strain in the gravy to it. Let it boil a few minutes and it will be good.

To make strong Broth to keep for Use.

Take a part of a leg of beef, and the scrag end a neck of mutton, break the bones in pieces, and put to it as much water as will cover it, and a little salt; and when it boils skim it clean, and put in a whole onion stuck with cloves, a bunch of sweet herbs, some pepper, and a nutmeg quartered. Let these boil till the meat is boiled in pieces, and the strength boiled out of it; strain it out and keep it for use.

Green Peas-Soup.

Take a gallon of water, make it boil; then put in six onions, four turnips, two carrots, and two heads of celery cut in slices, four cloves, four blades of mace, four cabbage-lettuces cut small, stew them for an hour; then strain it off, and put in two quarts of old green peas, and boil them in the liquor till tender; then beat or bruise them, and mix them up with the broth, and rub them through a tammy or cloth, and put it in a clean pot, and boil it up fifteen minutes; season with pepper and salt to your liking; then put your soup in your tureen, with small dices of bread toasted very hard.

A Peas-Soup for Winter.

Take about four pounds of lean beef, cut it in small pieces, about a pound of lean bacon, or pickled pork, set it on the fire with two gallons of water, let it boil, and skim it well; then put in six onions, two turnips, one carrot, and four heads of celery cut small, twelve corns of all-spice, and put in a quart of split peas, boil it gently for three hours, then strain them through a sieve, and rub the peas well through; then put your soup in a clean pot, and put in some dried mint rubbed very fine to powder; cut the white of four heads of celery, and two turnips in dices, and boil them in a quart of water for fifteen minutes ; then strain them off, and put them in your soup ; take about a dozen of small rashers of bacon fried, and put them in your soup, season with pepper and salt to your liking ; boil it up for fifteen minutes, then put it in your tureen, with dices of bread fried very crisp.

Another way to make it.

When you boil a leg of pork, or a good piece of beef, save the liquor. When it is cold take off the fat ; the next day boil a leg of mutton, save the liquor, and when it is cold take off the fat, set it on the fire, with two quarts of peas. Let them boil till they are tender, then put in the pork or beef liquor, with the ingredients as above, and let it boil till it is as thick as you would have it, allowing for the boiling again ; then strain it off, and add the ingredients as above. You may make your soup of veal or mutton gravy if you please, that is, according to your fancy.

To make Mutton-Broth.

Take a neck of mutton about six pounds, cut it in two, boil the scrag in a gallon of water, skim it well, then put in a little bundle of sweet herbs, an onion, and a good crust of bread. Let it boil an hour, then put in the other part of the mutton, a turnip or two, some dried marigolds, a few shives chopped fine, a little parsley chopped small ; then put these in, about a quarter of an hour before your broth is enough. Season it with salt ; or you may put in a quarter of a pound of barley or rice at first. Some love it thickened with oatmeal, and some with bread ; and some love it seasoned with mace, instead of sweet herbs and onion. All this is fancy, and different palates. If you boil turnips for sauce, do not boil all in the pot, it makes the broth too strong of them, but boil them in a sauce-pan.

Beef Broth.

Take a leg of beef, crack the bone in two or three parts, wash it clean, put it in a pot with a gallon of water, skim it clean, then put in two or three blades of mace, a little bundle of parsley, and a good crust of bread. Let it boil till the beef is quite tender, and the sinews, toast some bread and cut it in dices, and put it in your tureen; lay in the meat, and pour the soup in.

To make Scotch Barley-Broth.

Take a leg of beef, chop it all to pieces, boil it in three gallons of water with a piece of carrot and a crust of bread, till it is half boiled away; then strain it off, and put it into the pot again with half a pound of barley, four or five heads of celery washed clean and cut small, a large onion, a bundle of sweet herbs, a little parsley chopped small, and a few marigolds. Let this boil an hour. Take a cock, or large fowl, clean picked and washed, and put into the pot; boil it till the broth is quite good, then season with salt, and send it to table, with the fowl in the middle. This broth is very good without the fowl. Take out the onion and sweet herbs before you send it to table.

Some make this broth with a sheep's head instead of a leg of beef, and it is very good: but you must chop the head all to pieces. The thick flank (about six pounds to six quarts of water) makes good broth: then put the barley in with the meat, first skim it well, boil it an hour very softly, then put in the above ingredients, with turnips and carrots clean scraped and pared, and cut in little pieces. Boil all together softly, till the broth is very good; then season it with salt, and send it to table, with the beef in the middle, turnips and carrots round, and pour the broth over all.

Rules to be observed in making Soups or Broths.

First take care the pots or sauce-pans, and covers, be very clean, and free from all grease and sand, and that they be well tinned, for fear of giving the broth and soups any brassy taste. If you have time to stew as softly as you can, it will both have a finer flavour, and the meat will be tenderer. But then observe, when you make soups or broth for present use, if it is to be done softly, do not put much more water than you intend to have soup or broth; and if you have the convenience of an earthen pan or pipkin, set it on wood embers till it boils, then skim it, and put in your seasoning; cover it close, and set it on embers, so that it may do very softly for some time, and both the meat and broths will be delicious. You must observe in all broths and soups that one thing does not taste more than another; but that the taste be equal, and it has a fine agreeable relish, according to what you design it for; and you must be sure, that all the greens and herbs you put in be cleaned, washed, and picked.

OF PUDDINGS.

An Oat-Pudding to bake.

Of oats decorticated take two pounds, and new milk enough to drown it, eight ounces of raisins of the sun stoned, an equal quantity of currants neatly picked, a pound of sweet suet finely shred, six new laid eggs well beat; season with nutmeg, beaten ginger, and salt; mix it all well together: it will make a better pudding than rice.

To make a Marrow Pudding.

Take a quart of cream or milk, and a quarter of a pound of Naples biscuit, put them on the fire in a stew-pan, and boil them up; then take the yolks of eight eggs, the whites of four beat up very fine, a little moist sugar, some marrow chopped, a small glass of brandy and sack, a very little orange flower-water; mix all well together, and put them on the fire, keep it stirring till it is thick, and put it away to get cold; then have ready your dish rimmed with puff-paste, put your stuff in, sprinkle some currants that have been well washed in cold water, and rubbed clean in a cloth, some marrow cut in slices, and some candied-lemon, orange, and citron, cut in shreds, and send it to the oven; three quarters of an hour will bake it: send it up hot.

A boiled Suet-Pudding.

Take a quart of milk, four spoonfuls of flour, a pound of suet shred small, four eggs, one spoonful of beaten ginger, a tea spoonful of salt; mix the eggs and flour with a pint of the milk very thick, and with the seasoning mix in the rest of the milk and suet. Let your batter be pretty thick, and boil it two hours.

A boiled Plumb Pudding.

Take a pound of suet cut in little pieces not too fine, a pound of currants, and a pound of raisins stoned, eight eggs, half the whites, half a nutmeg grated, and a tea-spoonful of beaten ginger, a pound of flour, a pint of milk: beat the eggs first, then half the milk, beat them together, and by degrees stir in the flour, then the suet, spice and fruit, and as much milk as will mix it well together very thick. Boil it five hours.

A Yorkshire Pudding.

Take a quart of milk, four eggs, and a little salt, make it up into a thick batter with flour, like pancake batter. You must have a good piece of meat at the fire; take a stew-pan and put some dripping in, set it on the fire; when it boils, pour in your pudding; let it bake on the fire till vothink it is nigh enough, then turn a plate upside down in the dripping-pan, that the dripping may not be blacked; set your stew-pan on it under your meat, and let the dripping drop on the pudding, and the heat of the fire come to it, to make it of a fine brown. When your meat is done and sent to table, drain all the fat from your pudding, and set it on the fire again to dry a little; then slide it as dry as you can into a dish; melt some butter, and pour it into a cup, and set it in the middle of the pudding. It is an excellent good pudding; the gravy of the meat eats well with it.

A Steak-Pudding.

Make a good crust, with suet shred fine with flour, and mix it up with cold water: season it with salt, and make a pretty stiff crust, about two pounds of suet to a quarter of a peck of flour. Let your steaks be either beef or mutton, well seasoned with pepper and salt; make it up as you do an apple-pudding, tie it in a cloth, and put it into the water boiling. If it be a large pudding, it will take five hours; if a small one, three hours. This is the best crust for an apple-pudding. Pigeons eat well this way.

Suet Dumplings.

Take a pint of milk, four eggs, a pound of suet, and a pound of currants, two tea spoonfuls of salt, three of ginger: first take half the milk, and mix it like a thick batter, then put the eggs, and the salt and ginger, then the rest of the milk by degrees, with the suet and currants, and flour, to make it like a light paste. When the water boils, make them in rolls as big as a large turkey's egg, with a little flour; then flat them, and throw them into boiling water. Move them softly, that they do not stick together; keep the water boiling all the time, and half an hour will boil them.

To make a Potatoe-Pudding.

Boil two pounds of potatoes, and beat them in a mortar fine, beat in half a pound of melted butter, boil it half an hour, pour melted butter over it, with a glass of white-wine, or the juice of a Seville orange, and throw sugar all over the pudding and dish.

To make an Orange-Pudding.

You must take sixteen yolks of eggs, beat them fine, mix them with half a pound of fresh butter melted, and half a pound of white sugar, half a pint of cream, a little rose-water, and a little nutmeg. Cut the peel of a fine large Seville orange so thin as none of the white appears, beat it fine in a mortar till it is like a paste, and by degrees mix in the above ingredients all together; then lay a puff paste all over the dish, pour in the ingredients, and bake it.

To make a Lemon-Pudding.

Take three lemons, and cut the rind off very thin, boil them in three separate waters till very tender, then pound them very fine in a mortar; have ready a quarter of a pound of Naples biscuit, boiled up in a quart of milk or cream; mix them and the lemon rind with it; beat up twelve yolks and six whites of eggs very fine, melt a quarter of a pound of fresh butter, half a pound of fine sugar, a little orange-flower-water; mix all well together, put it over the stove, and keep it stirring till it is thick, squeeze the juice of half a lemon in; put puff-paste round the rim of your dish, put the pudding stuff in, cut some candied sweet-meats and put over; bake it three quarters of an hour, and send it up hot.

To boil an Almond-Pudding.

Beat a pound of sweet-almonds as small as possible, with three spoonfuls of rose-water, and a gill of sack or white-wine, and mix in half a pound of fresh butter melted, with five yolks of eggs and two whites, a quart of cream, a quarter of a pound of sugar, half a nutmeg grated, one spoonful of flour, and three spoonfuls of crumbs of white bread; mix all well together, and boil it. It will take half an hour boiling.

To make a Sago-Pudding.

Let half a pound of sago be washed well in three or four hot waters, then put to it a quart of new milk, and let it boil together till it is thick; stir it carefully, (for it is apt to burn,) put in a stick of cinnamon when you set it on the fire; when it is boiled take it out; before you pour it out, stir in half a pound of fresh butter, then pour it into a pan, and beat up nine eggs, with five of the whites, and four spoonfuls of sack; stir all together, and sweeten to your taste. Put in a quarter of a pound of currants clean washed and rubbed, and just plumped in two spoonfuls of sack and two of rose-water; mix all well together, stir it well over a slow fire till it is thick, lay a puff paste over a dish, pour in the ingredients and bake it.

To make a Millet-Pudding

You must get half pound of millet-seed, and after it is washed and picked clean, put to it half pound of sugar, a whole nutmeg grated, and three quarts of milk. When you have mixed all well together, break in half a pound of fresh butter in your dish, pour it in and bake it.

To make a Quince, Apricot, or White-Pear Plumb Pudding.

Scald your quinces very tender, pare them very thin, scrape off the soft, mix it with sugar very sweet, put in a little ginger and a little cinamon. To a pint of cream you must put three or four yolks of eggs, and stir it into your quinces till they are of a good thickness. It must be pretty thick. So you may do apricots or white-pear plumbs. Butter your dish, pour it in and bake it.

To make an Apple-Pudding

Take twelve large pippins, pare them, and take out the cores, put them into a sauce-pan, with four or five spoonfuls of water: boil them till they are soft and thick; then beat them well, stir in a pound of loaf sugar, the juice of three lemons, the peel of two lemons, cut thin and beat fine in a mortar, the yolks of eight eggs beat; mix all well together, bake it in a slack oven; when it is near done, throw over a little fine sugar. You may bake it in a puff paste, as you do the other puddings.

A Rice-Pudding.

Get a half pound of rice, put to it three quarts of milk, stir in half a pound of sugar, grate a small nutmeg in, and break in half a pound of fresh butter; butter a dish, and pour it in and bake it. You may add a quarter of a pound of currants, for change. If you boil the rice and milk, and then stir in the sugar, you may bake it before the fire, or in a tin oven. You may add eggs, but it will be good without.

To boil a Custard Pudding.

Take a pint of cream, out of which take two or three spoonfuls, and mix with a spoonful of fine flour; set the rest to boil. When it is boiled, take it off, and stir in the cold cream and flour very well; when it is cold, beat up five yolks and two whites of eggs, and stir in a little salt and some nutmeg, and two or three spoonfuls of sack; sweeten to your palate; butter a wooden bowl, and pour it in, tie a cloth over it, and boil it half an hour. When it is enough, untie the cloth, turn the pudding out into your dish, and pour melted butter over it.

To make a Batter-Pudding.

Take a quart of milk, beat up six eggs, half the whites, mix as above, six spoonfuls of flour, a tea-spoonful of salt, and one of beaten ginger: then mix all together, boil it an hour and a quarter, and pour melted butter over it. You may put in eight eggs if you have plenty, for change, and half a pound of prunes or currants.

To make a Batter-Pudding without Eggs.

Take a quart of milk, mix six spoonfuls of flour with a little of the milk first, a tea-spoonful of beaten ginger, and two of the tincture of saffron; then mix all together, and boil it an hour. You may add fruit as you think proper.

To make a Bread-Pudding.

Cut off all the crust of a two-penny white loaf, and slice it thin into a quart of milk, set it over a chafing-dish of coals till the bread has soaked up all the milk, then put in a piece of butter, stir it round, let it stand till cold; or you may boil your milk, and pour over your bread, and cover it up close, does full as well: then take the yolks of six eggs, the whites of three, and beat them up with a little rose-water and nutmeg, a little salt and sugar, if you chuse it. Mix all well together. and boil it one hour.

To make a baked Bread-Pudding.

Take the crumb of a two-penny-loaf, as much flour, the yolks of four eggs and two whites, a tea-spoonful of ginger, half a pound of raisins stoned, half a pound of currants clean washed and picked, a little salt. Mix first the bread and flour, ginger, salt, and sugar to your palate; then the eggs, and as much milk as will make it like a good batter, then the fruit; butter the dish, pour it in and bake it.

To make a Chesnut-Pudding.

Put a dozen and a half of chesnuts into a skillet or sauce-pan of water, boil them a quarter of an hour, then blanch and peel them, and beat them in a marble mortar, with a little orange-flower or rose-water and sack, till they are a fine thin paste; then beat up twelves eggs, with half the whites, and mix them well, grate half a nutmeg, a little salt, mix them with three pints of cream and half a pound of melted butter; sweeten to your palate, and mix all together; put it over the fire, and keep stirring it till it is thick. Lay a puff-paste all over the dish, pour in the mixture and bake it. When you cannot get cream, take three pints of milk, beat up the yolks of four eggs, and stir into the milk, set it over the fire, stirring it all the time till it is scalding hot, then mix it in the room of the cream.

To make a fine plain baked Pudding.

You must take a quart of milk, and put three bay-leaves into it. When it has boiled a little, with fine flour, make it into a hasty-pudding, with a little salt, pretty thick; take it off the fire, and stir in half a pound of butter, a quarter of a pound of sugar; beat up twelve eggs, and half the whites, stir all well together, lay a puff-paste all over the dish, and pour in your stuff. Half an hour will bake it.

To make an apricot-Pudding.

Coddle six large apricots very tender, break them very small, sweeten them to your taste. When they are cold, add six eggs, only two whites well beat; mix them well together with a pint of good cream, lay a puff-paste all over your dish, and pour in your ingredients. Bake it half an hour; do not let the oven be too hot; when it is enough, throw a little fine sugar all over it, and send it to table hot.

To make a Bread and Butter Pudding.

Get a two-penny-loaf, and cut it into thin slices of bread and butter, as you do for tea. Butter your dish as you cut them, lay slices all over the dish, then strew a few currants clean washed and picked, then a row of bread and butter, then a few currants, and so on till all your bread and butter is in; then take a pint of milk, beat up four eggs, a little salt, half a nutmeg grated; mix all together with sugar to your taste; pour this over the bread, and bake it half an hour. A puff-paste under does best. You may put in two spoonfuls of rose-water.

To make a boiled Rice-Pudding.

Having got a quarter of a pound of the flour of rice, put it over the fire with a pint of milk, and keep it stirring constantly, that it may not clod nor burn. When it is of a good thickness, take it off, and pour it into an earthen pan; stir in half a pound of butter very smooth, and half a pint of cream or new milk, sweeten to your palate, grate in half a nutmeg and the outward rind of a lemon. Beat up the yolks of six eggs and two whites, mix all well together; boil it either in small china basons or wooden bowls. When boiled, turn them into a dish, pour melted butter over them, with a little sack, and throw sugar all over.

To make a cheap Rice-Pudding.

Get a quarter of a pound of rice, and half a pound of raisins stoned, and tie them in a cloth. Give the rice a great deal of room to swell. Boil it two hours; when it is enough, turn it into your dish, and pour melted butter and sugar over it, with a little nutmeg.

To make a cheap baked Rice-Pudding.

You must take a quarter of a pound of rice,

boil it in a quart of new milk, stir it that it does not burn; when it begins to be thick, take it off, let it stand till it is a little cool, then stir in well a quarter of a pound of butter, and sugar to your palate; grate a small nutmeg, butter your dish, pour it in, and bake it.

To make a Quaking-Pudding.

Take a pint of good cream, six eggs, and half the whites, beat them well, and mix with the cream; grate a little nutmeg in, add a little rose-water, if it be agreeable; grate in the crumb of a half penny-roll, or a spoonful of flour; first mixed with a little of the cream, or a spoonful of the flour of rice, which you please. Butter a cloth well, and flour it; then put in your mixture, tie it not too close, and boil it half an hour fast. Be sure the water boils before you put it in.

To make a Cream-Pudding.

Take a quart of cream, boil it with a blade of mace, and half a nutmeg grated, let it cool; beat up eight eggs, and three whites, strain them well, mix a spoonful of flour with them, a quarter of a pound of almonds blanched, and beat very fine, with a spoonful of orange-flower or rose-water, mix with the eggs, then by degrees mix in the cream, beat all well together; take a thick cloth, wet it and flour it well, pour in your stuff, tie it close, and boil it half an hour. Let the water boil all the time fast; when it is done, turn it into your dish, pour melted butter over, with a little sack, and throw fine sugar all over it.

To make a Prune-Pudding.

Take a quart of milk, beat six eggs, half the whites, with half a pint of the milk, and four spoonfuls of flour, a little salt, and two spoonfuls of beaten ginger; then by degrees mix in all the milk, and a pound of prunes, tie it in a cloth, boil it an hour, melt butter and pour over it. Damsons eat well done this way in the room of prunes.

To make an Apple-Pudding.

Make a good puff-paste, roll it out half an inch thick, pare your apples, and core them, enough to fill the crust, and close it up, tie it in a cloth and boil it. If a small pudding, two hours; if a large one, three or four hours. When it is enough, turn it into your dish cut a piece of the crust out of the top, butter and sugar it to your palate; lay on the crust again, and send it to table hot. A pear-pudding make the same way. And thus you may make a damson-pudding, or any sort of plumbs, apricots, cherries, or mulberries, and they are very fine.

To make Yeast-Dumplings.

First make a light dough as for bread with flour, water, salt, and yeast, cover with a cloth, and set it before the fire half an hour; then have a sauce-pan of water on the fire, and when it boils take the dough and make it into little round balls, as big as a large hen's egg; then flat them with your hand, put them into the boiling water; a few minutes boils them. Take great care they do not fall to the bottom of the pot or sauce-pan, for then they will be heavy; and be sure to keep the water boiling all the time. When they are enough, take them up, (which they will be in ten minutes or less,) lay them in your dish, and have melted butter in a cup. As good a way as any to save trouble, is to send to the baker's for half a quartern of dough, (which will make a great many,) and then you have only the trouble of boiling it.

To make Norfolk-Dumplings.

Mix a good thick batter, as for pancakes; take half a pint of milk, two eggs, a little salt, and make it into a batter with flour. Have ready a clean sauce-pan of water boiling, into which drop this batter. Be sure the water boils fast, and two or three minutes will boil them; then throw them into a sieve to drain the water away; then turn them into a dish, and stir a lump of fresh butter into them: eat them hot, and they are very good.

To make Hard Dumplings.

Mix flour and water, with a little salt, like a paste roll them in balls, as big as a turkey's eggs, roll them in a little flour, have the water boiling, throw them in the water, and half an hour will boil them. They are best boiled with a good piece of beef. You may add, for change, a few currants. Have melted butter in a cup.

To make Apple-Dumplings.

Make a good puff-paste, pare some large apples, cut them in quarters, and take out the cores very nicely; take a piece of crust, and roll it round, enough for one apple; if they are big, they will not look pretty, so roll the crust round each apple, and make them round like a ball, with a little flour in your hand. Have a pot of water boiling, take a clean cloth, dip it in the water, and shake flour over it; tie each dumpling by itself, and put them in the water boiling, which keep boiling all the time; and if your crust is light and good, and the apples not too large, half an hour will boil them, but if the apples be large, they will take an hour's boiling. When they are enough, take them up, and lay them in a dish; throw fine sugar all over them, and send them to table. Have good fresh butter melted in a cup, and fine beaten sugar in a saucer.

Rules to be observed in making Puddings, &c.

In boiled puddings, take great care the bag or cloth be very clean, not soapy, but dipped in hot water, and well floured. If a bread-pudding, tie it loose; if a batter-pudding, tie it close; and be sure the water boils when you put the pudding in; and you should move the puddings in the pot now and then, for fear they stick. When you make a batter-pudding, first mix the flour well with a little milk, then put in the ingredients by degrees, and it will be smooth and not have lumps; but for a plain batter-pudding, the best way is to strain it through a coarse hair sieve, that it may neither have lumps, nor the treadles of the eggs: and for all other puddings, strain the eggs when they are beat. If you boil them in wooden bowls, or china-dishes, butter the inside before you put in your batter; and for all baked puddings, butter the pan or dish before the pudding is put in.

OF PIES.

To make a savory Lamb or Veal Pie.

Make a good puff paste crust, cut your meat into pieces, season it to your palate with pepper, salt, mace, cloves, and nutmegs finely beat; lay it into your crust with a few lamb-stones and sweetbreads seasoned as your meat; also some oysters and force-meat balls, hard yolks of eggs, and the tops of asparagus two inches long, first boiled green; put butter all over the pie, put on the lid, and set it in a quick oven an hour and a half, and then have ready the liquor, made thus: take a pint of gravy, the oyster liquor, a gill of red wine, and a little grated nutmeg: mix all together with the yolks of two or three eggs beat, and keep it stirring one way all the time. When it boils, pour it into your pie; put on the lid again. Send it hot to table. You must make liquor according to your pie.

To season an Egg-Pie.

Boil twelve eggs hard, and shred them with one pound of beef-suet, or marrow shred fine. Season them with a little cinnamon and nutmeg beat fine, one pound of currants clean washed and picked, two or three spoonfuls of cream, and a little sack and rose-water mixed all together, and fill the pie. When it is baked stir in half a pound of fresh butter, and the juice of a lemon.

To make a Mutton Pie.

Take a loin of mutton, pare off the skin and fat of the inside, cut it into steaks, season it well with pepper and salt to your palate. Lay it into your crust, fill it, pour in as much water as will almost fill the dish; then put on the crust, and bake it well.

A Beef-Steak-Pie.

Take fine rump-steaks, beat them with a rolling-pin, then season them with pepper and salt, according to your palate. Make a good crust, lay in your steaks, fill your dish, then pour in as much water as will half fill the dish. Put on the crust, and bake it well.

A Ham-Pie.

Take some cold boiled ham, and slice it about half an inch thick, make a good crust, and thick, over the dish, and lay a layer of ham, shake a little pepper over it; then take a large young fowl clean picked, gutted, washed, and singed; put a little pepper and salt in the belly, and rub a very little salt on the outside; lay the fowl on the ham; boil some eggs hard, put in the yolks, and cover all with ham, then shake some pepper on the ham, and put on the top-crust. Bake it well; have ready when it comes out of the oven some very rich beef-gravy, enough to fill the pie: lay on the crust again, and send it to table hot. A fresh ham will not be so tender; so that I always boil my ham one day, and bring it to table, and the next day make a pie of it. It does better than an unboiled ham. If you put two large fowls in, they will make a fine pie; but that is according to your company, more or less. The larger the pie, the finer the meat eats. The crust must be the same you make for a venison-pasty. You should pour a little strong gravy into the pie when you make it, just to bake the meat, and then fill it up when it comes out of the oven. Boil some truffles and morels and put into the pie, which is a great addition, and some fresh mushrooms, or dried ones.

To make a Pigeon Pie.

Make a puff-paste crust, cover your dish, let your pigeons be very nicely picked and cleaned, season them with pepper and salt, and put a good piece of fine fresh butter, with pepper and salt, in their bellies: lay them in your pan; the necks, gizzards, livers, pinions, and hearts, lay between, with the yolk of a hard egg and a beef-steak in the middle; put as much water as will almost fill the dish, lay on the top crust, and bake it well. This is the best way to make a pigeon-pie; but the French fill the pigeons with a very high force-meat, and lay force-meat balls round the inside, with asparagus tops, artichoke bottoms, mushrooms, truffles, and morels, and season high; but that is according to different palates.

To make a Giblet-Pie.

Take two pair of giblets nicely cleaned, put all but the livers into a sauce-pan, with two quarts of water, twenty corns of whole pepper, three blades of mace, a bundle of sweet herbs, and a large onion; cover them very close, and let them stew very softly till they are quite tender; then have a good crust ready, cover your dish, lay a fine rump steak at the bottom, seasoned with pepper and salt, then lay in your giblets with the livers, and strain the liquor they were stewed in. Season it with salt, and pour into your pie, put on the lid, and bake it an hour and a half.

To make a Duck-Pie.

Make a puff-paste crust, take two ducks, scald them, and make them very clean, cut off the feet, the pinions, the neck and head, all clean picked and scalded with the gizzards, livers, and hearts; pick out all the fat of the inside; lay a crust all over the dish, season the ducks with pepper and salt, inside and out, lay them in your dish, and the giblets at each end seasoned; put in as much water as will almost fill the pie, lay on the crust, and bake it, but not too much.

To make a Chicken-Pie.

Make a puff-paste crust, take two chickens, cut them to pieces, season them with pepper and salt, a little beaten mace, lay a force-meat made thus round the side of the dish: take half a pound of veal, half a pound of suet, beat them quite fine in a marble mortar, with as many crumbs of bread; season it with a very little pepper and salt, an anchovy with the liquor, cut the anchovy to pieces, a little lemon-peel cut very fine and shred small, a very little thyme; mix all together with the yolk of an egg; make some into round balls, about twelve, the rest lay round the dish. Lay in one chicken over the bottom of the dish; take two sweetbreads, cut them into five or six pieces, lay them all over, season them with pepper and salt, strew over them half an ounce of truffles and morels, two or three artichoke bottoms cut to pieces, a few cocks-combs, if you have them, a palate boiled tender, and cut to pieces; then lay on the other part of the chickens, put half a pint of water in, and cover the pie; bake it well, and when it comes out of the oven, fill it with good gravy, lay it on the crust, and send it to table.

To make a Cheshire Pork Pie.

Take a loin of pork, skin it cut it into steaks, season it with salt, nutmeg, and pepper; make a good crust, lay a layer of pork, then a larger layer, of pippins, pared and cored, a little sugar, enough to sweeten the pie, then another layer of pork; put in half a pint of white wine, lay some butter on the top, and close your pie. If your pie be large, it will take a pint of white wine.

To make a Goose Pie.

Half a peck of flour will make the walls of a goose-pie, made as in the receipts for crust. raise your crust just big enough to hold a large goose; first have a pickled dried tongue boiled tender enough to peel, cut off the root; bone a goose and a large fowl; take half a quarter of an ounce of mace beat fine, a large tea-spoonful of beaten pepper, three tea-spoonfuls of salt; mix all together, season your fowl and goose with it, then lay the fowl in the goose, and the tongue in the fowl, and the goose in the same form as if whole. Put half a pound of butter on the top, and lay on the lid. This pie is delicious, either hot or cold, and will keep a great while. A slice of this pie cut down across makes a pretty little side-dish for supper.

To make a Venison-Pasty.

Take a neck and breast of venison, bone it, season it with pepper and salt, according to your palate. Cut the breast in two or three pieces; but do not cut the fat of the neck if you can help it. Lay in the breast and neck-end first, and the best end of the neck on the top, that the fat may be whole; make a good rich puff-paste crust, let it be very thick on the sides, a good bottom crust, and thick at top; cover the dish, then lay in your venison, put in half a pound of butter, about a quarter of a pint of water, close your pasty, and let it be baked two hours in a very quick oven. In the mean time set on the bones of the venison in two quarts of water, with two or three blades of mace, an onion, a little piece of crust baked crisp and brown, a little whole pepper; cover it close, and let it boil softly over a slow fire till about half is wasted, then strain it off. When the pasty comes out of the oven, lift up the lid, and pour in the gravy. When your venison is not fat enough, take the fat of a loin of mutton, steeped in a little rape vinegar and red wine twenty-four hours, then lay it on the top of the venison, and close your pasty. It is a wrong notion of some people to think venison cannot be baked enough, and will first bake it in a false crust, and then bake it in the pasty ; by this time the fine flavour of the venison is gone. No ; if you want it to be very tender, wash it in warm milk and water, dry it in clean cloths till it is very dry, then rub it all over with vinegar, and hang it in the air. Keep it as long as you think proper, it will keep thus a fortnight good ; but be sure there be no moistness about it ; if there is, you must dry it well, and throw ginger over it, and it will keep a long time. When you use it, just dip it in luke-warm water and dry it. Bake it in a quick oven : if it is a large pastey, it will take three hours ; then your venison will be tender, and have all the fine flavour. The shoulder makes a pretty pasty, boned and made as above with the mutton fat.

A loin of mutton makes a fine pasty: take a large fat loin of mutton, let it hang four or five days, then bone it, leaving the meat as whole as you can ; lay the meat twenty-four hours in half a pint of red wine and half a pint of rape vinegar ; then take it out of the pickle, and order it as you do a pasty, and boil the bones in the same manner, to fill the pasty, when it comes out of the oven.

To make Mince-Pies the best Way.

Take three pounds of suet shred very fine, and chopped as small as possible ; two pounds of raisins stoned, and chopped as fine as possible ; two pounds of currants nicely picked, washed, rubbed, and dried at the fire ; half a hundred of fine pippins, pared, cored, and chopped small ; half a pound of fine sugar pounded fine ; a quarter of an ounce, of mace, a quarter of an ounce of cloves, two large nutmegs, all beat fine; put all together into a great pan, and mix it well together with half a pint of brandy, and half a pint of sack; put it down close in a stone pot, and it will keep good four months. When you make your pies, take a little dish, something bigger than a soup plate, lay a very thin crust all over it, lay a thin layer of meat, and then a thin layer of citron cut very thin, then a layer of mince-meat, and a layer of orange-peel cut thin, over that a little meat, squeeze half the juice of a fine Seville orange or lemon, lay on your crust, and bake it nicely. These pies eat finely cold. If you make them in little patties, mix your meat and sweet-meats accordingly. If you chuse meat in your pies, parboil a neat's-tongue, peel it, chop the meat as fine as possible, and mix with the rest; or two pounds of the inside of a surloin of beef boiled.

To make Orange or Lemon Tarts.

Take six large lemons, and rub them very well with salt, and put them in water for two days, with a handful of salt in it; then change them into fresh water every day (without salt) for a fortnight, then boil them for two or three hours till they are tender, then cut them into half-quarters, and then cut them three-corner-ways, as thin as you can: take six pippins pared, cored, and quartered, and a pint of fair water. Let them boil till the pippins break; put the liquor to your orange or lemon, and half the pulp of the pippins well broken, and a pound of sugar. Boil these together a quarter of an hour, then put it in a gallipot, and squeeze an orange in it: if it be a lemon tart, squeeze a lemon; two spoonfuls is enough for a tart. Your patty-pans must be small and shallow. Put fine puff-paste, and very thin; a little while will bake it. Just as your tarts are going into the oven, with a feather or brush, rub them over with melted butter, and then sift double refined sugar over them; and this is a pretty iceing on them.

To make different Sorts of Tarts.

If you bake in tin patties, butter them, and you must put a little crust all over, because of the taking them out; if in china, or glass, no crust but the top one. Lay fine sugar at the bottom, then your plumbs, cherries, or any other sort of fruit, and sugar at top; then put on your lid, and bake them in a slack oven. Mince-pies must be baked in tin patties, because of taking them out, and puff-paste is best for them. For sweet tarts the beaten crust is best; but as you fancy. You have the receipt for the crust in this chapter. Apple, pear, apricot, &c. make thus: apples and pears, pare them, cut them into quarters and core them; cut the quarters across again, set them on in a sauce-pan, with just as much water as will barely cover them, let them simmer on a slow fire just till the fruit is tender; put a good piece of lemon-peel in the water with the fruit, then have your patties ready. Lay fine sugar at bottom, then your fruit, and a little sugar at top; that you must put in at your discretion. Pour over each tart a tea-spoonful of lemon juice, and three tea spoonfuls of the liquor they were boiled in; put on your lid, and bake them in a slack oven. Apricots do the same way, only do not use lemon.

As to preserved tarts, only lay in your preserved fruit, and put a very thin crust at top, and let them be baked as little as possible; but if you would make them very nice, have a large patty, the size you would have your tarts. Make your sugar crust, roll it as thick as a half-penny; then butter your patties, and cover it. Shape your upper crust on a hollow thing on purpose, the size of your patty, and mark it with a marking-iron for that purpose, in wh it shape you please, to be hollow and open to see the fruit through; then bake your crust in a very slack oven not to discolour it, but to have it crisp. When the crust is cold, very carefully take it out, and fill it with what fruit you please lay on the lid, a d it is done; therefore if the tart is not eat, your sweet meat is not the worse, and it looks genteel.

Paste for Tarts.

One pound of flour, three quarters of a pound of butter, mix up together, and beat well with a rolling-pin.

Puff-Paste.

Take a quarter of a peck of flour, rub in a pound of butter very fine, make it up in a light paste with cold water, just stiff enough to work it up; then roll it out about as thick as a crown-piece, put a layer of butter all over, sprinkle on a little flour, double it up, and roll it out again; double it, and roll it out seven or eight times; then it is fit for all sorts of pies and tarts that require a puff-paste.

A good Crust for great Pies.

To a peck of flour, add the yolks of three eggs; then boil some water, and put in half a pound of fried suet, and a pound and a half of butter. Skim off the butter and suet and as much of the liquor as will make it a light good crust; work it up well, and roll it out.

A Dripping Crust.

Take a pound and half of beef dripping, boil it in water, strain it, then let it stand to be cold, and take off the hard fat: scrape it, boil it so four or five times, then work it well up into three pounds of flour, as fine as you can, and make it up into paste with cold water. It makes a very fine crust.

A Crust for Custards.

Take half a pound of flour, six ounces of butter, the yolks of two eggs, three spoonfuls of cream; mix them together, and let them stand a quarter of an hour, then work it up and down, and roll it very thin.

Paste for Crackling Crust.

Blanch four handfuls of almonds, and throw them into water, then dry them in a cloth and pound them in a mortar very fine, with a little orange flower water, and the white of an egg. When they are well pounded, pass them through a coarse hair sieve, to clear them from all the lumps or clods; then spread it on a dish till it is very pliable; let it stand for a while, then roll out a piece for the under crust, and dry it in the oven on the pie pan, while other pastry works are making, as knots, cyphers, &c. for garnishing your pies.

To make an Apple Pie.

Make a good puff paste crust, lay some round the sides of the dish, pare and quarter apples, and take out the cores, lay a row of apples thick, throw in half the sugar you design for your pie, mince a little lemon peel fine, throw over, and squeeze a little lemon over them, then a few cloves, here and there one, then the rest of your apples, and the rest of your sugar. You must sweeten to your palate, and squeeze a little more lemon. Boil the peeling of the apples and the cores in some fair water, with a blade of mace, till it is very good; strain it, and boil the syrup with a little sugar, till there is but very little and good, pour it into your pie, put on your upper-crust and bake it. You may put in a little quince or marmalade, if you please.

Thus make a pear pie, but do not put in any quince. You may butter them when they come out of the oven, or beat up the yolks of two eggs, and half a pint of cream, with a little nutmeg, sweetened with sugar, put it over a slow fire, and keep stirring it till it just boils up, take off the lid, and pour in the cream. Cut the crust in little three-corner pieces, stick about the pie, and send it to table.

To make a Cherry-Pie.

Make a good crust, lay a little round the sides of your dish, throw sugar at the bottom; and lay in your fruit and sugar at top; a few red currants does well with them; put on your lid, and bake in a slack oven.

Make a plum pie the same way, and a gooseberry pie. If you would have it red, let it stand a good while in the oven after the bread is drawn. A custard is very good with the gooseberry pie.

To make a Soal-Pie.

Make a good crust, cover your dish, boil two pounds of eels tender, pick all the flesh clean from the bones; throw the bones into the liquor you boil the eels in, with a little mace and salt, till it is very good, and about a quarter of a pint, then strain it. In the mean time cut the flesh of your eel fine, with a little lemon peel shred fine, a little salt, pepper, and nutmeg, a few crumbs of bread, chopped parsley, and an anchovy; melt a quarter of a pound of butter, and mix with it, then lay it in the dish; cut the flesh of a pair of large soals. or three pair of very small ones, clean from the bones and fins, lay it on the force meat, and pour in the broth of the eels you boiled; put the lid of the pie on, and bake it. You should boil the bones of the soals, with the eels bones, to make it good

If you boil the soal bones with one or two little eels, without the force-meat, your pie will be eery good. And thus you may do a turbot.

To make an Eel-Pie.

Make a good crust; clean, gut, and wash your eels very well, then cut them in pieces half as long as your finger; season them with pepper, salt and a little beaten mace to your palate, either high or low. Fill your dish with eels, and put as much water as the dish will hold; put on your cover and bake them well.

To make a Flounder-Pie.

Gut some flounders, wash them clean, dry them in a cloth, just boil them, cut off the meat clean, from the bones, lay a good crust over the dish, and lay a little fresh butter at the bottom, and on that the fish; season with pepper and salt to your mind. Boil the bones in the water your fish was boiled in, with a little bit of horse-raddish, a little parsley, a very little bit of lemon-peel, and a crust of bread, Boil it till there is just enough liquor for the pie then strain it, and put it into your pie: put on the top-crust and bake it.

To make a Salmon-Pie.

Make a good crust, cleanse a piece of salmon well, season it with salt, mace, and nutmeg, lay a piece of butter at the bottom of the dish, and lay your salmon in. Melt butter according to your pie; take a lobster, boil it, pick out all the flesh, chop it small, bruise the body, mix it well with the butter, which must be very good; pour it over your salmon, put on the lid, and bake it well.

To make a Lobster-Pie.

Take two or three lobsters, and boil them; take the meat out of the tails whole, cut them in four pieces long ways: take out all the spawn, and the meat of the claws, beat it well in a mortar; season it with pepper salt, two spoonfuls of vinegar, and a little anchovy liquor; melt half a pound of fresh butter, stir all together, with the crumbs of a penny roll rubbed through a fine cullender, and the yolks of two eggs; put a fine puff-paste over your dish, lay in your tails and the rest of the meat over them; put on your cover, and bake it in a slow oven.

VARIETY OF DISHES FOR LENT.

To make an Eel-Soup.

Take eels according to the quantity of soup you would make; a pound of eels will make a pint of good soup: so to every pound of eels put a quart of water, a crust of bread, two or three blades of mace, a little whole pepper, an onion, and a bundle of sweet herbs; cover them close, and let them boil till half the liquor is wasted; then strain it, and toast some bread, cut it small, lay the bread in the dish, and pour in your soup. If you have a stew-hole, set the dish over it for a minute, and send it to table. If you find your soup not rich enough, you must let it boil till it is as strong as you would have it. You may make this soup as rich and good as if it was meat: you may add a piece of carrot to brown it.

To make a Rice-Soup.

Take two quarts of water, a pound of rice, a little cinnamon ; cover it close, and let it simmer very softly till the rice is quite tender, take out the cinnamon, then sweeten it to your palate ; grate half a nutmeg, and let it stand till it is cold; then beat up the yolks of three eggs, with half a pint of white wine, mix them very well, then stir them into the rice, set them on a slow fire, and keep stirring all the time for fear of curdling, When it is of a good thickness, and boils, take it up. Keep stirring it till you put it into your dish.

To make a Barley-Soup.

Take a gallon of water, half a pound of barley a blade or two of mace, a large crust of bread, and a lemon peel. Let it boil till it comes to two quarts, then add half a pint of white wine, and sweeten to your palate.

To make Peas-Porridge.

Take a quart of green peas, put to them a quart of water, a bundle of dried mint, and a little salt. Let them boil till the peas are quite tender ; then put in some beaten pepper, a piece of butter as big as a walnut rolled in flour, stir it all together, and let it boil a few minutes ; then add two quarts of milk, let it boil a quarter of an hour, take out the mint, and serve it up.

To make Rice-Milk.

Take half a pound of rice, boil it in a quart of water, with a little cinnamon. Let it boil till the water is all wasted; take great care it does not burn; then add three pints of milk, and the yolk of an egg beat up. Keep it stirring, and when it boils take it up. Sweeten to your palate.

To make an Orange-Fool.

Take the juice of six oranges, and six eggs well beaten, a pint of cream, a quarter of a pound of sugar, a little cinnamon and nutmeg. Mix all together, and keep stirring over a slow fire till it is thick, then put in a little piece of butter, and keep stirring till cold, and dish it up.

To make Plum-Porridge, or Barley-Gruel.

Take a gallon of water half a pound of barley, a quarter of a pound of raisins clean washed, a quarter of a pound of currants washed and picked. Boil these till above half the water is wasted, with two or three blades of mace; then sweeten it to your palate, and add half a pint of white wine.

To make Hasty-Pudding

Take a quart of milk, and four bay-leaves, set it on the fire to boil, beat up the yolks of two eggs and stir in a little salt. Take two or three spoonfuls of milk, and beat up with your eggs, and stir in your milk, then with a wooden spoon in one hand, and the flour in the other, stir it in till it is of a good thickness, but not too thick. Let it boil, and keep it stirring, then pour it into a dish, and stick pieces of butter here and there. You may omit the egg if you do not like it; but it is a great addition to the pudding; and a little piece of butter stirred in the milk makes it eat short and fine. Take out the bay-leaves before you put in the flour.

To make Apple-Fritters.

Beat the yolks of eight eggs, and the whites of four well together and strain them into a pan; then take a quart of cream, make it as hot as you can bear your finger in it; then put to it a quarter of a pint of sack, three quarters of a pint of ale, and make a posset of it. When it is cool, put it to your eggs, beating it well together; then put in nutmeg, ginger, salt, and flour, to your liking. Your batter should be pretty thick, then put in pippins sliced or scraped, and fry them in a deal of butter quick.

To make Pancakes.

Take a quart of milk, beat in six or eight eggs, leaving half the whites out; mix it well till your batter is of a fine thickness. You must observe to mix your flour first with a little milk, then add the rest by degrees; put in two spoonfuls of beaten ginger, a glass of brandy, a little salt; stir all together; make your stew-pan very clean, put in a piece of butter as big as a walnut, then pour in a ladleful of batter, which will make a pancake, moving the pan round that the batter be all over the pan: shake the pan, and when you think that side is enough, toss it; if you cannot, turn it cleverly; and when both sides are done lay it in a dish before the fire, and so do the rest. You must take care they are dry; when you send them to table, strew a little sugar over them.

To bake Apples whole.

Put your apples into an earthen pan, with a few cloves, a little lemon-peel, some coarse sugar, a glass of red wine: put them into a quick oven, and they will take an hour baking.

To stew Pears.

Pare six pears, and either quarter them or do them whole; they make a pretty dish with one whole, the rest cut in quarters, and the cores taken out. Lay them in a deep earthen pot, with a few cloves, a piece of lemon-peel, a gill of red wine, and a quarter of a pound of fine sugar. If the pears are very large, they will take half a pound of sugar, and half a pint of red wine; cover them close with brown paper, and bake them till they are enough. Serve them hot or cold, just as you like them, and they will be very good with water in the place of wine.

To make a Tansey.

Take a pint of cream, and half a pint of blanched almonds, beat fine, with rose and orange-flower water, stir them together over a slow fire; when it boils take it off, and let it stand till cold; then beat in ten eggs, grate in a small nutmeg, four Naples biscuits, a little grated bread; sweeten to your taste, and if you think it is too thick, put in some more cream, and the juice of spinach to make it green; stir it well together, and either fry it or bake it. If you fry it, do one side first, and then with a dish turn the other.

Stewed Spinach and Eggs.

Pick and wash your spinach very clean, put it into a sauce-pan, with a little salt; cover it close shake the pan often ; when it is just tender, and whilst it is green, throw it into a sieve to drain, lay it in your dish. In the mean time have a stew-pan of water boiling. Break as many eggs into cups as you would poach. When the water boils put in the eggs, have an egg-slice ready to take them out with, lay them on the spinach, and garnish the dish with orange cut into quarters, with melted butter in a cup.

To collar Eels.

Take your eel and scour it well with salt, wipe it clean ; then cut it down the back, take out the bone, cut the head and tail off, put the yolk of an egg over it, and then take four cloves, two blades of mace, half a nutmeg beat fine, a little pepper and salt, some chopped parsley, and sweet herbs chopped very fine ; mix them all together, and sprinkle over it, roll the eel up very tight, and tie it in a cloth ; put on water enough to boil it, and put in an onion, some cloves and mace, and four bay leaves ; boil it up with the bones, head, and tail for half an hour, with a little vinegar and salt ; then take out the bones, &c. and put in your eels ; boil them, if large, two hours ; lesser in proportion : when done put them away to cool ; then take them out of the liquor and cloth, and cut them in slices, or send them whole, with raw parsley under and over.

N. B. You must take them out of the cloth, and put them in the liquor, and tie them close down to keep.

To pickle or bake Herrings.

Scale and wash them clean, cut off the heads, take out the roes, or wash them clean, and put them in again as you like. Season them with a little mace and cloves beat, a very little beaten pepper and salt, lay them in a deep pan, lay two or three bay-leaves between each layer, put in half vinegar and half water, or rape vinegar. Cover it close with a brown paper, and send it to the oven to bake; let it stand till cold. Thus do sprats. Some use only alspice, but that is not so good.

To souse Muckerel

You must wash them clean, gut them, and boil them in salt and water till they are enough; take them out, lay them in a clean pan, cover them with the liquor, add a little vinegar; and when you send them to table, lay fennel over them.

OF HOGS-PUDDINGS SAUSAGES, &c.

To make Black Puddings.

First, before you kill your hog get a peck of grits, boil them half an hour in water, then drain them, and put them into a clean tub or large pan; then kill your hog, and save two quarts of the blood of the hog, and keep stirring it till the blood is quite cold; then mix it with your grits, and stir them well together. Season with a large spoonful of salt, a quarter of an ounce of cloves, mace and nutmeg together, an equal quantity of each; dry it, beat it well and mix in. Take a little winter savory, sweet marjorum, and thyme, penny-royal stripped of, the stalks, and chopped very fine, just enough to season them, and to give them a flavour, but no more. The next day take the leaf of the hog and cut into dice, scrape and wash the gut very clean, then tie one end, and begin to fill them; mix in the fat as you fill them; be sure put in a good deal of fat, fill the skins three parts full, tie the other end, and make your puddings what length you please; prick them with a pin, and put them into a kettle of boiling water. Boil them very softly an hour; then take them out, and lay them on clean straw,

In Scotland they make a pudding with the blood of a goose. Chop off the head, and save the blood; stir it till it is cold, then mix it with grits, spice, salt, and sweet herbs, according to their fancy, and some beef suet chopped. Take the skin off the neck, then pull out the wind-pipe and fat, fill the skin, tie it at both ends; so make a pie of the giblets, and lay the pudding in the middle.

To make Sausages.

Take three pounds of nice pork, fat and lean together, without skin or gristles, chop it as fine as possible, season it with a tea-spoonful of beaten pepper, and two of salt, some sage shred fine, about three spoonfuls; mix it well together; have the guts very nicely cleaned, and fill them; or put them down, in a pot, so roll them of what size you please, and fry them. Beef makes very good sausages.

To make Bologna Sausages.

Take a pound of bacon, fat and lean together, a pound of beef, a pound of veal, a pound of pork a pound of beef suet, cut them small and chop them fine; take a small handful of sage, pick off the leaves, chop it fine with a few sweet herbs; season pretty high, with pepper and salt. You must have a large gut, and fill it, then set on a sauce-pan of water: when it boils put it in, and pick the gut for fear of bursting. Boil it softly an hour, then lay it on clean straw to dry.

TO CURE HAMS, &c.

To Collar Beef.

Take a piece of thin flank of beef, and bone it; cut the skin off, then salt it with two ounces of salt petre, two ounces of salt prunella, two ounces of bay salt; half a pound of coarse sugar, and two pounds of white salt, beat the hard salts fine, and mix all together; turn it every day and rub it with the brine well for eight days: then take it out of the pickle, wash it, and wipe it dry; and then take a quarter of an ounce of cloves, and a quarter of an ounce of mace, twelve corns of alspice, and a nutmeg beat very fine, with a spoonful of beaten pepper, a large quantity of chopped parsley, with some sweet herbs chopped fine; sprinkle it on the beef, and roll it up very tight, put a coarse cloth round, and tie it very tight with beggars tape; boil it in a large copper of water; if a large collar, six hours; if a small one, five hours; take it out, and put it in a press till cold; if you have never a press, put it between two boards, and a large weight upon it till it is cold; then take it out of the cloth and cut it into slices. Garnish with raw parsley.

To make Dutch Beef.

Take the lean of a buttock of beef raw, rub it well with brown sugar all over, and let it lie in a pan or tray two or three hours, turning it two or three times; then salt it well with common salt and salt petre, and let it lie a fortnight, turning it every day; then roll it very strait in a coarse cloth, put it in a cheese-press a day and a night, and hang it to dry in a chimney, When you boil it, you must put it in a cloth; when it is cold, it will cut in slices as dutch beef.

To pickle pork.

Bone your pork, cut it into pieces of a size fit to lie in the tub or pan you design it to lie in, rub your pieces well with salt-petre, then take two parts of common salt, and two of bay salt, and rub every piece well; put a layer of common salt in the bottom of your vessel, cover every piece over with common salt, lay them one upon another as close as you can, filling the hollow places on the sides with salt, As your salt melts on the top, strew on more; lay a coarse cloth over the vessel, a board over that, and a weight on the board to keep it down. Keep it close covered; it will, thus ordered, keep the whole year. Put a pound of salt petre and two pounds of bay salt to a hog.

A pickle for Pork which is to be eat soon

You must take two gallons of pump water, one pound of bay-salt, one pound of coarse sugar, six ounces of salt-petre; boil it all together, and skim it when cold. Cut the pork in what pieces you please, lay it down close, and pour the liquor over it. Lay a weight on it to keep it close, and cover it close from the air, and it will be fit to use in a week. If you find the pickle begins to spoil, boil it again, and skim it; when it is cold, pour it on your pork again.

To make Mutton Hams,

You must take a hind-quarter of mutton, cut it like a ham; take an ounce of salt-petre, a pound of coarse sugar, a pound of common salt; mix them, and rub your ham, lay it in a hollow tray with the skin downwards, baste it every day for a fortnight, then roll it in saw-dust, and hang it in the wood-smoke a fortnight; then boil it, and hang it in a dry place, and cut it out in rashers. It does not eat well boiled, but eats finely broiled.

To make Pork-Hams.

You must take a fat hind-quarter of pork, and cut off a fine ham. Take two ounces of salt-petre, a pound of coarse sugar, a pound of common salt, and two ounces of salt prunella; mix all together, and rub it well. Let it lie a month in this pickle, turning and basting it every day, then hang it in wood smoke as you do beef, in a dry place, so as no heat comes to it; and if you keep them long, hang them a month or two in a damp place, so as they will be mouldy, and it will make them cut fine and short. Never lay these hams in water till you boil them, and then boil them in a copper, if you have one, or the biggest pot you have. Put them in the cold water, and let them be four or five hours before they boil. Skim the pot well and often, till it boils. If it is a very large one, three hours will boil it; if a small one, two hours will do, provided it be a great while before the water boils. Take it up half an hour before dinner, pull off the skin, and throw raspings finely sifted all over. Hold a red-hot fire-shovel over it, and when dinner is ready, take a few raspings in a sieve, and sift all over the dish; then lay in your ham, and with your finger make figures round the edge of the dish. Be sure to boil your ham in as much water as you can, and to keep it skimming all the time till it boils. It must be at least four hours before it boils.

This pickle does finely for tongues; afterwards to lie in it a fortnight, and then hang in the wood-smoke a fortnight, or to boil them out of the pickle.

Yorkshire is famous for hams; and the reason is this; their salt is much finer than ours in London, it is a large clear salt, and gives the meat a fine flavour. I used to have it from Malden in Essex, and that salt will make any ham as fine as you can desire. It is by much the best salt for salting of meat. A deep hollow wooden tray is better than a pan, because the pickle swells about it.

When you broil any of these hams in slices, or bacon, have some boiling water ready, and let the slices lie a minute or two in the water, then broil them; it takes out the salt, and makes them eat finer.

To make Bacon.

Take a side of pork, then take off all the inside fat, lay it on a long board or dresser, that the blood may run away, rub it well with good salt on both sides, let it lie thus a day; then take a pint of bay salt, a quarter of a pound of salt-petre, beat them fine, two pounds of coarse sugar, and a quarter of a peck of common salt. Lay your pork in something that will hold the pickle, and rub it well with the above ingredients. Lay the skinny side downward, and baste it every day with the pickle for a fortnight; then hang it in wood-smoke as you do beef, and afterwards hang it in a dry place, but not hot. You are to observe, that all hams and bacon should hang clear from every thing, and not against a wall.

Observe to wipe off all the old salt before you put it into this pickle, and never keep bacon or hams in a hot kitchen, or in a room where the sun comes. It makes them all rusty.

SEVERAL NEW RECEIPTS ADAPTED TO THE AMERICAN MODE OF COOKING.

To make a baked Indian Pudding.

One quart of boiled milk to five spoonfuls of Indian Meal, one gill of molasses, and salt to your taste ; putting it in the oven to bake when it is cold.

An Indian Pudding boiled.

One quart of milk, and three half-pints of Indian meal, and a gill of molasses, then put it in a cloth, and let it boil seven or eight hours. The water boiling when it is put in.

Water may be used instead of milk in case you have none.

To make Mush.

Boil a pot of water, according to the quantity you wish to make, and then stir in the meal till it becomes quite thick, stirring it all the time to keep out the lumps, season with salt, and eat it with milk or molasses.

Buck-Wheat Cakes.

Take milk-warm water, a little salt, a table spoonful of yeast, and then stir in your buck-wheat till it becomes of the thickness of batter ; and then let it enjoy a moderate warmth for one night to raise it, bake the same on a griddle, greasing it first to prevent them from sticking.

To make Pumpkin-Pie.

Take the Pumpkin and peel the rind off, then stew it till it is quite soft, and put thereto one pint of pumpkin, one pint of milk, one glass of malaga wine, one glass of rose-water, if you like it, seven eggs, half a pound of fresh butter, one small nutmeg, and sugar and salt to your taste.

Dough Nuts.

To one pound of flour, put one quarter of a pound of butter, one quarter of a pound of sugar and two spoonfuls of yeast; mix them all together in warm milk or water of the thickness of bread, let it raise, and make them in what form you please, boil your fat (consisting of hog's lard), and put them in.

To make Sausages.

Take your pork, fat and lean together, and mince it fine, then season it with ground pepper, salt, and sage pounded, then have the offals well cleaned, and fill them with the above; they are then fit for use. When you put them in your pan remember to prick them to prevent them from bursting.

To make Blood Puddings.

Take your Indian meal (according to the quantity you wish to make), and scald it with boiled milk or water, then stir in your blood, straining it first, mince the hog's lard and put it in the pudding, then season it with treacle and pounded penny-royal to your taste, put it in a bag and let it boil six or seven hours.

To make Cranberry Tarts.

To one pound of flour three quarters of a pound

of butter, then stew your cranberry's to a jelly, putting good brown sugar in to sweeten them, strain the cranberry's and then put them in your patty pans for baking in a moderate oven for half an hour.

To pickle Peppers.

Take your peppers and cut a slit in the side of them, put them in cold salt and water for twelve hours, then take them out and put them in fresh salt and water, and hang them over the fire in a brass kettle, letting the water be as hot as you can bear your hand in, let them remain over the fire till they turn yellow, when they turn yellow, shift the water and put them in more salt and water of the same warmth; then cover them with the cabbage leaves till they turn green, when they are done, drain the salt and water off, then boil your vinegar, and pour it over them: they will be fit for use in three days.

To Pickle Beets.

Put into a gallon of cold vinegar as many beets as the vinegar will hold, and put thereto half an ounce of whole pepper, half an ounce of allspice, a little ginger, if you like it, and one head of garlic.

Note. Boil the beets in clear water, with their dirt on as they are taken out of the earth, then take them out and peel them and when the vinegar is cold put them in, and in two days they will be fit for use. The spice must be boiled in the vinegar.

To make Peach Sweetmeats.

To one pound of Peaches put half a pound of good brown sugar, with half a pint of water to dissolve it, first clarifying it with an egg; then boil the peaches and sugar together, skimming the egg off, which will rise on the top, till it is of the thickness of a jelly. If you wish to do them whole, do not peel them, but put them into boiling water, and give them a boil, then take them out and wipe them dry.—Pears are done the same way.

Quince Sweetmeats.

To one pound of quinces put three quarters of a pound of good brown sugar ; the quinces boiled. With respect to the rest follow the above receipt.

Green Gage Sweetmeats.

Make a syrup just as you do for quinces, only allowing one pound of sugar, to one pound of gages.—Plumbs and damsons are made the same way.

A receipt to make Maple Sugar.

Make an incision in a number of maple trees, at the same time, about the middle of February, and receive the juice of them in wooden or earthen vessels. Strain this juice (after it is drawn from the sediment) and boil it in a wide mouthed kettle. Place the kettle directly over the fire, in such a manner that the flame shall not play upon its sides. Skim the liquor when it is boiling. When it is reduced to a thick syrup and cooled, strain it again, and let it settle for two or three days, in which time it will be fit for granulating. This operation is performed by filling the kettle half full of syrup, and boiling it a second time. To prevent its boiling over, add to it a piece of fresh butter or fat of the size of a walnut You may easily determine when it is sufficiently boiled to granulate, by cooling a little of it. It must then be put into bags or baskets, through which the water will drain. This sugar if refined by the usual process, may be made into as good single or double refined loaves, as were ever made from the sugar obtained from the juice of the West India cane.

To make Maple Molasses

This may be done three ways, 1. From the thick syrup, obtained by boiling after it is strained for granulation. 2. From the drainings of the sugar after it is granulated. 3, From the last runnings of the tree [which will not granulate] reduced by evaporation to the consistence of molasses.

To make Maple Beer.

To every four gallons of water when boiling, add one quart of maple molasses. When the liquor is cooled to blood heat, put in as much yeast as is necessary to ferment it. Malt or bran may be added to this beer, when agreeable. If a table spoonful of the essence of spruce be added to the above quantities of water and molasses, it makes a most delicious and wholesome drink.

Receipt to make the famous Thieves Vinegar.

Take of wormwood, thyme, rosemary, lavender, sage, rue and mint, each a handful; pour on them a quart of the best wine vinegar, set them eight days in moderate hot ashes, shake them now and then thoroughly, then squeeze the juice out of the contents through a clean cloth; to which add two ounces of camphire. The use therefore is to rinse the mouth, and wash therewith under the arm pits, neck and shoulders, temples, palms of the hands, and feet, morning and evening; and to smell frequently thereat, has its salutary effects.

N. B. The above receipt did prove an efficacious remedy against the plague in London, when it raged there in the year 1665.

Method of destroying the putrid Smell which Meat acquires during hot Weather.

Put the meat intended for making soup, into a sauce-pan full of water, scum it when it boils, and then throw into the sauce-pan a burning pit coal, very compact and destitute of smoke, leave it there for two minutes, and it will have contracted all the smell of the meat and soup.

If you wish to roast a piece of meat on the spit, you must put it into water until it boils, and after having scummed it, throw a burning pit coal into the boiling water as before; at the end of two minutes, take out the meat, and having wiped it well in order to dry it, put it upon the spit.

To make Spruce Beer out of the Essence.

For a cask of eighteen gallons take seven ounces of the Essence of Spruce, and fourteen pounds of molasses; mix them with a few gallons of hot water put into the cask; then fill the cask with cold water, stir it well, make it about lukewarm; then add about two parts of a pint of good yeast or the grounds of porter; let it stand about four or five days to work, then bung it up tight, and let stand two or three days, and it will be fit for immediate use after it has been bottled.

To make Spruce Beer out of Shed Spruce.

To one quart of Shed Spruce, two gallons of cold water, and so on in proportion to the quantity you wish to make, then add one pint of molasses to every two gallons, let it boil four or five hours and stand till it is luke-warm, then put one pint of yeast to ten gallons, let it work, then put it into your cask, and bung it up tight, and in two days it will be fit for use.

To make an Eel Pie.

Skin your eels and parboil them, then season them with pepper and salt, and put them into your paste, with half a dozen raw oysters, one quarter of a pound of butter, and water.

To make a Pork pie

Take fresh pork and cut it into thin slices, season it with pepper and salt, and put it into your paste.

To make a raised Pork pie.

Take six ounces of butter to one pound of flour and so on in proportion, boil the butter in a sufficient quantity of water to mix with the flour hot, let the paste be stiff and form it in a round shape with your hands ; then put in your pork, seasoned to your taste with pepper and salt, and then bake it for about an hour.

To make a Bath Pudding.

Take one pint of new milk, six eggs beat well in the milk, four table spoonfuls of fine flour, three table spoonfuls of yeast, three spoonfuls of rose water, and three spoonfuls of Malaga wine ; grate into it a small nutmeg, sweetened with fine soft sugar to your taste ; mix them all well together, and let them stand one hour before they are to be baked ; bake them in eight small patty-pans, and one large one for the middle of the dish ; butter the patty pans ; put them in a fierce oven, and in fifteen minutes they will be done.

To make a pot Pie.

Make a crust and put it round the sides of your pot, then cut your meat in small pieces, of whatever kind the pot pie is to be made of, and season it with pepper and salt, then put it in the pot and fill it with water, close it with paste on the top ; it will take three hours doing.

To make Short Gingerbread

One pound of superfine flour, to half a pound of good fresh butter, and so on in proportion to the quantity you wish to make, beat your butter till it froths, half an ounce of ginger, a few carraway seeds, and one pound of sugar, roll it out thin and bake it. Common gingerbread is made the same way, only molasses instead of sugar.

To make Whafles

One pound of sugar, one pound of flour, one pound of butter, half an ounce of cinnamon, one glass of rose water ; make it in balls as big as a nutmeg, and put them in your whafle iron to bake.

To make Crullers.

One pound of flour to half a pound of good brown sugar and half a pound of butter, let your hog's lard be boiling, then make them into what form you please, and put them in to fry.

The following curious Method of rearing Turkeys to advantage, translated from a Swedish Book, entitled Rural Oeconomy.

Many of our housewives, says this ingenious author, have long despaired of success in rearing turkey's, and complained, that the profit rarely

OF PICKLING.

To pickle Walnuts Green.

Take the largest and clearest you can get, pare them as thin as you can, have a tub of spring-water standing by you, and throw them in as you do them. Put into the water a pound of bay-salt, let them lie in the water twenty-four hours, take them out; then put them into a stone jar, and between every layer of walnuts lay a layer of vine-leaves at the bottom and top, and fill it up with cold vinegar. Let them stand all night, then pour the vinegar from them into a copper, with a pound of bay-salt; set it on the fire, let it boil, then pour it hot on your nuts, tie them over with a woollen cloth, and let them stand a week; then pour that pickle away, rub your nuts clean with a piece of flannel, then put them again in your jar, with vine-leaves, as above, and boil fresh vinegar. Put into your pot to every gallon of vinegar, a nutmeg sliced, cut four large races of ginger, a quarter of an ounce of mace, the same of cloves, a quarter of an ounce of whole black-pepper, the like of Ordingal pepper; then pour your vinegar boiling hot on your walnuts, and cover them with a woollen cloth. Let it stand three or four days, so do two or three times, when cold put in half a pint of mustard-seed, a large stick of horse-raddish sliced, tie them down close with a bladder, and then with a leather. They will be fit to eat in a fortnight. Take a large onion, stick the cloves in, and lay in the middle of the pot. If you do them for keeping, do not boil your vinegar, but then they will not be fit to eat under six months, and the next year you may boil the pickle this way

They will keep two or three years good and firm.

To pickle Walnuts White

Take the largest nuts you can get, just before the shell begins to turn, pare them very thin till the white appears, and throw them into spring-water, with a handful of salt as you do them. Let them stand in that water six hours, lay on them a thin board to keep them under the, water then set a stew-pan on a charcoal fire, with clean spring water ; take your nuts out of the other and put them into the stew-pan. Let them simmer four or five minutes, but not boil, then have ready by you a pan of spring-water, with a handful of white salt in it, stir it with your hand till the salt is melted, then take your nuts out of the stew-pan with a wooden ladle, and put them into the cold water and salt. Let them stand a quarter of an hour, lay the board on them as before ; if they are not kept under the liquor they turn black, then lay them on a cloth and cover them with another to dry, then carefully wipe them with a soft cloth put them into your jar or glass, with some blades of mace and nutmeg sliced thin. Mix your spice between your nuts, and pour distilled vinegar over them ; first let your glass be full of nuts, pour mutton-fat over them and tie a bladder and then a leather.

To pickle Walnuts black.

You must take large full grown nuts, at their full growth before they are hard, lay them in salt and water ; let them lie two days, then shift them into fresh water ; let them lie two days, longer ; then shift them again, and let them lie three in your pickling jar. When the jar is half full, put in a large onion stuck with cloves. To a hundred of walnuts put in half a pint of mustard seed, a quarter of an ounce of mace, half an ounce of black pepper, half an ounce of all-spice, six bay-leaves, and a stick of horse-radish; then fill your jar, and pour boiling vinegar over them. Cover them with a plate, and when they are cold, tie them down with a bladder and leather, and they will be fit to eat in about two or three months. The next year, if any remains, boil up your vinegar again, and skim it; when cold pour it over your walnuts. This is by much the best pickle for use; therefore you may add more vinegar to it, what quantity you please. If you pickle a great many walnuts, and eat them fast, make your pickle for a hundred or two, the rest keep in strong brine of salt and water, boiled till it will bear an egg, and as your pot empties, fill them up with those in the salt and water. Take care they are covered with pickle.

In the same manner you may do a smaller quantity; but if you can get rape-vinegar, use that instead of salt and water. Do them thus: put your nuts into the jar you intend to pickle them in, throw in a good handful of salt, and fill the pot with rape vinegar.—Cover it close, and let them stand a fortnight; then pour them out of the pot, wipe it clean, and just rub the nuts with a coarse cloth, and then put them in the jar with the pickle, as above. If you have the best sugar-vinegar of your own making, you need not boil it the first year, but pour it on cold; and the next year, if any remains, boil it again, skim it, put fresh spice to it, and it will do again.

To pickle Gerkins.

Take five hundred gerkins, and have ready a large earthen pan of spring water and salt, to every gallon of water two pounds of salt; mix it well together, and throw in your gerkins, wash them out in two hours, and put them to drain, let them be drained very dry, and put them into a jar; in the mean time get a bell-metal pot, with a gallon of the best white-wine vinegar, half an ounce of cloves and mace, one ounce of all-spice, one ounce of mustard seed, a stick of horse-radish cut into slices, six bay leaves, a little dill, two or three races of ginger, cut in pieces, a nutmeg cut in pieces, and a handful of salt; boil it up in the pot all together, and put it over the gerkins; cover them close down, and let them stand twenty-four hours; then put them in your pot, and simmer them over the stove till they are green; be careful not to let them boil, if you do, you will spoil them; then put them in a jar, and cover them close down till cold; then tie them over with a bladder, and a leather over that; put them in a cold dry place. Mind always to keep your pickles tied down close, and take them out with a wooden spoon, or a spoon kept on purpose.

To pickle large Cucumbers in slices.

Take the large cucumbers before they are two ripe, slice them the thickness of crown pieces in a pewter dish; to every dozen of cucumbers slice two large onions thin, and so on till you have filled the dish, with a handful of salt between every row; then cover them with another pewter dish, and let them stand twenty four hours then put them into a cullender, and let them drain very well; put them in a jar, cover them over with white wine vinegar, and let them stand four hours ; pour the vinegar from them into a copper sauce-pan, and boil it with a little salt; put to the cucumbers a little mace, a little whole pepper, a large race of ginger sliced, and then pour the boiling vinegar on. Cover them close, and when they are cold tie them down. They will be fit to eat in two or three days

To pickle Asparagus.

Take the largest asparagus you can get, cut off the white ends, and wash the green ends in spring-water, then put them in another clean water, and let them lie two or three hours in it ; then have a large broad stew pan full of spring water with a good large handful of salt ; set it on the fire, and when it boils put in the asparagus, not tied up but loose, and not too many at a time, for fear you break the heads.—Just scald them, and no more, take them out with a broad skimmer and lay them on a cloth to cool.—Then for your pickle take a gallon, or more according to your quantity of asparagus, of white wine vinegar, and one ounce of bay-salt, boil it, and put your asparagus in your jar ; to a gallon of pickle, two nutmegs, a quarter of an ounce of mace, the same of whole white-pepper, and pour the pickle hot over them. Cover them with a linen cloth, three or four times double, let them stand a week longer, boil the pickle again, and pour it on hot as before. When they are cold, cover them close with a bladder and leather.

To pickle Peaches.

Take your peaches when they are at their full growth, just before they turn to be ripe ; be sure they are not bruised ; then take spring-water, as much as you think will cover them, make it salt enough to bear an egg, with bay and comm on salt an equal quantity of each ; then put in your peaches, and lay a thin board over them to keep them under the water. Let them stand three days, and then take them out and wipe them very carefully with a fine soft cloth and lay them in your glass or jar, then take as much white-wine vinegar as will fill your glass or jar : to every gallon put one pint of the best well make mustard, two or three heads of garlick, a good deal of ginger sliced, half an ounce of cloves, mace and nutmeg ; mix your pickle well together, and pour over your peaches. Tie them close with a bladder and leather ; they will be fit to eat in three months. You may with a fine pen-knife cut them across ; take out the stone, fill them with made mustard and garlick, and horse-radish and ginger ; tie them together. You may pickle nectarines and apricots the same way

To pickle French Beans

Make a strong pickle, with cold spring-water and bay-salt, strong enough to bear an egg, then put your pods in, and lay a thin board on them, to keep them under water. Let them stand ten days, then drain them in a sieve, and lay them on a cloth to dry ; then take white-wine vinegar, as much as you think will cover them, boil it, and put your pods in a jar with ginger, mace, cloves, and Jamaica pepper.—Pour your vinegar boiling hot on, cover them with a coarse cloth, three or four times double, that the steam may come through a little, and let them stand two days. Repeat this two or three times ; when it is cold, put in a pint of mustard-seed, and some horse-radish : cover it close.

Another way to pickle French Beans.

Pickle your beans as you do the gerkins.

To pickle Cauliflowers.

Take the largest and closest you can get; pull them in sprigs; put them in an earthen dish, and sprinkle salt over them. Let them stand twenty-four hours to draw out all the water, then put them in a jar, and pour salt and water boiling over them; cover them close, and let them stand till the next day; then take them out, and lay them on a coarse cloth to drain; put them into glass jars, and put in a nutmeg sliced, two or three blades of mace in each jar; cover them with distilled, vinegar and tie them down with a bladder, and over that a leather. They will be fit for use in a month.

To pickle Beet-root.

Set a pot of spring-water on the fire, when it boils put in your beets, and let them boil till they are tender; take them out, and with a knife take off all the outside, cut them in pieces according to your fancy; put them in a jar, and cover them with cold vinegar, and tie them down close; when you use the beet take it out of the pickle, and cut it into what shape you like; put it in a little dish with some of the pickle over it You may use it for sallads, or garnish.

To pickle White Plums,

Take the large white plums; and if they have stalks, let them remain on, and do them as you do your peaches. See page 149.

To pickle Onions.

Take your onions when they are dry enough to lay up for winter, the smaller they are the better they look; put them into a pot, and cover them with spring-water, with a handful of white salt, let them boil up; then strain them off, and take three coats off; put them in a cloth, and let two people take hold of it, one at each end, and rub them backward and forwards till they are very dry; then put them in your bottles, with some blades of mace and cloves, a nutmeg cut in pieces; have some double distilled white-wine vinegar; boil it up with a little salt; let it be cold, and put it over the onions; cork them close and tie a bladder and leather over it.

To pickle Lemons.

Take twelve lemons, scrape them with a piece of broken glass, then cut them across in two, four parts downright, but none quite through, but that they will hang together; put in as much salt as they will hold, rub them well, and strew them over with salt. Let them lie in an earthen dish three days, and turn them every day; slit an ounce of ginger very thin, and salted for three days a small handful of mustard seeds bruised and searced through a hair sieve, and some red Indian pepper; take your lemons out of the salt, sqeeze them very gently, put them into a jar with the spice and ingredients and cover them with the best white wine vinegar. Stop them up very close, and in a month's time they will be fit to eat.

To pickle Mushrooms White.

Take small buttons, cut the stalk, and rub off the skin with flannel dipped in salt, and throw them into milk and water: drain them out, and put them into a stew-pan, with a handful of salt over them; cover them close, and put them over a gentle stove for five minutes, to draw out all the water, then put them on a coarse cloth to drain till cold.

To make Pickle for Mushrooms.

Take a gallon of the best vinegar, put it into a cold still; to every gallon of vinegar, put half a pound of bay-salt, a quarter of a pound of mace, a quarter of an ounce of cloves, a nutmeg cut in quarters, keep the top of the still covered with a wet cloth. As the cloth dries put on a wet one. Do not let the fire be too large, lest you burn the bottom of the still. Draw it as long as you taste the acid, and no longer. When you fill your bottles, put in you mushrooms, here and there put in a few blades of mace, and a slice of nutmeg; then fill the bottle with pickle, and melt some mutton fat, strain it and pour over it. It will keep them better than oil.

You must put your nutmeg over the fire in a little vinegar, and give it a boil. While it is hot you may slice it as you please. When it is cold, it will not cut, for it will crack to pieces.

To pickle Codlings.

Gather your codlings when they are the size of a large double walnut; take a pan, and put vine, leaves thick at the bottom. Put in your codlings, and cover them well with vine-leaves and spring-water; put them over a slow fire till you can peel the skin off; take them carefully up in a hair-sieve, peel them very carefully with a pen-knife; put them into the same water again, with the vine-leaves as before. Cover them close, and set them at a distance from the fire, till they are of a fine green; drain hem in a cullender till cold; put them in jars, with some mace and a clove or two of garlick; cover them with distilled vinegar; pour some mutton fat over, and tie them with a bladder and leather down very tight.

To pickle Fennel.

Set spring-water on the fire, with a handful of salt, when it boils, tie your fennel in bunches, and put them into the water, just give them a scald, lay them on a cloth to dry; when cold, put in a glass, with a little mace and nutmeg, fill it with cold vinegar, lay a bit of green fennel on the top, and over that a bladder and leather.

To pickle Grapes.

Get grapes at the full growth, but not ripe; cut them in small bunches fit for garnishing, put them in a stone jar, with vine-leaves between every layer of grapes; then take as much spring-water as you think will cover them, put in a pound of bay-salt, and as much white salt as will make it bear an egg. Dry your bay-salt and pound it, it will melt the sooner; put it into a bell-metal or copper pot, boil it and skim it very well; as it boils, take all the black scum off, but not the white scum. When it has boiled a quarter of an hour, let it stand to cool and settle; when it is almost cold pour the clear liquor on the grapes, lay vine-leaves on the top, tie them down close with a linen cloth, and cover them with a dish. Let them stand twenty four hours; then take them out, and lay them on a cloth, cover them over with another, let them be dried between the cloths; then take two quarts of vinegar, one quart of spring-water and one pound of coarse sugar. Let it boil a little while, skim it as it boils very clean, let it stand till it is quite cold, dry your jar with a cloth, put fresh vine-leaves at the bottom, and between every bunch of grapes, and on the top; then pour the clear off the pickle on the grapes fill your jar that the pickle may be above the grapes, tie a thin bit of board in a piece of flannel, lay it on the top of the jar, to keep the grapes under the pickle; tie them out with a bladder, and then a leather; take them down with a wooden spoon. Be sure to make pickle enough to cover them.

To pickle Barberries.

Take white wine vinegar; to every quart of vinegar, put in half a pound of sixpenny sugar, then pick the worst of your barberries, and put into this liquor and the best into glasses; then boil your pickle with the worst of your barberries, and skim it very clean. Boil it till it looks of a fine colour, then let it stand to be cold before you strain; then strain it through a cloth, wringing it to get all the colour you can from the barberries. Let it stand to cool and settle, then pour it clear into the glasses in a little of the pickle; boil a little fennel; when cold, put a little bit at the top of the pot or glass, and cover close with a bladder and leather. To every half pound of sugar put a quarter of a pound of white salt.

Red currants is done the same way. Or you may do barberries thus: pick them clean from leaves and spotted ones; put them into jars; mix spring water and salt pretty strong, and put over them, and when you see the scum rise, change the salt and water, and they will keep a long time.

To pickle Red Cabbage.

Slice the cabbage very fine cross-ways; put it on an earthen dish, and sprinkle a handful of salt over it, cover it with another dish, and let it stand twenty-four hours; then put it in a cullender to drain, and lay it in your jar; take white-wine vinegar enough to cover it, a little cloves, mace, and all-spice, put them in whole, with one pennyworth of cochineal bruised fine: boil it up, and put it over hot or cold, which you like best, and cover it close with a cloth till cold; then tie it over with leather

To pickle Golden Pippins

Take the finest pippins you can get free from spots and bruises, put them into a preserving-pan of cold spring water, and set them on a charcoal fire. Keep them turning with a wooden spoon till they will peel; do not let them boil When they are enough peel them, and put them into the water again with a quarter of a pint of the best vinegar, and a quarter of an ounce of alum, cover them close with a pewter-dish, and set them on the charcoal fire again, a slow fire, not to boil. Let them stand, turning them now and then, till they look green; then take them out and lay them on a cloth to cool; when cold make your pickle as for the peaches, only instead of made mustard, this must be mustard seed whole. Cover them close, and keep them for use.

To pickle Nastertium Berries and Limes; you pick them off the Lime Trees in Summer.

Take nastertium berries gathered as soon as as the blossom is off, or the limes, and put them in cold spring-water and salt ; change the water for three days successively. Make a pickle of white wine vinegar, mace, nutmeg, slice six shalots six blades of garlick, some pepper-corns, salt, and horse raddish, cut in slices. Make your pickle very strong, drain your berries very dry, and put them in bottles. Mix your pickle up well together, but you must not boil it ; put it over the berries or limes, and tie them down close.

To pickle Oysters, Cockles, and Muscles

Take two hundred oysters, the newest and best you can get, be careful to save the liquor in some pan as you open them, cut off the black verge saving the rest put them into their own liquor ; then put all the liquor and oysters into a kettle, boil them about half an hour on a very gentle fire, do them very slowly, skimming them as the scum rises, then take them off the fire, take out the oysters, strain the liquor through a fine cloth ; then put in the oysters again ; then take out a pint of the liquor whilst it is hot, put thereto three quarters of an ounce of mace, and half an ounce of cloves. Just give it one boil, then put it to the oysters, and stir up the spices well among them ; then put in about a spoonful of salt, three quarters of a pint of the best white wine vinegar, and a quarter of an ounce of whole pepper ; then let them stand till they are cold ; then put the oysters, as many as you well can, into the barrel ; put in as much liquor as the barrel will hold, letting them settle a while, and they will soon be fit to eat. Or you may put them in stone-jars, cover them close with a bladder and leather, and be sure they be quite cold before you cover them up. Thus do cockles and muscles ; only this, cockles are small, and to this spice you must have at least two quarts. There is nothing to pick off them. Muscles you must have two quarts ; take great care to pick the crab out under the tongue, and a little fus which grows at the root of the tonge. The two latter, cockles, and muscles, must be washed in several waters, to clean them from the grit ; put them in a stew-pan by themselves, cover them close, and when they are open, pick them out of the shells and strain the liquor.

To pickle young Suckers, or young Artichokes, before the Leaves are hard.

Take young suckers, pare them very nicely, all the hard ends of the leaves and stalks, just scald them in salt and water, and when they are cold put them into little glass bottles, with two or three large blades of mace, and a nutmeg sliced thin ; fill them either with distilled vinegar, or the sugar-vinegar of your own making, with half spring-water.

To pickle Artichoke-Bottoms.

Boil artichokes till you can pull the leaves off, then take off the chokes, and cut them from the stalk ; take great care you do not let the knife touch the top, throw them into salt and water for an hour, then take them out and lay them on a cloth to drain, then put them into large wide-mouthed glasses ; put a little mace and sliced nutmeg between, fill them either with distilled vinegar, or sugar-vinegar and spring-water ; cover them with mutton fat fried, and tie them down with a bladder and leather.

To pickle Samphire.

Take the samphire that is green, lay it in a clean pan, throw two or three handfuls of salt over, then cover it with spring-water. Let it lie twenty-four hours, then put it into a clean brass sauce-pan, throw in a handful of salt, and cover it with good vinegar. Cover the pan close, and set it over a very slow fire; let it stand till it is just green and crisp; then take it off in a moment, for if it stands to be soft it is spoiled, put it in your pickling pot, and, cover it close. When it is cold, tie it down with a bladder and leather, and keep it for use. Or you may keep it all the year in a very strong brine of salt and water, and throw it into vinegar just before you use it.

To pickle Mock Ginger.

Take the largest cauliflowers you can get, cut off all the flowers from the stalks, and peel them, throw them into strong spring water and salt for three days, then drain them in a sieve pretty dry; put them in a jar, boil white wine vinegar with cloves, mace, long pepper, and all-spice, each half an ounce, forty blades of garlic, a stick of horse-radish cut in slices, a quarter of an ounce of Cayenne pepper, and a quarter of a pound of yellow turmarick, two ounces of bay-salt, pour it boiling over the stalks; cover it down close till the next day, then boil it again, and repeat it twice more, and when cold tie it down close.

To pickle Melon Mangoes.

Take as many green melons as you want, and slit them two-thirds up the middle, and with a spoon take all the seeds out; put them in strong spring-water and salt for twenty four hours, then drain them in a sieve; mix half a pound of white mustard, two ounces of long pepper, the same of all-spice, half an ounce of cloves and mace, a good quantity of garlic, and horse-radish cut in slices, and a quarter of an ounce of Cayenne pepper; fill the seed holes full of this mixture; put a small skewer through the end, and tie it round with pack thread close to the skewer, put them in a jar, and boil up vinegar with some of the mixture in it, and pour over the melons. Cover them down close, and let them stand till next day, then green them the same way as you do gerkins. You may do large cucumbers the same way. Tie them down close when cold, and keep them for use.

Elder-shoots, in imitation of Bamboo.

Take the largest and youngest shoots of elder, which put out in the middle of May, the middle stalks are most tender and bigest; the small ones are not worth doing. Peel off the outward peel or skin. and lay them in a strong brine of salt and water for one night, then dry them in a cloth, piece by piece. In the mean time, make your pickle of half white-wine and half beer vinegar; to each quart of pickle you must put an ounce of white or red pepper, an ounce of ginger sliced, a little mace, and a few corns of Jamaica pepper. When the spice has boiled in the pickle, pour it hot upon the shoots, stop them close immediately, and set the jar two hours before the fire, turning it often. It is as good a way of greening pickles as often boiling. Or you may boil the pickle two or three times, and pour it on boiling hot, just as you please. If you make the pickle of the sugar-vinegar you must let one half be spring water.

RULES to be observed in PICKLING.

Always use stone-jars for all sorts of pickles that require hot pickle to them. The first charge is the least; for these not only last longer, but keep the pickle better: for vinegar and salt will penetrate through all earthen vessels; stone and glass are the only things to keep pickle in. Be sure never to put your hands in to take pickles out, it will soon spoil it. The best method is, to every pot tie a wooden spoon, full of little holes, to take the pickles out with.

OF MAKING CAKES, &c.

To make a Rich Cake.

Take four pounds of flour dried and sifted, seven pounds of currant washed and rubbed, six pounds of the best fresh butter, two pounds of Jordan almonds blanched, and beaten with orange-flower water, and sack till fine; then take four pounds of eggs, put half the whites away, three pounds of double-refined sugar beaten and sifted, a quarter of an ounce of mace, the same of cloves and cinnamon, three large nutmegs, all beaten fine, a little ginger, half a pint of sack, half a pint of right French brandy, sweet-meats to your liking, they must be orange, lemon, and citron. Work your butter to a cream with your hands, before any of your ingredients are in, then put in your sugar, and mix it well together, let your eggs be well beat and strained through a sieve, work in your almonds first, then put in your eggs, beat them together till they look white and thick; then put in your sack, brandy, and spices, shake your flour in by degrees, and when your oven is ready, put in your currants, and sweet-meats as you put in your hoop. It will take four hours baking in a quick oven. You must keep it beating with your hand all the while you are mixing of it, and when your currants are well washed and cleaned, let them be kept before the fire, so that they may go warm into your cake. This quantity will bake best in two hoops.

To ice a great Cake.

Take the whites of twenty four eggs and a pound of double refined sugar beat and sifted fine; mix both together in a deep earthen pan, and with a whisk, whisk it well for two or three hours, till it looks white and thick, then with a thin broad board, or bunch of feathers, spread it all over the top and sides of the cake; set it at a proper distance before a good clear fire, keep turning it continually for fear of its changing colour; but a cool oven is best, and an hour will harden it. You may perfume the icing with what perfume you please.

To make a Pound Cake.

Take a pound of butter, beat it in an earthern pan with your hand one way, till it is like a fine thick cream: then have ready twelve eggs, but half the whites; beat them well, and beat them up with the butter, a pound of flour beat in it, a pound of sugar, and a few carraways. Beat it all well together for an hour with your hand, or a great wooden spoon, butter a pan and put it in, and then bake it an hour in a quick oven.

For change you may put in a pound of currants, clean washed and picked.

To make a cheap Seed Cake.

You must take half a peck of flour, a pound and a half of butter, put it into a sauce-pan with a pint of new milk, set it on the fire, take a pound of sugar, half an ounce of all-spice beat fine, and mix them with the flour. When the butter is melted, pour the milk and butter in the middle of the flour, and work it up like paste. Pour in with the milk half a pint of good ale yeast, set it before the fire to rise, just before it goes to the oven. Either put in some currants or carraway-seeds, and bake it in a quick oven. Make it into two cakes. They will take an hour and a half baking.

To make a Butter-Cake.

You must take a dish of butter, and beat it like cream with your hands, two pounds of sugar well beat, three pounds of flour well dried, and mix them in with the butter, twenty-four eggs, leave out half the whites, and then beat all together for an hour. Just as you are going to put it into the oven, put in a quarter of an ounce of mace, a nutmeg beat, a little sack or brandy, and seeds or currants, just as you please.

To make Ginger-Bread Cakes.

Take three pounds of flour, one pound of sugar, one pound of butter rubbed in very fine, two ounces of ginger beat fine, a large nutmeg grated then take a pound of treacle, a quarter of a pint of cream, make them warm together, and make up the bread stiff, roll it out, and make it up into thin cakes, cut them out with a tea-cup, or small glass, or roll them round like nuts, and bake them on tin-plates in a slack oven.

To make a fine Seed or Saffron Cake.

You must take a quarter of a peck of fine flour, a pound and a half of butter, three ounces of carraway-seeds, six eggs beat well, a quarter of an ounce of cloves and mace beat together very fine, a penny-worth of cinnamon beat, a pound of sugar a penny-worth of rose water, a penny-worth of saffron, a pint and a half of yeast, and a quart of milk; mix it all together, lightly with your hands thus: first boil your milk and butter, then skim off the butter, and mix with your flour and a little of the milk, stir the yeast into the rest and strain it, mix it with the flour, put in your seed and spice, rose-water, tincture of saffron, sugar, and eggs, beat it all up well with your hands lightly, and bake it in a hoop or pan, but be sure to butter the pan well. It will take an hour and a half in a quick oven. You may leave out the seed if you choose it, and I think it rather better without it; but that you may do as you like.

To make a rich Seed-Cake called the Nun's Cake.

You must take four pounds of the finest flour, and three pounds of double refined sugar beaten and sifted; mix them together, and dry them by the fire till you prepare the other materials. Take four pounds of butter, beat it with your hand till it is soft like cream; then beat thirty-five eggs, leave out sixteen whites, strain off your eggs from the threads, and beat them and the butter together till all appears like butter. Put in four or five spoonfuls of rose or orange flower water, and beat again; then take your flour and sugar with six ounces of caraway-seeds, and strew them in by degrees, beating it up all the time for two hours together. You may put in as much tincture of cinnamon or ambergrease as you please ; butter your hoop, and let it stand three hours in a moderate oven. You must observe always, in beating of butter, to do it with a cool hand, and beat always one way in a deep earthen dish.

To make pepper Cakes.

Take half a gill of sack, half a quarter of an ounce of whole white-pepper, put it in, and boil it together a quarter of an hour ; then take the pepper out, and put in as much double refined sugar as will make it like a paste ; then drop it in what shape you please on plates, and let it dry itself.

To make Portugal Cakes

Mix into a pound of fine flour, a pound of loaf sugar beat and sifted, then rub it into a pound of pure sweet butter till it is thick like grated white-bread, then put it to two spoonfuls of rose-water, two of sack, ten eggs, whip them very well with a whisk, then mix it into eight ounces of currants, mixed all well together, butter the tin-pans, fill them but half full, and bake them, if made without currants they will keep half a year ; add a pound of almonds blanched, and beat with rose-water, as above, and leave out the flour. These are another sort, and better.

To make a pretty Cake.

Take five pounds of flour well dried, one pound of sugar, half an ounce of mace, as much nutmeg : beat your spice very fine, mix the sugar and spice in the flour, take twenty-two eggs, leave out six whites, beat them, put a pint of ale-yeast and the eggs in the flour, take two pounds and a half of fresh butter, a pint and a half of cream, set the cream and butter over the fire till the butter is melted, let it stand till it is blood-warm. Before you put it into the flour, set it an hour by the fire to rise; then put it in seven pounds of currants, which must be plumped in half a pint of brandy, and three quarters of a pound of candied peels. It must be an hour and a quarter in the oven. You must put two pounds of chopped raisins in the flour, and a quarter of a pint of sack. When you put the currants in, bake it in a hoop.

To make Ginger-Bread.

Take three quarts of fine flour two ounces of beaten ginger, a quarter of an ounce of nutmeg, cloves, and mace beat fine, but most of the last; mix all together, three quarters of a pound of fine sugar, two pounds of treacle, set it over the fire, but do not let it boil; three-quarters of a pound of butter melted in the treacle, and some candied lemon and orange-peel cut fine; mix all these together well. An hour will bake it in a quick oven.

To make little fine Cakes.

One pound of butter beaten to cream, a pound and a quarter of flour, a pound of fine sugar beat fine, a pound of currants clean washed and picked, six eggs, two whites left out; beat them fine, mix the flour, sugar, and eggs by degrees into the batter, beat it all well with both hands; either make it into little cakes, or bake it in one.

Another Sort of little Cakes.

A Pound of flour, and half a pound of sugar: beat half a pound of butter with your hand, and mix them well together. Bake it in little cakes.

To make Drop-Biscuits

Take eight eggs, and one pound of double refined sugar beaten fine, twelve ounces of fine flour well dried, beat your eggs very well, then put in your sugar and beat it, and then your flour by degrees, beat it all very well together without ceasing: your oven must be as hot as for halfpenny bread; then flour some sheets of tin, and drop your biscuits, of what bigness you please, put them into the oven as fast as you can, and when you see them rise, watch them: if they begin to colour, take them out and put in more, and if the first is not enough, put them in again. If they are right done, they will have a white ice on them. You may, if you chuse, put in a few carraways; when they are all baked, put them in the oven again to dry, then keep them in a very dry place.

To make common Biscuits

Beat up six eggs, with a spoonful of rose-water and a spoonful of sack; then add a pound of fine powdered sugar, and a pound of flour, mix them into the eggs by degrees, and an ounce of coriander-seeds, mix all well together, shape them on white thin paper, or tin molds, in any form you please. Beat the white of an egg, with a feather rub them over, and dust fine sugar over them. Set them in an oven moderately heated, till they rise and come to a good colour, take them out, and when you have done with the oven, if you have no stove to dry them in, put them in the oven again, and let them stand all night to dry.

To make French Biscuits

Having a pair of clean scales ready, in one scale put three new-laid eggs, in the other scale put as much dried flour an equal weight with the eggs, take out the flour, and as much fine powdered sugar; first beat the whites of the eggs up well with a wisk till they are of a fine froth, then whip in half an ounce of candied lemon-peel cut very thin and fine and beat well, then by degrees whip in the flour and sugar, then slip in the yolks, and with a spoon temper it well together; then shape your biscuits on fine white paper with your spoon, and throw powdered sugar over them. Bake them in a moderate oven, not too hot, giving them a fine colour on the top. When they are baked, with a fine knife cut them off from the paper, and lay them in boxes for use.

To make Mackeroons

Take a pound of almonds, let them be scalded, blanched, and thrown into cold water, then dry them in a cloth, and pound them in a mortar, moisten them with orange-flower water, or the white of an egg, lest they turn to oil, afterwards take an equal quantity of fine powder sugar, with three or four whites of eggs, and a little musk, beat all well together, and shape them on a wafer-paper, with a spoon round. Bake them in a gentle oven on tin plates.

To make Shrewsbury Cakes.

Take two pounds of flour, a pound of sugar finely searced, mix them together (take out a quarter of a pound to roll them in); take four eggs beat; four spoonfuls of cream, and two spoonfuls of rose-water; beat them well together and mix them with the flour into a paste, roll them into thin cakes, and bake them in a quick oven.

To make Madling Cakes.

To a quarter of a peck of flour, well dried at the fire, add two pounds of mutton-suet fried and strained clear off: when it is a little cool, mix it well with the flour, some salt, and a very little all-spice beat fine; take half a pint of good yeast, and put in half a pint of water, stir it well together, strain it and mix up your flour, into a paste of moderate stiffness. You must add as much cold water as will make the paste of a right order: make it into cakes about the thickness and bigness of an oat-cake; have ready some currants clean washed and picked, strew some just in the middle of your cakes between your dough, so that none can be seen till the cake is broke. You may leave the currants out, if you do not chuse them.

To make light Wigs.

Take a pound and half of flour, and half a pint of milk made warm, mix these together, cover it up, and let it lie by the fire half an hour; then take half a pound of sugar and half a pound of butter then work these into a paste, and make it into wigs, with as little flour as possible. Let the oven be pretty quick and they will rise very much. Mind to mix a quarter of a pint of good ale-yeast in milk.

To make very good Wigs.

Take a quarter of a peck of the finest flour, rub it into three quarters of a pound of fresh butter till it is like grated bread, something more than half a pound of sugar, half a nutmeg, half a race of ginger grated, three eggs, yolks and whites beat very well, and put to them half a pint of thick ale-yeast, three or four spoonfuls of sack, make a hole in the flour, and pour in your yeast and eggs, as much milk, just warm, as will make it into a light paste. Let it stand before the fire to rise half an hour, then make it into a dozen and a half of wigs, wash them over with eggs just as they go into the oven. In a quick oven half an hour will bake them.

To make Buns.

Take two pounds of fine flour, a pint of good ale yeast, put a little sack in the yeast, and three eggs beaten, knead all these together with a little warm milk, a little nutmeg, and a little salt; and lay it before the fire till it rises very light, then knead in a pound of fresh butter, a pound of rough carraway-comfits, and bake them in a quick oven in what shape you please on floured paper.

To make little Plum-Cakes.

Take two pounds of flour dried in the oven, or at a great fire, and a half a pound of sugar finely powdered, four yolks of eggs, two whites, half a pound of butter washed with rose-water, six spoonfuls of cream warmed, a pound and half of currants unwashed, but pickled and rubbed very clean in a cloth; mix all well together, then make them up into cakes, bake them in an oven, almost as hot as for a manchet, and let them stand half an hour till they are coloured on both sides, then take down the oven-lid, and let them stand to soak. You must rub the butter into the flour very well, then the egg and cream, and then the currants.

OF CHEESECAKES, CREAMS, JELLIES WHIP-SYLLABUBS, &c.

To make fine Cheese-Cakes.

Take a pint of cream, warm it, and put to it five quarts of milk warm from the cow, then put runnet to it, and give it a stir about; and when it is come, put the curd in a linen bag or cloth, let it drain well away from the whey, but do not squeeze it much; then put it into a mortar, and break the curd as fine as butter; put to your curd half a pound of sweet almonds blanched and beat exceeding fine, and half a pound of mackeroons beat very fine. If you have no mackeroons, get Naples biscuits; then add to it the yolks of nine eggs beaten, a whole nutmeg grated, two perfumed plums dissolved in rose, or orange-flower water, half a pound of fine sugar; mix all well together, then melt a pound and quarter of butter and stir it well in it, and half a pound of currants plumped, to let stand to cool till your use it; then make your puff-paste thus: take a pound of fine flour, wet it with cold water, roll it out, put into it by degrees a pound of fresh butter, and shake a little flour on each coat as you roll it. Make it just as you use it.

You may leave out the currants for change; nor need you put in the perfumed plums, if you dislike them: and for variety, when you make them of mackeroons, put in as much tincture of saffron as will give them a high colour, but no currants. This we call saffron cheesecakes; the other without currants, almond cheesecakes; with currants, fine cheesecakes; with mackeroons, mackeroon cheesecakes.

To make Lemon Cheesecakes.

Take the peel of two large lemons, boil it very tender; then pound it well in a mortar, with a quarter of a pound or more of loaf-sugar, the yolks of six eggs, and a half pound of fresh butter, and a little curd beat fine; pound and mix all together, lay a puff paste in your patty-pans, fill them half full and bake them. Orange cheesecakes are done the same way, only you boil the peel in two or three waters, to take out the bitterness.

A second Sort of Lemon Cheesecakes.

Take two large lemons, grate off the peel of both, and squeeze out the juice of one, and add to it half a pound of double-refined sugar, twelve yolks of eggs, eight whites well beaten, then melt half a pound butter in four or five spoonfuls of cream, then stir it all together and set it over the fire, stirring it till it begins to be pretty thick; then take it off, and when it is cold, fill your patty-pans little more than half full. Put a paste very thin at the bottom of your patty-pans. Half an hour, with a quick oven, will bake them.

To make Almond Cheesecakes.

Take half a pound of Jordan almonds, and lay them in cold water all night; the next morning blanch them into cold water; then take them out, and dry them in a clean cloth, beat them very fine in a little orange flower water, then take six eggs, leave out four whites, beat them and strain them, then half a pound of white sugar with a little beaten mace; beat them well together in a marble mortar, take ten ounces of good fresh butter, melt it, a little grated lemon-peel, and put them in the mortar with the other ingredients; mix all well together, and fill your patty-pans.

To make Fairy Butter.

Take the yolks of two hard-eggs, and beat them in a marble mortar, with a large spoonful of orange-flower water, and two tea-spoonfuls of fine sugar beat to powder; beat this all together till it is a fine paste, then mix it up with about as much fresh butter out of the churn, and force it through a fine strainer full of little holes into a plate. This is a pretty thing to set off a table at supper.

To make Almond Custards.

Take a pint of cream, blanch and beat a quarter of a pound of almonds fine, with two spoonfuls of rose-water. Sweeten to your palate, beat up the yolks of four eggs, stir all together one way over the fire till it is thick, then pour it out into cups. Or you may bake it in little china cups.

To make baked Custards.

One pint of cream boiled with mace and cinnamon; when cold, take four eggs, two whites left out, a little rose and orange flower water and sack, nutmeg and sugar to your palate; mix them well together, and bake them in china cups.

To make plain Custards.

Take a quart of new milk, sweeten it to your taste, grate in a little nutmeg, beat up eight eggs, leave out half the whites, beat them up well, stir them into the milk, and bake it in china basons, or put them in a deep china dish, have a kettle of water boiling, set the cup in, let the water come above half way, but do not let it boil too fast for fear of its getting into the cups, and take a hot iron and colour them at the top. you may add a little rose-water.

To make Orange-Butter.

Take the yolks of ten eggs beat very well, half a pint of Rhenish, six ounces of sugar, and the juice of three sweet oranges ; set them over a gentle fire, stirring them one way till it is thick. When you take it off, stir in a piece of butter as big as a large walnut.

To make Steeple Cream.

Take five ounces of hartshorn, and two ounces of ivory, and put them in a stone-bottle, fill it up with fair water to the neck, put in a small quantity of gum-arabic, and gum-dragon ; then tie up the bottle very close, and set it into a pot of water, with hay at the bottom. Let it stand six hours, then take it out, and let it stand an hour before you open it, lest it fly in your face ; then strain it and it will be a strong jelly, then take a pound of blanched almonds, beat them very fine, mix it with a pint of thick cream, and let it stand a little ; then strain it out and mix it with a pound of jelly, set it over the fire till it is scalding hot, sweeten it to your taste with double refined sugar, then take it off, put in a little amber, and pour it into small high gallipots, like a sugar-loaf at top ; when it is cold, turn them, and lay cold whipt-cream about them in heaps. Be sure it does not boil when the cream is in.

Lemon-Cream.

Take five large lemons, pare them as thin as possible, steep them all night in twenty spoonfuls of spring water, with the juice of the lemons, then strain it through a jelly-bag into a silver sauce-pan, if you have one, the whites of six eggs beat well, ten ounces of double refined sugar, set over a very slow charcoal fire, stir it all the time one way, skim it, and when it is hot as you can bear your fingers in, pour it into glasses.

A second Lemon-Cream.

Take the juice of four large lemons, half a pint of water, a pound of double-refined sugar beaten fine, the whites of seven eggs, and the yolk of one beaten very well, mix all together, strain it, and set it on a gentle fire, stirring it all the while, and skim it clean, put into it the peel of one lemon, when it is very hot, but do not boil, take out the lemon-peel, and pour it into China dishes. You must observe to keep it stirring one way all the time it is over the fire.

Jelly of Cream.

Take four ounces of hartshorn, put it on in three pints of water, let it boil till it is a stiff jelly, which you will know by taking a little in a spoon to cool; then strain it off, and add to it half a pint of cream, two spoonfuls of rose-water, two spoonfuls of sack, and sweeten it to your taste; then give it a gentle boil, but keep stirring it all the time, or it will curdle; then take it off and stir it till it is cold; then put it into broad bottomed cups, let them stand all night, and turn them out in a dish; take half a pint of cream, two spoonfuls of rose-water. and as much sack, sweeten it to your palate, and pour over them.

To make Orange-Cream.

Take and pare the rind of a Seville orange very fine, and squeeze the juice of four oranges; put them into a stew-pan, with half a pint of water, and half a pound of fine sugar, beat the whites of five eggs, and mix into it, and set them on a slow fire; stir it one way till it grows thick and white, strain it through a gauze, and stir it till cold; then beat the yolks of five eggs very fine, and put into your pan with the cream; stir it over a gentle fire till it is ready to boil; then put it in a bason and stir it till it is cold, and then put it in your glasses.

To make Gooseberry cream.

Take two quarts of gooseberries, put to them as much water as will cover them, scald them, and then run them through a sieve with a spoon; to a quart of pulp you must have six eggs well beaten; and when the pulp is hot, put in an ounce of fresh butter, sweeten it to your taste, put in your eggs, and stir them over a gentle fire till they grow thick, then set it by; and when it is almost cold, put into it two spoonfuls of juice of spinach, and a spoonful of orange-flower water or sack; stir it well together, and put it into your bason. When it is cold, serve it to the table.

To make Barley-Cream.

Take a small quantity of pearl-barley, boil it in milk and water till it is tender, then strain the liquor from it, put your barley into a quart of cream, and let it boil a little; then take the whites of five eggs and the yolk of one, beaten with a spoonful of fine flour, and two spoonfuls of orange-flower-water; then take the cream off the fire, and mix in the eggs by degrees and set it over the fire again to thicken. Sweeten to your taste, pour it into basons, and when it is cold serve it up.

To make Pistachio-Cream.

Take half a pound of Pistachio nuts, break them, and take out the kernels; beat them in a stew-pan with a pint of good cream, and the yolks of two eggs beat very fine; stir it gently over a slow fire till it is thick, but be sure it do not boil; then put it into a soup-plate; when it is cold, stick some kernels, cut long-ways, all over it, and send it to table.

Hartshorn Cream.

Take four ounces of hartshorn shavings, and boil it in three pints of water till it is reduced to half a pint, and run it through a jelly-bag; put to it a pint of cream and four ounces of fine sugar, and just boil it up; put it into cups or glasses and let it stand till quite cold. Dip your cups or glasses in scalding water, and turn them out into your dish; stick sliced almonds on them. It is generally eat with white wine and sugar.

To make Almond-Cream.

Take a quart of cream, boil it with a nutmeg grated, a blade or two of mace, a bit of lemon-peel, and sweeten to your taste; then blanch a quarter of a pound of almonds, beat them very fine with a spoonful of rose or orange-flower water, take the white of nine eggs well beat, and strain them to your almonds, beat them together, rub them very well through a coarse hair-sieve; mix all together with your cream, set it on the fire, stir it all one way all the time till it almost boils; pour it into a bowl, and stir it till cold, and then put it in cups or glasses, and send it to table.

To make a fine Cream.

Take a quart of cream, sweeten it to your palate, grate a little nutmeg, put in a spoonful of orange-flower-water and rose-water, and two spoonfuls of sack, beat up four eggs, but two whites: stir it all together one way over the fire till it is thick; have cups ready and pour it in.

To make Ratafia Cream.

Take six large laurel-leaves, boil them in a quart of thick cream; when it is boiled throw away the leaves, beat the yolks of five eggs with a little cold cream, and sugar to your taste, then thicken the cream with your eggs, set it over the fire again but do not let it boil; keep it stirring all the while one way, and pour it into china dishes. When it is cold, it is fit for use.

To make Whipt Cream.

Take a quart of thick cream, and the whites of eight eggs beat well, with half a pint of sack; mix it together, and sweeten it to your taste, with double refined sugar. You may perfume it if you please, with a little musk or ambergrease tied in a rag, and steeped a little in the cream; whip it up with a whisk, and some lemon-peel tied in the middle of the whisk; take the froth with a spoon, and lay it in your glasses or basons. This does well over a fine tart.

To make Whipt-Syllabubs

Take a quart of thick cream, and half a pint of

sack, the juice of two Seville oranges or lemons, grate in the peel of two lemons, half a pound of double-refined sugar, pour it into a broad earthen pan, and whisk it well, but first sweeten some red-wine or sack, and fill your glasses as full as you chuse, then as the froth rises take it off with a spoon, and lay it on a sieve to drain, then lay it carefully into your glasses till they are as full as they will hold. Do not make these long before you use them. Many use cyder sweetened, or any white wine you please, or lemon, or orange whey made thus: squeeze the juice of a lemon or orange, into a quarter of a pint of milk, when the curd is hard, pour the whey clear of, and sweeten it to your palate. You may colour some with the juice of spinach, some with saffron, and some with cochineal, just as you fancy.

To make Everlasting Syllabubs.

Take five half pints of thick cream, half a pint of Rhenish, half a pint of sack, and the juice of two large Seville oranges; grate in just the yellow rind of three lemons, and a pound of double-refined sugar, well beat and sifted: mix all together with a spoonful of orange-flower water; beat it well together with a whisk half an hour, then with a spoon take it off, and lay it on a sieve to drain, then fill your glasses. These will keep above a week and it is better made the day before. The best way to whip syllabub is, have a fine large chocolate mill, which you must keep on purpose, and a large deep bowl to mill them in. It is both quicker done, and the froth stronger. For the thin that is left at the bottom, have ready some calf's-foot jelly boiled and clarified, there must be nothing but the calf's foot boiled to a hard jelly: when cold, take off the fat, clear it with the whites of eggs, run it through a flannel bag, and mix it with the clear, which you saved of the syllabubs. Sweeten it to your palate, and give it a boil; then pour it into basons, or what you please. When cold turn it out, and it is a fine flummery.

To make Solid Syllabub.

To a quart of rich cream put a pint of white-wine, the juice of two lemons, the rind of one grated, sweeten it to your taste, mill it with a chocolate mill till it is all of a thickness; then put it in glasses, or a bowl, and set it in a cool place till next day.

To make a Trifle.

Cover the bottom of your dish or bowl with Naples biscuits broke in pieces, mackeroons broke in halves, and ratafia cakes. Just wet them all through with sack, then make a good boiled custard, not too thick and when cold pour it over it, then put a syllabub over that. You may garnish it with ratafia cakes, currant jelly, and flowers, and stew different coloured nonpareils over it. Note, these are bought at the confectioners.

To make Hartshorn Jelly.

Boil half a pound of hartshorn in three quarts of water over a gentle fire, till it becomes a jelly. If you take out a little to cool, and it hangs on the spoon, it is enough. Strain it while it is hot, put it in a well tinned sauce-pan, put to it a pint of Rhenish wine, and a quarter of a pound of loaf sugar; beat the whites of four eggs or more to a froth; stir it all together that the whites mix well with the jelly, and pour it in, as if you were cooling it. Let it boil two or three minutes: then put in the juice of three of four lemons; let it boil a minute or two longer. When it is finely curdled and a pure white colour, have, ready a swan-skin jelly bag over a china bason, pour in your jelly, and pour back again till it is as clear as rock-water; then set a very clean china bason, under, have your glasses as clean as possible, and with a clean spoon fill your glasses. Have ready some thin rind of the lemons, and when you have filled half your glasses, throw your peel into your bason; and when the jelly is all run out of the bag, with a clean spoon fill the rest of the glasses, and they will look of a fine amber colour. Now in putting in the ingredients there is no certain rule. You must put in lemon and sugar to your palate. Most people love them sweet; and indeed they are good for nothing unless they are.

Orange Jelly.

Take half a pound of hartshorn shavings, or four ounces of isinglass, and boil it in spring-water till it is of a strong jelly; take the juice of three Seville oranges, three lemons, and six China oranges, and the rind of one Seville orange, and one lemon pared very thin; put them to your jelly, sweeten it with loaf sugar to your palate; beat up the whites of eight eggs to a froth, and mix well in, then boil it for ten minutes, then run it through a jelly-bag till it is very clear, and put it in moulds till cold, then dip your mould in warm water, and turn it out into a china dish, or a flat glass, and garnish with flowers.

To make Ribband-Jelly.

Take out the great bones of four calves feet, put the feet into a pot with ten quarts of water, three ounces of hartshorn, three ounces of ising-glass, a nutmeg quartered, and four blades of mace; then boil this till it comes to two quarts strain it through a flannel bag, let it stand twenty-four hours, then scrape off all the fat from the top very clean, then slice it, put to it the whites of six eggs, beaten to a froth, boil it a little, and strain it through a flannel bag, then run the jelly into little high glasses, run every colour as thick as your finger, one colour must be thorough cold before you put another on, and that you put on must be but blood-warm, for fear it mix together. You must colour red with cochineal, green with spinach, yellow with saffron, blue with syrup of violets, white with thick cream, and sometimes the jelly by itself. You may add orange-flower water, or wine and sugar, and lemon, if you please; but this is all fancy.

To make Calve's-Feet Jelly.

Boil two calve's feet in a gallon of water, till it comes to a quart, then strain it, let it stand till cold, skim off all the fat clean, and take the jelly up clean. If there is any settling in the bottom, leave it; put the jelly into a sauce pan, with a pint of mountain wine, half a pound of loaf sugar, the juice of four large lemons; beat up six or eight whites of eggs with a whisk, then put them into a sauce-pan, and stir all together well till it boils. Let it boil a few minutes. Have ready a large flannel bag, pour it in, it will run through thick, pour it in again till it runs clear, then have ready a large china bason, with the lemon-peels cut as thin as possible, let the jelly run into that bason; and the peels both give it a fine amber colour, and also a flavour; with a clean silver spoon fill your glasses.

To make Currant Jelly.

Strip the currants from the stalks, put them in a stone jar, stop it close, set it in a kettle of boiling water, half way the jar, let it boil half an hour, take it out, and strain the juice through a coarse hair-sieve; to a pint of juice put a pound of sugar, set it over a fine clear fire in your preserving-pan or bell-metal skillet; keep stirring it all the time till the sugar is melted, then skim the scum off as fast as it rises. When your jelly is very clear and fine, pour it into gallipots; when cold, cut white paper just the bigness of the top of the pot and lay on the jelly, dip those papers in brandy; then cover the top close with white paper, and prick it full of holes; set it in a dry place, put some into glasses, and paper them.

To make Rasberry-Jam.

Take a pint of this currant-jelly, and a quart of rasberries, bruise them well together, set them over a slow fire, keeping them stirring all the time till it boils. Let it boil gently half an hour, and stir it round very often to keep it from sticking, and rub it through a cullender; pour it into your gallipots, paper as you do the currant jelly, and keep it for use. They will keep for two or three years, and have the full flavour of the rasberry.

To make Hartshorn Flummery.

Boil half a pound of the shavings of hartshorn in three pints of water till it comes to a pint, then strain it through a sieve into a bason, and set it by to cool; then set it over the fire, let it just melt, and put to it half a pint of thick cream, scalded and grown cold again, a quarter of a pint white-wine, and two spoonfuls of orange flower water; sweeten with sugar, and beat it for an hour and an half, or it will not mix well, nor look well; dip your cups in water before you put in the flummery, or else it will not turn out well. It is best when it stands a day or two before you turn it out. When you serve it up, turn it out of the cups, and stick blanched almonds, cut in long narrow bits, on the top. You may eat them either with wine or cream.

A second Way to make Hartshorn Flummery.

Take three ounces of hartshorn, and put to it two quarts of spring water, let it simmer over the fire six or seven hours, till half the water is consumed, or else put it in a jug, and set it in the oven with houshold bread, then strain it through a sieve, and beat half a pound of almonds very fine, with some orange-flower water in the beating; when they are beat, mix a little of your jelly with it, and some fine sugar, strain it out, and mix it with your other jelly, stir it together, till it is little more than blood-warm, then pour it into half-pint basons or dishes for the purpose, and fill them up half full. When you use them turn them out of the dish as you do flummery. If it does not come out clean, set your bason a minute or two in warm water. You may stick almonds in or not, just as you please. Eat it with wine and sugar. Or make your jelly this way; put six ounces of hartshorn in a glazed jug with a long neck, and put to it three pints of soft water, cover the top of the jug close, and put a weight on it to keep it steady; set it in a pot or kettle of water twenty-four hours, let it not boil, but be scalding hot, then strain it out, and make your jelly.

To make a fine Syllabub from the Cow.

Make your syllabub of either cyder or wine, sweeten it pretty sweet, and grate nutmeg in; then milk the milk into the liquor; when this is done, pour over the top half a pint of cream, according to the quantity of syllabub you make.

You may make this syllabub at home, only have new milk; make it as hot as milk from the cow, and out of a tea-pot or any such thing pour it in, holding your hand very high, and strew over some currants well washed and picked, and plumped before the fire.

To make a Hedge-Hog.

Take two pounds of blanched almonds, beat them well in a mortar, with a little canary and orange-flower water, to keep them from oiling. Make them into stiff paste, then beat in the yolks of twelve eggs, leave out five of the whites, put to it a pint of cream sweetened with sugar, put in half a pound of sweet butter melted, set it on a furnace or slow fire, and keep it constantly stirring till it is stiff enough to be made in the form of a hedge-hog: then stick it full of blanched almonds slit and stuck up like the bristles of a hedge-hog; then put it into a dish; take a pint of cream and the yolks of four eggs beat up, sweeten with sugar to your palate. Stir them together over a slow fire till it is quite hot ; then pour it round the hedge-hog in a dish, and let it stand till it is quite cold, and serve it up. Or a rich calf's foot jelly made clear and good, poured into the dish round the hedge-hog ; when it is cold it looks pretty, and makes a neat dish ; or it looks pretty in the middle of a table for supper.

To make French Flummery.

Take a quart of cream, and half an ounce of isinglass, beat it fine, and stir it into the cream. Let it boil softly over a slow fire a quarter of an hour, keep it stirring all the time ; then take it off, sweeten it to your palate and put in a spoonful of rose water, and a spoonful orange-flower water ; strain it, and pour it into a glass or bason, or what you please, and when it is cold turn it out. It makes a fine side-dish. You may eat it with cream, wine, or what you please. Lay round it baked pears. It both looks very pretty, and eats fine.

A Buttered Tart,

Take eight or ten large codlings, and scald them, when cold skin them, take the pulp and beat it as fine as you can with a silver spoon ; then mix in the yolks of six eggs and the whites of four, beat all well together : squeeze in the juice of a Seville orange. and shred the rind as fine as possible, with some grated nutmeg and sugar to your taste : melt some fine fresh butter, and beat up with it according as it wants, till it is all like a fine thick cream, and then make a fine puff-paste, have a large tin-patty that will just hold it, cover the patty with the paste, and pour in the ingredients. Do not put any cover on, bake it a quarter of an hour, then slip it out of the patty on a dish, and throw fine sugar well beat all over it. It is a very pretty side-dish for a second course. You may make this of any large apples you please.

Moon-Shine.

First have a piece of tin, made in the shape of a half moon, as deep as a half pint bason, and one in the shape of a large star, and two or three less ones. Boil two calves feet in a gallon of water till it comes to a quart, then strain it off, and when cold skim off the fat, take half the jelly, and sweeten it with sugar to your palate, beat up the whites of four eggs, stir all together over a slow fire till it boils; then run it through a flannel bag till clear, put it in a clean sauce-pan, and take an ounce of sweet almonds blanched and beat very fine in a marble mortar, with two spoonfuls of rose-water, and two of orange flower water; then strain it through a coarse cloth; mix it with the jelly, stir in four large spoonfuls of thick cream, stir it all together till it boils; then have ready the dish you intend it for, lay the tin in the shape of a half-moon in the middle and the stars round it; lay little weights on the tin to keep them in the places you would have them lie; then pour in the above blanch-manger into the dish, and when it is quite cold take out the tin linings, and mix the other half of the jelly with half a pint of good white-wine, and the juice of two or three lemons, with loaf sugar enough to make it sweet, and the whites of eight eggs beat it in, stir it all together over a slow fire till it boils then run it through a flannel bag till it is quite clear into a china bason, and very carefully fill up the places where you took the tin out, let it stand till cold, and send it to table.

Note. You may for change fill the dish with fine thick almond custard; and when it is cold, fill up the half moon and stars with a clear jelly.

The Floating Island, a pretty Dish for the Middle of a Table at a Second Course or for Supper.

You may take a soup-dish, according to the size and quantity you would make, but a pretty deep glass is best, and set it on a china dish; first take a quart of the thickest cream you can get, make it pretty sweet with fine sugar, pour in a gill of sack, grate the yellow rind of a lemon in, and mill the cream till it is all of a thick froth; then carefully pour the thin from the froth, into a dish; take a French roll, or as many as you want cut it as thin as you can, lay a layer of that as light as possible on the cream, then a layer of currant-jelly, then a very thin layer of roll, and then hartshorn-jelly, then French roll, and over that whip your froth which you saved off the cream very well milled up, and lay at top as high as you can heap it; and as for the rim of the dish, set it round with fruit or sweetmeats, according to your fancy. This looks very pretty in the middle of a table with candles round, and you may make it of as many different colours as you fancy, and according to what jellies and jams, or sweetmeats you have, or at the bottom of your dish you may put the thickest cream you can get; but that is as you fancy.

OF MADE-WINES, BREWING, FRENCH BREAD, &c.

To make Raisin Wine.

Take two hundred of raisins, stalks and all, and put them into a large hogshead, fill it with water, let them steep a fortnight, stirring them every day; then pour off all the liquor, and press the raisins. Put both liquors together in a nice clean vessel that will just hold it, for it must be full; let it stand till it has done hissing, or making the least noise, then stop it close, and let it stand six months. Peg it, and if you find it quite clear rack it off in another vessel; stop it close and let it stand three months longer; then bottle it, and when you use it rack it off into a decanter.

To make Elder Wine.

Pick the elder berries when full ripe, put them into a stone jar, and set them in the oven, or a kettle of boiling water till the jar is hot through; then take them out and strain them through a coarse cloth, wringing the berries, and put the juice into a clean kettle; to every quart of juice put a pound of fine Lisbon sugar, let it boil, and skim it well. When it is clear and fine pour it into a jar; when cold, cover it close, and keep it till you make raisin wine; then when you tun your wine, to every gallon of wine put half a pint of the elder-syrup.

To make Orange-Wine.

Take twelve pounds of the best powder sugar, with the whites of eight or ten eggs well beaten, into six gallons of spring-water, and boil three quarters of an hour. When cold, put into it six spoonfuls of yeast, and the juice of twelve lemons, which, being pared must stand with two pounds of white sugar in a tankard, and in the morning skim off the top, and then put it into the water: then add the juice and rinds of fifty oranges, but not the white parts of the rinds, and so let it work all together two days and two nights; then add two quarts Renish or white-wine, and put it into your vessel.

To make Orange Wine with Raisins.

Take thirty pounds of new Malaga raisins picked clean, chop them small, take twenty large Seville oranges, ten of them you must pare as thin as for preserving; boil about eight gallons of soft water till a third be consumed, let it cool a little, then put five gallons of it hot upon your raisins and orange peel, stir it well together, cover it up, and when it is cold let it stand five days, stirring it once or twice a day; then pass it through a hair sieve, and with a spoon press it as dry as you can, put in a runlet fit for it, and put it to the rind of the other ten oranges, cut as thin as the first; then make a syrup of the juice of twenty oranges, with a pound of white sugar. It must be made the day before you turn it up; stir it well together, and stop it close; let it stand two months to clear, then bottle it up. It will keep three years, and is better for keeping.

To make Elder-Flower Wine, very like Frontiniac.

Take six gallons of spring-water, twelve pounds of white-sugar, six pounds of raisins of the sun chopped. Boil these together one hour, then take the flowers of elder, when they are falling, and rub them off to the quantity of half a peck. When the liquor is cold, put them in, the next day put in the juice of three lemons, and four spoonfuls of good ale yeast. Let it stand covered up two days; then strain it off, and put it in a vessel fit for it. To every gallon of wine put a quart of Rhenish, and put your bung lightly on a fortnight, then stop it down close. Let it stand six months; and if you find it is fine, bottle it off.

To make Gooseberry-Wine.

Gather your gooseberries in dry weather, when they are half ripe, pick them, and bruise a peck in a tub, with a mallet; then take a horse hair-cloth, and press them as much as possible, without breaking the seeds. When you have pressed out all the juice, to every gallon of gooseberries put three pounds of fine dry powder sugar, stir it all together till the sugar is dissolved, then put it in a vessel or cask which must be quite full. If ten or twelve gallons, let it stand a fortnight; if a twenty gallon cask, five weeks. Set it in a cool place, then draw it off from the lees, clear the vessel of the lees, and pour in the clear liquor again. If it be a ten gallon cask, let it stand three months; if a twenty gallon four months, then bottle it off.

To make Cu rant-Wine.

Gather your currants on a fine dry day, when the fruit is full ripe; strip them, put them in a large pan, and bruise them with a wooden pestle. Let them stand in a pan or tub twenty-four hours to ferment; then run it through a hair-sieve, and do not let your hand tuch the liquor. To every gallon of this liquor, put two pounds and a half of white sugar, stir it well together, and put it into your vessel. To every six gallons put in a quart of brandy, and let it stand six weeks. If it is fine, bottle it; if it is not, draw it off as clear as you can, into another vessel, or large bottles; and in a fortnight, bottle it in small bottles.

To make Cherry-Wine.

Pull your cherries when full ripe off the stalks and press them through a sieve. To every gallon of liquor put two pounds of lump sugar beat fine, stir it together, and put it into a vessel; it must be full: when it has done working and making any noise, stop it close for three months, and bottle it off.

To make Birch-Wine.

The season for procuring the liquor from the birch-trees is in the begining of March, while the sap is rising, and before the leaves shoot out; for when the sap is come forward, and the leaves appear, the juice, by being long digested in the bark, grows thick and coloured, which before was thin and clear.

The method of procuring the juice is, by boring holes in the body of the tree, and putting in fossets, which are commonly made of the branches of elder, the pith being taken out. You may without hurting the tree, if large, tap it in several places, four or five at a time, and by that means save from a good many trees several gallons every day: if you have not enough in one day, the bottles in which it drops must be corked close, and rosined or waxed; however, make use of it as soon as you can.

Take the sap and boil it as long as any scum

rises, skimming it all the time; to every gallon of liquor put four pounds of good sugar, the thin peel of a lemon, boil it afterwards half an hour, skimming it very well, pour it into a clean tub, and when it is almost cold, set it to work with yeast spread upon a toast, let it stand five or six days, stirring it often; then take such a cask as will hold the liquor, fire a large match dipped in brimstone, and throw it into the cask, stop it close till the match is extinguished, tun your wine, lay the bung on light till you find it has done working; stop it close and keep it three months, then bottle it off.

To make Quince-Wine.

Gather the quinces when dry and full ripe; take twenty large quinces, wipe them clean with a coarse cloth, and grate them with a large grater or rasp as near the core as you can, but none of the core; boil a gallon of spring water, throw in your quinces, let it boil softly about a quarter of an hour; then strain them well into an earthen pan on two pounds of double-refined sugar, pare the peel of two large lemons, throw in and squeeze the juice through a sieve, stir it about till it is very cool, then toast a little bit of bread very thin and brown, rub a little yeast on it, let it stand close covered twenty-four hours, then take out the toast and lemon, put it up in a keg, keep it three months, then bottle it. If you make a twenty gallon cask, let it stand six months before you bottle it; when you strain your quinces, you are to wring them hard in a coarse cloth.

To make Cowslip or Clary-Wine.

Take six gallons of water, twelve pounds of

sugar, the juice of six lemons, the whites of four eggs beat very well, put all together in a kettle, let it boil half an hour, skim it very well: take a peck of cowslips; if dry ones, half a peck; put them into a tub, with the thin peeling of six lemons, then pour on the boiling liquor, and stir them about: when almost cold, put in a thin toast baked dry and rubbed with yeast. Let it stand two or three days to work. If you put in before you tun it six ounces of syrup of citron or lemons, with a quart of Rhenish wine, it will be a great addition; the third day strain it off, and squeeze the cowslips through a coarse cloth; then strain it through a flannel bag, and tun it up; lay the bung loose for two or three days to see if it works, and if it does not, bung it down tight; let it stand three months, then bottle it.

To make Turnip-Wine.

Take a good many turnips, pare, slice, and put them in a cyder-press, and press out all the juice very well. To every gallon of juice have three pounds of lump-sugar, have a vessel ready, just big enough to hold the juice, put your sugar into a vessel, and also to every gallon of juice half a pint of brandy. Pour in the juice, and lay something over the bung for a week to see if it works. If it does, you must not bung it down till it has done working; then stop it close for three months, and draw it off in another vessel. When it is fine, bottle it off.

To make Rasberry Wine.

Take some fine rasberries, bruise them with the back of a spoon, then strain them through a flannel bag into a stone-jar. To each quart of juice put a pound of double-refined sugar, stir it well together, and cover it close; let it stand three days, then pour it off clear. To a quart of juice put two quarts of white-wine, bottle it off; it will be fit to drink in a week. Brandy made thus is a very fine dram, and a much better way than steeping the rasberries.

RULES for BREWING.

Care must be taken, in the first place, to have the malt clean; and after it is ground, it ought to stand four or five days.

For strong October, five quarters of malt to three hogsheads, and twenty-four pounds of hops. This will afterwards make two hogsheads of good keeping small-beer, allowing five pounds of hops to it.

For middling beer, a quarter of malt makes a hogshead of ale, and one of small beer; or it will make three hogsheads of good small beer, allowing eight pounds of hops. This will keep all the year. Or it will make twenty gallons of strong ale, and two hogsheads of small beer that will keep all the year.

If you intend your ale to keep a great while, allow a pound of hops to every bushel; if to keep six months, five pounds to a hogshead, and the softest and clearest water you can get.

Observe the day before to have all your vessels very clean, and never use your tubs for any other use except to make wines.

Let your cask be very clean the day before with boiling water; and if your bung is big enough, scrub them well with a little birch-broom or brush; but if they be very bad, take out the heads, and let them be scrubbed clean with a hand-brush, sand, and fullers-earth. Put on the head again, and scald them well, throw into the barrel a piece of unslacked lime, and stop the bung close.

The first copper of water, when it boils, pour into your mash-tub, and let it be cool enough to see your face in, then put in your malt, and let it be well mashed, have a copper of water boiling in the mean time, and when your malt is well mashed, fill your mashing-tub, stir it well again, and cover it over with the sacks. Let it stand three hours, set a broad shallow tub under the cock, let it run very softly, and if it is thick throw it up again till it runs fine; then throw a handful of hops in the under tub, let the mash run into it, and fill your tubs till all is run off. Have water boiling in the copper, and lay as much more on as you have occasion for, allowing one third for boiling and waste. Let that stand an hour, boiling more water to fill the mash-tub for small beer, let the fire down a little, and put it into tubs enough to fill your mash. Let the second mash be run off, and fill your copper with the first wort; put in part of your hops and make it boil quick. About an hour is long enough, when it is half boiled, throw in a handful of salt. Have a clean white wand and dip it into the copper, and if the wort feels clammy it is boiled enough, then slacken your fire, and take off your wort. Have ready a large tub, put two sticks across, and set your straining basket over the tub on the sticks, and strain your wort though it. Put your other wort on to boil with the rest of the hops; let your mash be covered again with water, and thin your wort that is cooled in as many thing as you can; for the thinner it lies, and the quicker it cools the better. When quite cool, put it into the tunning-tub. Throw a handfull of salt into every boil. When the mash has stood an hour draw it off, then fill your mash with cold water, take off the wort in the copper and order it as before. When cool, add to it the first in the tub; so soon as you empty one copper, fill the other, so boil your small-beer well. Let the last mash run off, and when both are boiled with fresh hops, order them as the two first boilings, when cool empty the mash tub, and put the small-beer to work there. When cool enough work it, set a wooden bowl full of yeast in the beer, and it will work over, with a little of the beer in the boil. Stir your tun up every twelve hours, let it stand two days; then turn it, taking off the yeast. Fill your vessels full, and save some to fill your barrels, let it stand till it has done working, then lay on your bung lightly for a fortnight, after that stop it as close as you can. Mind you have a vent-peg at the top of the vessel, in warm weather, open it, and if your drink hisses, as it often will, loosen till it has done, then stop it close again. If you can boil your ale in one boiling it is best, if your copper will allow of it; if not, boil it as conveniency serves.

When you come to draw your beer, and find it is not fine, draw off a gallon, and set it on the fire, with two ounces of isinglass cut small and beat. Dissolve it in the beer over the fire, when it is all melted, let it stand till it is cold, and pour it in at the bung, which must lie loose on till it has done fermenting, then stop it close for a month.

Take great care your casks are not musty, or

have any ill taste; if they have, it is a hard thing to sweeten them.

You are to wash your casks with cold water before you scald them, and they should lie a day or two soaking, and clean them well, then scald them.

The best Thing for rope.

Mix two handfuls of bean-flower, and one handful of salt, throw this into a kilderkin of beer, do not stop it close till it has done fermenting, then let it stand a month, and draw it off, but sometimes nothing will cure it.

When a Barrel of Beer has turned Sour.

To a kilderkin of beer throw in at the bung a quart of oat-meal, lay the bung on loose two or three days, then stop it down close, and let it stand a month. Some throw in a piece of chalk as big as a turkey's egg, and when it has done working stop it close for a month, then tap it.

BAKING.

To make White-Bread after the London Way.

Take a bushel of the finest flour well dressed, put it in the kneading-trough at one end, take a gallon of water (which we call liquor) and some yeast, stir it into the liquor till it looks of a good brown colour and begins to curdle, strain and mix it with your flour till it is about the thickness of a seed-cake; then cover it with the lid of the trough, and let it stand three hours, and as soon as you see it begin to fall, take a gallon more of liquor, weigh three quarters of a pound of salt, and with your hand mix it well with the water, strain it, and with the liquor make your dough of a moderate thickness, fit to make up into loaves, then cover it again with the lid, and let it stand three hours more. In the mean time, put the wood into the oven and heat it. It will take two hours heating. When your spunge has stood its proper time, clear the oven and begin to make your bread, Set it in the oven, and close it up, and three hours will bake it. When once it is in, you must not open the oven till the bread is baked, and observe in summer that your water be milk-warm; and in winter as hot as you can bear your finger in it.

Note. As to the quantity of liquor your dough will take, experience will teach you in two or three times making, for all flour does not want the same quantity of liquor; and if you make any quantity it will raise up the lid and run over.

To make French Bread.

Take three quarts of water, and one of milk, in winter scalding hot, in summer a little more than milk-warm. Season it well with salt, then take a pint and a half of good ale-yeast not bitter, lay it in a gallon of water the night before, pour it off the water, stir in your yeast into the milk and water, then with your hand break in a little more than a quarter of a pound of butter, work it well till it is dissolved, then beat up two eggs in a bason, and stir them in, have about a peck and a half of flour, mix it with your liquor; in winter make your dough pretty stiff, in summer more slack, so that you may use a little more or less flour, according to the stiffness of your dough; mix it well, but the less you work the better. Make it into rolls, and have a very quick oven. When they have lain about a quarter of an hour turn them on the other side, let them lie about a quarter longer, take them out and chip all your French bread with a knife, which is better than rasping it, and make it look spungy and of a fine yellow, whereas the rasping takes off all that fine colour, and makes it look two smooth. You must stir your liquor into the flour as you do for pie-crust. After your dough is made cover it with a cloth, and let it lie to rise while the oven is heating.

To make Muffins.

To a bushel of Hertfordshire white flour, take a pint and a half of good ale-yeast, from pale-malt, if you can get it, because it is whitest, let the yeast lie in water all-night, the next day pour off the water clear, make two gallons of water just milk-warm, not to scald your yeast, and two ounces of salt, mix your water, yeast, and salt well together for about a quarter of an hour, then strain it and mix up your dough as light as possible, and let it lie in your trough an hour to rise, then with your hand roll it, and pull it into little pieces about as big as a large walnut, roll them with your hand like a ball, lay them on your table, and as fast as you do them lay a piece of flannel over them, and be sure to keep your dough covered with flannel; and when you have rolled out all your dough begin to bake the first, and by that time they will be spread out in the right form; lay them on your iron; as one side begins to change colour turn to the other, take great care they do not burn, or be too much discoloured, but that you will be a judge of in two or three makings. Take care the middle of the iron is not too hot, as is apt to be: but then you may put a brick-bat or two in the middle of the fire to slacken the heat. The thing you bake on must be made thus;

Build a place as if you were going to set a copper, and in the stead of a copper, a piece of iron all over the top fixed in form just the same as the bottom of an iron pot, and make your fire underneath with coal as in a copper. Observe, muffins are made the same way, only this, when you pull them to pieces roll them in a good deal of flour and with a rolling-pin roll them thin, cover them with a piece of flannel, and they will rise to a proper thickness, and if you find them too big or too little, you must roll dough accordingly. These must not be the least discoloured. When you eat them, toast them crisp on both sides, then with your hand pull them open, and they will be like a honey-comb, lay in as much butter as you intend to use, then clap them together again, and set it by the fire. When you think the butter is melted turn them, that both sides may be buttered alike, but do not touch them with a knife, either to spread or cut them open, if you do they will be as heavy as lead, only when they are buttered and done, you may cut them across with a knife.

Note. Some flour will soak up a quart or three pints more water, then other flour, then you must add more water or shake in more in making up, for the dough must be as light as possible.

A Receipt for making Bread without Yeast by the help of a Leaven.

Take a lump of dough about two pounds of your last making, which has been raised by yeast, keep it by you in a wooden vessel, and cover it well with flour. This is your leaven, then the night before you intend to bake, put the said leaven to a peck of flour, and work them well together with warm water. Let it lie in a dry wooden vessel, well covered with a linen cloth and a blanket, and keep it in a warm place. This dough kept warm will rise again next morning, and will be sufficient to mix with two or three bushels of flour, being worked up with warm water, and a little salt. When it is well worked up, and thoroughly mixed with all the flour, let it be well covered with the linen and blanket, until you find it rise, then knead it well, and work it up into bricks or loaves, making the loaves broad, and not so thick and high as is frequently done, by which means the bread will be better baked. Then bake your bread.

Always keep by you two or more pounds of the dough of your last baking well covered with flour, to make leaven to serve from one baking day to another; the more leaven is put to the flour, the lighter and spungier the bread will be. The fresher leaven, the bread will be the less sour.

From the Dublin Society.

A Method to preserve a Large Stock of Yeast, which will keep and be of use for several Months either to make Bread or Cakes.

When you have yeast in plenty, take a quantity of it, stir and work it well with a whisk until it becomes liquid and thin, then get a large wooden platter, cooler, or tub, clean and dry, and, with a soft brush lay a thin layer of the yeast on the tub, and turn the mouth downwards that no dust may fall upon it but so that the air may get under to dry it. When that coat is very dry, then lay on another till you have a sufficient quantity, even two or three inches thick, to serve for several months, always taking care the yeast in the tub be very dry before you lay more on. When you have occason to use this yeast cut a piece off, and lay it in warm water; stir it together, and it will be fit for use. If it is for brewing, take a large handful of birch tied together, and dip it into the yeast and hang it up to dry; take great care no dust comes to it, and so you may do as many as you please. When your beer is fit to set to work, throw in one of these, and it will make it work as well as if you had fresh yeast.

You must whip it about in the wort, and then let it lie; when the vat works well, take out the broom, and dry it again, and it will do for the next brewing.

Note. In the building of your oven for baking, observe you make it round, low roofed, and a little mouth; then it will take less fire, and keep in the heat better than a long oven and high roofed, and will bake the bread better.

JARRING CHERRIES, and PRESERVES, &c.

To jar Cherries, Lady North's Way.

Take twelve pounds of cherries, stone them, put them in your preserving pan, with three pounds of double-refined sugar and a quart of water; then set them on the fire till they are scalding hot, take them off a little while, and set on the fire again. Boil them till they are tender, then sprinkle them with half a pound of double-refined sugar pounded, and skim them clean. Put them all together in a China bowl, let them stand in a syrup three days; drain them through a sieve, take them out one by one, with the holes downwards on a wicker sieve, then set them in a stove to dry, as they dry turn them upon clean sieves. When they are enough, put a clean white sheet of paper in a preserving pan, then put all the cherries in with another clean white sheet of paper on the top of them; cover them close with a cloth, and set them over a cool fire till they sweat. Take them off the fire, then let them stand till they are cold, and put them in boxes or jars to keep.

To dry Cherries.

To four pounds of cherries put one pound of sugar, and just put as much water to the sugar as will wet it; when it is melted, make it boil; stone your cherries, put them in, and make them boil; skim them two or three times, take them off, and let them stand in the syrup two or three days, then boil your syrup and put to them again, but do not boil your cherries any more. Let them stand three or four days longer, then take them out, lay them in sieves to dry, and lay them in the sun, or in a slow oven to dry; when dry, lay them in rows in papers, and so a row of cherries, and a row of white paper in boxes.

To preserve Cherries with the Leaves and Stalks green.

First dip the stalks and leaves in the best vinegar boiling hot, stick the sprigs upright in a sieve till they are dry; in the mean time boil some double-refined sugar to syrup, and dip the cherries, stalks and leaves, in the syrup, and just let them scald: lay them on a sieve, and boil the sugar to a candy height, then dip the cherries, stalks, leaves, and all; then stick the branches in sieves, and dry them as you do other sweetmeats. They look very pretty at candle-light in a dessert.

To make Orange Marmalade.

Take the clearest Seville oranges, and cut them in two; take out all the pulp and juice into a pan, and pick all the skins and seeds out; boil the rinds in hard water till they are quite tender, and change the water three times while they are boiling, and then pound them in a mortar, and put in the juice and pulp; put them in a preserving pan, with double their weight of loaf-sugar, set it over a slow fire, boil it gently forty minutes, put it into pots. Cover it with brandy-paper and tie it down close.

To make White Marmalade.

Pare and core the quinces as fast as you can, then take to a pound of quinces (being cut to pieces, less than half quarters) three quarters of a pound of double-refined sugar beat small, then throw half the sugar on the raw quinces, set it on a slow fire till the sugar is melted, and the quinces are tender; then put in the rest of the sugar, and boil it up as fast as you can. When it is almost enough, put in some jelly and boil it apace; then put it up, and when it is quite cold, cover it with white paper.

To make Red Marmalade.

Take full ripe quinces, pare and cut them in quarters, and core them; put them in a saucepan, cover with the parings, fill the sauce-pan nearly full of spring-water, cover it close and stew them gently till they are quite soft, and a deep pink colour; then pick out the quinces from the parings, and beat them to a pulp in a mortar; take their weight in loaf-sugar, put in as much of the water they were boiled in as will dissolve it, and boil and skim it well: put in your quinces and boil them gently three quarters of an hour; keep stirring them all the time, or it will stick to the pan and burn; put it into flat pots, and when cold tie it down close.

To preserve Oranges whole.

Take the best Bermudas or Seville oranges you can get, and pare them with a pen-knife very thin, and lay your oranges in water three or four days, shifting them every day: then put them in a kettle with fair water, and put a board on them to keep them down in the water, and have a skillet on the fire with water, that may be ready to supply the kettle with boiling water; as it wastes it must be filled up three or four times, while the oranges are doing, for they will take up seven or eight hours boiling; they must be boiled till a white straw will run through them, then take them out, and scoop the seeds out of them, very carefully by making a little hole in the top, and weigh them. To every pound of oranges put a pound and three quarters of double-refined sugar, beat well and sifted through a clean lawn sieve, fill your oranges with sugar, and strew some on them. Let them lie a little while, and make your jelly thus.

Take two dozen of pippins or John-apples, and slice them into water, and when they are boiled tender, strain the liquor from the pulp, and to every pound of oranges you must have a pint and a half of this liquor and put to it three quarters of the sugar you left in filling the oranges, set it on the fire, and let it boil, skim it well, and put it into a clean earthen pan till it is cold, then put it into your skillet; put in your oranges; with a small bodkin job your oranges as they are boiling to let the syrup into them, strew on the rest of your sugar whilst they are boiling, and when they look clear take them up and put them in your glasses, put one in a glass just fit for them, and boil the syrup till it is almost a jelly, then fill up your glasses. When they are cold paper them up, and keep them in a dry place.

Or thus: Cut a hole out of the stalk end of your orange, as big as a sixpence, scoop out all the pulp very clean, tie them singly in muslin, and lay them two days in spring-water; change the water twice a day, and boil them in the muslin till tender; be careful you keep them covered with water, weigh the oranges before you scoop them: to every pound add two pounds of double-refined sugar, and a pint of water; boil the sugar and water with the orange juice to a syrup, skim it well, let it stand till it is cold, take the oranges out of the muslin, and put them in, and boil them till they are quite clear, and put them by till cold; then pare and core some green pippins, and boil them in water till it is very strong of the pippin; do not stir them, put them down gently with the back of a spoon, and strain the liquor through a jelly-bag, till it is clear. Put to every pint of liquor a pound of double-refined sugar, and the juice of a lemon, strained as clear as you can; boil it to a strong jelly; drain the oranges out of your syrup, and put them in glass or white stone jars, of the size of the orange, and pour the jelly on them. Cover them with brandy-papers, and tie them over with a bladder. You may do lemons in the same manner.

Quinces whole.

Take your quinces and pare them ; cut them in quarters, or leave them whole, which you please. Put them into a sauce-pan, and cover them with hard water ; lay your parings over them, to keep them under water ; cover your sauce-pan close, that no steam can come out ; set them over a slow fire till they are soft and a fine pink colour ; then let them stand till cold. Make a syrup of double-refined sugar, with as much water as will wet it ; boil and skim it well. Put in your quinces, let them boil ten minutes ; take them off, and let them stand three hours ; then boil them till the syrup is thick, and the quinces clear ; then put them in deep jars, and when cold put brandy paper over them, and tie them down close.

To make Conserve of Red Roses, or any other Flowers.

Take rose-buds, or any other flowers, and pick them ; cut off the white part from the red, and put the red flowers, and sift them through a sieve, to take out the seeds ; then weigh them, and to every pound of flowers take two pounds and a half of loaf sugar ; beat the flowers pretty fine in a stone mortar, then by degrees put the sugar to them, and beat it very well, till it is well incorporated together ; then put it into gallipots, tie it over with paper, over that a leather, and it will keep seven years.

To make Conserve of Hips.

Gather hips before they grow soft, cut off the heads and stalks, slit them in halves, take out all the seeds and white that is in them very clean, then put them in an earthen pan, and stir them every day, or they will grow mouldy. Let them stand till they are soft enough to rub them through a coarse hair-sieve; as the pulp comes take it off the sieve; they are a dry berry, and will require pains to rub them through. Then add its weight in sugar, mix them well together without boiling, and keep it in deep gallipots for use.

To make Syrup of Roses.

Infuse three pounds of damask rose-leaves in a gallon of warm water, in a well-glazed earthen pot, with a narrow mouth, for eight hours, which stop so close that none of the virtue may exhale. When they have infused so long, heat the water again, squeeze them out, and put in three pounds more of rose-leaves to infuse, for eight hours more; then press them out very hard; then to every quart of this infusion add four pounds of fine sugar, and boil it to a syrup.

To make Syrup of Citron.

Pare and slice your citrons thin, lay them in a bason, with layers of fine sugar. The next day pour off the liquor into a glass, skim it, clarify it over a gentle fire.

To make Syrup of Clove-Gilliflowers.

Clip your gilliflowers, sprinkle them with fair water, put them into an earthen pot, stop it up very close, set it in a kettle of water, and let it boil for two hours; then strain out the juice, put it into a skillet, set it on the fire, keep it stirring till the sugar is all melted, do not let it boil; then set it by to cool, and put it into bottles.

To make Syrup of Peach-Blossoms.

Infuse peach-blossoms in hot water, as much as will handsomely cover them. Let them stand in balneo, or in sand, for twenty-four hours covered close; then strain the flowers from the liquor and put in fresh flowers. Let them stand to infuse as before, then strain them out and to the liquor put fresh peach blossoms the third time, and, if you please, a fourth time. Then to every pound of your infusion add two pounds of double-refined sugar; and setting it in sand, or balneo, make a syrup, which keep for use.

To make Syrup of Quinces.

Grate quinces, pass their pulp through a cloth to extract the juice, set their juices in the sun to settle, or before the fire, and by that means clarify it; for every four ounces of this juice take a pound of sugar boiled brown. If the putting in the juice of the quinces should check the boiling of the sugar too much, give the syrup some boiling till it becomes pearled; then take it off the fire, and when cold, put it into the bottles.

To preserve Apricots.

Take your apricots, stone and pare them thin, and take their weight in double-refined sugar, beaten and sifted; put your apricots in a silver cup or tankard, cover them over with sugar, and let them stand so all night. The next day put them in a preserving pan, set them on a gentle fire, and let them simmer a little while, then let them boil till tender and clear, taking them off sometimes to turn and skim. Keep them under the liquor as they are doing, and with a small clean bodkin, or great needle, job them, that the syrup may penetrate into them. When they are enough, take them up, and put them in glasses. Boil and skim your syrup; and when it is cold put in your apricots. Put brandy paper over, and tie them close.

To preserve Damsons whole.

You must take some damsons and cut them in pieces put them in a skillet over the fire, with as much water as will cover them. When they are boiled, and the liquor pretty strong, strain it out. Add for every pound of the damsons wiped clean, a pound of single-refined sugar, put the third part of your sugar into the liquor, set it over the fire and when it simmers, put in the damsons. Let them have one good boil, and take them off for half an hour, covered up close; then set them on again, and let them simmer over the fire after turning them; then take them out and put them in a bason, strew all the sugar that was left on them, and pour the hot liquor over them. Cover them up, and let them stand till next day, then boil them up again till they are enough. Take them up, and put them in pots; boil the liquor till it jellies, and pour it on them when it is almost cold; so paper them up.

To candy any Sort of Flowers

Take the best treble refined sugar, break it into humps, and dip it piece by piece into water, put them into a vessel of silver, and melt them over the fire; when it just boils, strain it, and set it on the fire again and let it boil till it draws in hairs, which you may perceive by holding up your spoon, then put in the flowers, and set them in cups or glasses. When it is of a hard candy, break it in lumps, and lay it as high as you please. Dry it in a stove, or in the sun, and it will look like sugar-candy.

To preserve Gooseberries whole without stoning.

Take the largest preserving gooseberries, and pick off the black eye, but not the stalk, then set them over the fire on a pot of water to scald, cover them very close, but do not boil or break, and when they are tender take them up into cold water, then take a pound and a half of double-refined sugar, to a pound of gooseberries, and clarify the sugar with water, a pint to a pound of sugar, and when your syrup is cold, put the gooseberries single in your preserving pan, put the syrup to them and set them on a gentle fire, let them boil, but not too fast, lest they break, and when they have boiled, and you perceive that the sugar has entered them, take them off, cover them with white paper, and set them by till the next day. Then take them out of the syrup, and boil the syrup till it begins to be ropy, skim it, and put it to them again, then set them on a gentle fire, and let them simmer gently, till you perceive the syrup will rope, then take them off, set them by till they are cold, cover them with paper, then boil some gooseberries in fair water, and when the liquor is strong enough, strain it out. Let it stand to settle, and to every pint take a pound of double-refined sugar, then make a jelly of it, put the gooseberries in glassse when they are cold: cover them with the jelly the next day, paper them wet, and then half dry the paper that goes in the inside, it closes down better, and then put white paper over the glass. Set it in your stove, or a dry place.

To preserve White Walnuts.

First pare your walnuts till the white appears, and nothing else. You must be very careful in the doing of them, that they do not turn black, and as fast as you do them, throw them into salt and water, and let them lie till your sugar is ready. Take three pounds of good loaf-sugar, put it into your preserving-pan, set it over a charcoal fire, and put as much water as will just wet the sugar. Let it boil, then have ready ten or a dozen whites of eggs strained and beat up to froth; cover your sugar with froth as it boils and skim it; then boil it, and skim it till it is as clear as crystal, then throw in your walnuts; just give them a boil till they are tender, then take them out, and lay them in a dish to cool; when cool put them in your preserving pan, and when the sugar is as warm as milk, pour it over them; when quite cold paper them down.

Thus clear your sugar for all preserves, apricots, peaches, gooseberries, currants, &c.

To preserve Walnuts green.

Wipe them very clean, and lay them in strong salt and water twenty four hours; then take them out, and wipe them very clean, have ready a skillet of water boiling, throw them in, let them boil a minute, and take them out. Lay them on a coarse cloth, and boil your sugar as above;

then just give your walnuts a scald in the sugar, take them up, and lay them to cool. Put them in your preserving pot, and pour on your syrup as above.

To preserve the large Green Plums.

First dip the stalks and leaves in boiling vinegar; when they are dry, have your syrup ready, and first give them a scald, and very carefully with a pin take off the skin: boil your sugar to a candy height, and dip in your plums, hang them by the stalk to dry and they will look finely transparent, and by hanging that way to dry, will have a clear drop at the top. You must take great care to clear your sugar nicely.

To preserve Peaches.

Take the largest peaches you can get, not over ripe, rub off the lint with a cloth, and run them down the seam with a pin skin deep; cover them with French brandy, tie a bladder over them, and let them stand a week. Make a strong syrup, and boil and skim it well; take the peaches out of the brandy, and put them in and boil them till they look clear; then take them out, and put them in glasses, mix the syrup with the brandy, and when cold pour it over your peaches. Tie them close down with a bladder and leather over it.

To make Quince Cakes.

You must let a pint of the syrup of quinces, with a quart or two of rasberries, be boiled and clarified over a clear gentle fire, taking care that it be well skimmed from time to time; then add a pound and a half of sugar, cause as much more to be brought to a candy height, and poured in hot. Let the whole be continually stirred about till it is almost cold, then spread it on plates, and cut it out into cakes.

TO make ANCHOVIES, VERMICELLI, CATCHUP, VINEGAR; and to keep ARTICHOKES, FRENCH BEANS, &c.

To make Anchovies.

To a peck of sprats, two pounds of common salt, a quarter of a pound of bay-salt, four pounds of salt-petre, two ounces of sal-prunella, two penny-worth of cochineal; pound all in a mortar, put them into a stone-pot, a row of sprats, a layer of your compound, and so on to the top alternately. Press them hard down, cover them close, let them stand six months, and they will be fit for use. Observe that your sprats be very fresh, do not wash or wipe them, but just take them as they come out of the water.

To Pickle Smelts, where you have plenty.

Take a quarter of a peck of smelts, half an ounce of pepper, half an ounce of nutmeg, a quarter of an ounce of mace, half an ounce of salt petre, a quarter of a pound of common salt, beat all very fine, wash and clean the smelts, gut them, then lay them in rows in a jar, and between every layer of smelts strew the seasoning with four or five bay-leaves, then boil red wine, and pour over them enough to cover them. Cover them with a plate, and when cold tie them down close. They exceed anchovies.

To make Vermicelli.

Mix yolks of eggs and flour together in a pretty stiff paste, so as you can work it up cleverly, and roll it as thin as it is possible to roll the paste. Let it dry in the sun ; when it is quite dry, with a very sharp knife cut it as thin as possible, and keep it in a dry place. It will run up like little worms, as vermicelli does ; though the best way is to run it through a coarse sieve, whilst the paste is soft. If you want some to be made in haste, dry it by the fire, and cut it small. It will dry by the fire in a quarter of an hour. This far exceeds what comes from abroad, being fresher.

To make catchup.

Take the largest flaps of mushrooms gathered dry, and bruise them ; put some at the bottom of an earthen pan , strew some salt over, then mushrooms, then salt, till you have done. Put in half an ounce of cloves and mace, and the like of all spice. Let them stand six days, stir them up every day, then send them to the oven, and bake them gently for four hours. Take them out, and strain the liquor through a cloth, or fine sieve. To every gallon of liquor add a quart of red wine. If not salt enough, add a little more, a race or two of ginger cut small, boil it till one quart is wasted : strain it into a pan, and let it be cold. Pour it from the settling ; bottle it, and cork it tight

Another Way to make Catchup.

Take the large flaps, and salt them as above ; boil the liquor, strain it through a little flannel bag ; to a quart of that liquor put a quart of stale beer a large stick of horse-radish but in little slips, five or six bay-leaves, an onion stuck with twenty or thirty cloves, a quarter of an ounce of mace, a quarter of an ounce of nutmegs, beat, a quarter of an ounce of black and white pepper, a quarter of an ounce of all-spice, and four or five races of ginger. Cover it close, and let it simmer very softly till about one third is wasted; then strain it through a flannel bag; when it is cold bottle it in pint bottles, cork it close, and it will keep a great while.

Artichokes to keep all the Year.

Boil as many artichokes as you intend to keep; boil them so as just the leaves will come out, then pull off the leaves and choke, cut them from the strings, lay them on a tin-plate, and put them in an oven where tarts are drawn; let them stand till the oven is heated again, take them out before the wood is put in, and set them in again, after the tarts are drawn; so do till they are as dry as a board, then put them in a paper bag, and hang them in a dry place. You should lay them in warm water, three or four hours before you use them, shifting the water often. Let the last water be boiling hot. They will be very tender, and eat as fine as fresh ones. You need not dry all your bottoms at once, as the leaves are good to eat, so boil a dozen at a time, and save the bottoms for this use,

To keep French Beans all the Year.

Take fine young beans, gather them on a very fine day, have a large stone jar ready, clean and dry, lay a layer of salt at the bottom, and then a layer of beans, then salt, and then beans, and so on till the jar is full; cover them with salt, tie a coarse cloth over them, and a board on that, and then a weight to keep it close from all air; set them in a dry cellar, and when you use them cover them close again; wash them you took out very clean, and let them lie in soft water twenty four hours, shifting the water often; when you boil them do not put any salt in the water. The best way of dressing them is, boil them with just the white heart of a small cabbage, then drain them, chop the cabbage, and put both into a sauce-pan with a piece of butter as big as an egg, rolled in flour, shake a little pepper, and put in a quarter of a pint of good gravy, let them stew ten minutes, and then dish them up for a side-dish. A pint of beans to the cabbage. You may do more or less, as you please.

To keep Green Peas till Christmas.

Take fine young peas, shell them throw them into boiling water with some salt in it, let them boil five or six minutes, throw them into a cullender to drain; then lay a cloth four or five times double on a table, and spread them on; dry them very well, and have your bottles ready, fill them and cover them with mutton-fat dried; when it is a little cool, fill the necks almost to the top, cork them, tie a bladder and a lath over them, and set them in a cool dry place. When you use them, boil your water, put in a little salt, some sugar, and a piece of butter; when they are boiled enough, throw them into a sieve to drain; then put them into a sauce pan with a good piece of butter, keep shaking it round all the time till the butter is melted, then turn them into a dish, and send them to table.

Another Way to preserve Green Peas.

Gather your peas on a very dry day, when they are neither old, nor too young, shell them and have ready some quart bottles with little mouths, being well dried; fill the bottles and cork them well, have ready a pipkin of rosin melted, into which dip the necks of the bottles, and set them in a very dry place that is cool.

To keep Green Gooseberries till Christmas.

Pick your large green gooseberries on a dry day, have ready your bottles clean and dry, fill the bottles and cork them in a kettle of water up to the neck, let the water boil very softly till you find the gooseberries are coddled, take them out and put in the rest of the bottles till all are done; then have ready some rosin melted in a pipkin, dip the necks of the bottles in, and that will keep all air from coming at the cork, keep them in a cold dry place where no damp is, and they will bake as red as a cherry. You may keep them without scalding, but then the skins will not be so tender, nor bake so fine.

To keep Red Gooseberries.

Pick them when full ripe; to each quart of gooseberries put a quarter of a pound of Lisbon sugar, and to each quarter of a pound of sugar put a quarter of a pint of water; let it boil, then put in your gooseberries, and let them boil softly two or three minutes, then pour them into little stone jars; when cold cover them up, and keep them for use; they make fine pies with little trouble. You may press them through a cullender; to a quart of pulp put half a pound of fine

Lisbon sugar, keep stirring over the fire till both be well mixed and boiled, and pour it into a stone jar: when cold cover it with white paper, and it makes very pretty tarts or puffs.

To keep Walnuts all the Year.

Take a large jar, a layer of sea-sand at the bottom, then a layer of walnuts, then sand, then the nuts, and so on till the jar is full; and be sure they do not touch each other in any of the layers. When you would use them, lay them in warm water for an hour, shift the water as it cools; then rub them dry, and they will peel well and eat sweet. Lemons will keep thus covered better than any other way.

Another Way to keep Lemons.

Take the fine large fruit that are quite sound and good, and take a fine packthread about a quarter of a yard long, turn it through the hard nib at the end of the lemon; then tie the string together, and hang it on a little hook in an airy dry place; so do as many as you please, but be sure they do not touch one another, nor any thing else, but hang as high as you can. Thus you may keep pears, &c. only tying the string to the stalk.

To keep White Bullice, Pear-Plums, or Damsons, &c. for Tarts or Pies.

Gather them when full grown, and just as they begin to turn. Pick all the largest out, save two-thirds of the fruit, the other third put as much water to as you think will cover the rest. Let them boil and skim them, when the fruit is boiled very soft, then strain it through a coarse sieve ; and to every quart of this liquor put a pound and a half of sugar, boil it and skim it very well ; then throw in your fruit, just give them a scald ; take them off the fire, and when cold put them into bottles with wide mouths ; pour your syrup over them, and cover them with oil. Be sure to take the oil well off when you use them, and do not put them in larger bottles than you think you shall make use of at a time, because all those sorts of fruits spoil with the air.

To make Vinegar.

To every gallon of water put a pound of coarse Lisbon sugar, let it boil, and keep skimming it as long as the scum rises ; then pour it into tubs, and when it is as cold as beer to work, toast a good toast, and rub it over yeast : Let it work twenty-four hours ; then have ready a vessel iron-hooped, and well painted, fixed in a place where the sun has full power, and fix it so as to have no occasion to move it. When you draw it off, then fill your vessels, lay a tile on the bung to keep the dust out. Make it in March, and it will be fit to use in June or July. Draw it off into little stone bottles the latter end of June or beginning of July, let it stand till you want to use it, and it will never foul any more ; but when you go to draw it off, and you find it not sour enough, let it stand a month longer before you draw it off. For pickles to go abroad use this vinegar alone ; but in England you will be obliged when you pickle, to put one half cold spring water to it, and then it will be full sour with this vinegar. You need not boil unless you please, for almost any sort of pickles ; it will keep them quite good. If will keep walnuts very fine without boiling, even to go to the Indies; but then do not put water to it. For green pickles you may pour it scalding hot on two or three times. All other sorts of pickles you need not boil it. Mushrooms only wash them clean, dry them, put them into little bottles with a nutmeg just scalded in vinegar, and sliced (whilst it is hot) very thin, and a few blades of mace; then fill up the bottles with the cold vinegar and spring water, pour the mutton fat fried over it and tie a bladder and leather over the top. These mushrooms will not be so white, but as finely tasted as if they were just gathered; and a spoonful of this pickle will give sauce a fine flavour.

White walnuts, suckers and onions, and all white pickles, do in the same manner, after they are ready for the pickles.

To fry Smelts.

Let your smelts be fresh caught, wipe them very dry with a cloth, beat up yolks of eggs and rub over them, strew crumbs of bread on, have some clear dripping boiling in a frying-pan, and fry them quick of a fine gold colour. Put them on a plate to drain; and lay them in your dish. Garnish with fried parsley, with plain butter in a cup.

To dress White Bait.

Take white-bait fresh caught, and put them in a cloth with a handful of flour, and shake them about till they are separated and quite dry; have some hog's lard boiling quick, fry them two minutes, drain them, and dish up with plain butter and soy.

To roast a Pound of Butter.

Lay it in salt and water two or three hours, then spit it, and rub it all over with crumbs of bread, with a little grated nutmeg, lay it to the fire, and as it roasts, baste it with the yolks of two eggs and then with crumbs of bread all the time it is roasting; but have ready a pint of oysters stewed in their own liquor, and lay it on your oysters. Your fire must be very slow.

DISTILLING.

To distil Walnut-Water.

Take a peck of fine green walnuts, bruise them well in a large mortar, put them in a pan, with a handful of balm bruised, put two quarts of good French brandy to them, cover them close, and let them lie three days; the next day distil them in a cold still; from this quantity draw three quarts, which you may do in a day.

How to use this Ordinary Still.

You must lay the plate, then wood ashes thick at the bottom, then the iron pan, which you are to fill with your walnuts and liquor, then put on the head of the still, make a pretty brisk fire till the still begins to drop then slacken it so as just to have enough to keep the still at work. Mind all the time to keep a wet cloth all over the head of the still all the time it is at work, and always observe not to let the still work longer than the liquor is good, and take great care you do not burn the still, and thus you may distil what you please. If you draw the still too far it will burn, and give your liquor a bad taste.

To make Treacle-Water.

Take the juice of green walnuts four pounds, of

rue, carduus, mary gold and balm, of each three pounds, roots of butter-bur half a pound, roots of burdock one pound, angelica and master-wort, of each half a pound, leaves of scordium six handfuls Venice treacle and mithridate of each half a pound, old Canary wine two pounds, white-wine vinegar six pounds, juice of lemon six pounds; and distil this in an alembic.

To make Black Cherry Water.

Take six pounds of black cherries, and bruise them small, then put to them the tops of rosemary, sweet marjoram, spearmint, angelica, balm, marygold flowers, of each a handful, dried violets one ounce, anise-seeds and sweet fennel seeds, of each half an ounce bruised, cut the herbs small, mix all together, and distil them off in a cold still.

To make Hysterical Water.

Take betony, roots of lovage, seeds of wild parsnips, of each two ounces, roots of single piony four ounces, of misletoe of the oak three ounces, myrrh a quarter of an ounce, castor half an ounce, beat all these together, and add to them a quarter of a pound of dried milliepedes; pour on these three quarts of mugwort water, and two quarts of brandy, let them stand in a close vessel eight days, then distil it in a cold still pasted up. You may draw off nine pints of water, and sweeten it to your taste. Mix all together, and bottle it up.

To distil Red Rose Buds.

Wet your roses in fair water, four gallons of roses will take near two gallons of water, then still them in a cold still; take the same stilled water, and put into it as many fresh roses as it will wet, then still them again.

Mint, balm, parsley, and penny-royal water, distil the same way.

To make Plague-water.

Roots.	Flowers.	Seeds.
Angelica,	Wormwood,	Hart's tongue,
Dragon,	Succory,	Horehound,
Maywort,	Hysop,	Fennel,
Mint,	Agrimony,	Melilot,
Rue,	Fennel,	St. John's wort,
Carduus,	Cowslips,	Comfrey,
Origany,	Poppies,	Fevervew,
Winter-savoury,	Plaintain,	Red rose leaves,
Broad thyme,	Setfoyl,	Wood-sorrel,
Rosemary,	Vocvain,	Pellitory of the wall
Pimpernell,	Maidenhair,	Heart's ease.
Sage,	Motherwort,	Centaury,
Fumatory,	Cowage,	Sea-drink, a good
Coltsfoot,	Golden-rod	handful of each of
Scabious,	Gromwell,	the aforesaid things
Borrage,	Dill,	Gentian-root,
Saxafrage,		Dock-root,
Betony,		Butter-bur root,
Liverwort		Piony-root,
Germander,		Bay-berries,
		Juniper-berries of each of these a pound.

One ounce of nutmegs, one ounce of cloves, and half an ounce of mace; pick the herbs and flowers, and shred them a little. Cut the roots, bruise the berries, and pound the spices fine, take a peck of green-walnuts, and chop them small, mix all these together, and lay them to steep in sack lees, or any white wine lees, if not in good spirits; but wine lees are best. Let them lie a week, or better, be sure to stir them once a day with a stick, and keep them close covered, then still them in an alembic with a slow fire, and take care your still does not burn. The first, second, and third running is good, and some of the fourth. Let them stand till cold, then put them together.

To make Surfeit-Water.

You must take scurvy-grass, brock-lime water-cresses, Roman wormwood, rue, mint, balm, sage, clivers, of each one handful; green merery two handfuls; poppies, if fresh half a peck; if dry a quarter of a peck; cochineal, six penny-worth, saffron, six penny-worth; anise-seeds, carraway-seeds, coriander-seeds, cardamom-seeds of each an ounce; liquorice two ounces scraped, figs split a pound, raisins of the sun stoned a pound, juniper berries an ounce bruised, nutmeg an ounce beat, sweet fennel-seeds an ounce bruised, a few flowers of rosemary, marygold and sage flowers; put those into a large stone-jar, and put to them three gallons of French brandy, cover it close, and let it stand near the fire for three weeks. Stir it three times a week, and be sure to keep it close stopped, and then strain it off; bottle your liquor, and pour on the ingredients a gallon more of French brandy. Let it stand a week, stirring it once a day, then distil it in a cold still, and this will make a fine white surfeit-water.

You may make this water at any time of the year, if you live in London, because the ingredients are always to be had either green or dry; but it is the best made in summer.

To make Milk-Water.

Take two good handfuls of worm-wood, as much carduus, as much rue, four handfuls of mint, as much balm, half as much angelica, cut these a little, put them into a cold still, and put to them three quarts of milk. Let your fire be quick till your still drops, and then slacken your fire. You may draw off two quarts. The first quart will keep all the year.

To dress a Turtle the West India Way.

Take the turtle out of the water the night before you dress it, and lay it on its back, in the morning cut its head off, and hang it up by its hind-fins for it to bleed till the blood is all out, then cut the callapee, which is the belly, round, and raise it up; cut as much meat to it as you can, throw it into spring-water with a little salt, cut the fins off, and scald them with the head; take off all the scales, cut all the white meat out, and throw it into spring-water and salt, the guts and lungs must be cut out, wash the lungs very clean from the blood, then take the guts and maw and slit them open, wash them very clean, and put them on to boil in a large pot of water, and boil them till they are tender, then take off the inside skin, and cut them in pieces of two or three inches long; have ready a good veal broth made as follows: take one large, or two small knuckles of veal, and put them on in three gallons of water, let it boil, skim it well, season with turnips, onions, carrots, and cellery, and a good large bundle of sweet herbs, boil it till it is half wasted, then strain it off. Take the fins, and put them in a stew-pan, cover them with veal broth, season with an onion chopped fine, all sorts of sweet herbs chopped very fine, half an ounce of cloves and mace, half a nutmeg beat very fine, stew it very gently till tender; then take the fins out, and put in a pint of Madeira wine, and stew it for fifteen minutes, beat up the whites of six eggs with the juice of two lemons; put the liquor in and boil it up, run it through a flannel bag. Make it hot, wash the fins very clean, and put them in. Take a piece of butter and put at the bottom of a stew-pan, put your white meat in and sweat it gently till it is almost tender. Take the lungs and heart, and cover them with veal broth, with an onion, herbs, and spice, as for the fins, stew them till tender, take out the lungs strain the liquor off, thicken it, and put in a bottle of Madeira wine, season with Cayenne pepper, and salt pretty high; put in the lungs, and white meat stew them up gently for fifteen minutes, have some force-meat balls made out of the white part instead of veal, as for Scotch collops, if any eggs, scald them; if not, take twelve hard yolks of eggs, made into egg-balls; have your calapash or deep shell done round the edges with paste, season it in the inside with Cayenne pepper and salt, and a little Madeira wine, bake it half an hour, then put in the lungs and white meat, force meat, and eggs, over, and bake it half an hour. Take the bones, and three quarts of veal broth, seasoned with an onion, a bundle of sweet herbs, two blades of mace, stew it an hour, strain it through a sieve, thicken it with flour and butter, put in half a pint of Madeira wine, stew it half an hour, season with Cayenne pepper and salt to your liking: this is the soup. Take the callapee, run your knife between the meat and shell, and fill it full of force-meat, season it all over with sweet herbs chopped fine, a shalot chopped, Cayenne pepper and salt, and a little Madeira wine, put a paste round the edge, and bake it an hour and a half. Take the guts and maw, put them in a stew-pan, with a little broth, a bundle of sweet herbs, two blades of mace beat fine, thicken with a little butter rolled in flour, stew them gently for half an hour, season with Cayenne pepper and salt, beat up the yolks of two eggs in half a pint of cream, put it in, and keep stirring it one way till it boils up; then dish them up as follows:

Calapee.

Fricasee. Soup. Fins.

Callapash.

The fins eat fine when cold put by in the liquor.

Another Way to dress a Turtle.

Kill your turtle as before, then cut the belly-shell clean off, cut off the fins, take all the white meat out, and put it into spring water, take the guts and lungs out; do the guts as before; wash the lungs well, scald the fins, head, and belly-shell; take a saw, and saw the shell all round abut two inches deep, scald it, and take the shell off, cut it in pieces. Take the shells, fins, and head, and put them in a pot, cover them with veal-broth; season with two large onions chopped fine, all sorts of sweet herbs chopped fine, half an ounce of cloves and mace, a whole nutmeg, stew them till tender; take out all the meat, and strain the liquor through a sieve, cut the fins in two or three pieces; take all the brawn from the bones, cut it in pieces about two inches square; take the white meat, put some butter at the bottom of the stew-pan, put your meat in, and sweat it gently over a slow fire till almost done; take it out of the liquor, and cut it in pieces about the bigness of a goose's egg; take the lungs and heart, and cover them with veal broth; season with an onion, sweet herbs, and a little beat spice (always observe to boil the liver by itself); stew it till tender, take the lungs out, and cut them in pieces; strain off the liquor through a sieve; take a pound of butter and put it in a large stew-pan, big enough to hold all the turtle, and melt it; put half a pound of flour in, and stir it till it is smooth; put in the liquor, and keep stirring it till it is well mixed, if lumpy strain it through a sieve; put in your meat of all sorts, a great many force-meat balls and egg-balls, and put in three pints of Madeira wine; season with pepper and salt, and Cayenne pepper pretty high; stew it three quarters of an hour, add the juice of two lemons; have your deep shell baked, put some into the shells, and bake it or brown it with a hot iron, and serve the rest in tureens.

N. B. This is for a turtle of sixty pounds weight.

To make a Mock Turtle.

Take a large calf's head with the skin on, well scalded and cleaned, boil it three quarters of an hour; take it out, and slit it down the face, take all the skin and meat from the bones as clean as possible, be careful you do not break off the ears; lay it on a dresser, and fill the ears full of force-meat, tie them round with a cloth; take out the eyes, and pick all the meat from the bones, put it in a large stew-pan with the best and fattest parts of another head without the skin, boiled as long as the above, and three quarts of veal-gravy; lay the skin on the meat, with the flesh side up, and cover the pan close, and let it stew one hour over a moderate fire; put in three sweet-breads cut in pieces, two ounces of truffles and morels, four artichoke bottoms, boiled and cut in four pieces each, an anchovy boned and chopt small, season it pretty high with salt and Cayenne pepper, put in half a lemon, three pints of Madeira wine, two spoonfuls of catchup, one of lemon pickle, half a pint of pickle or fresh mushrooms, a quarter of a pound of butter rolled in flour, and let it all stew half an hour longer; take the yolks of four eggs boiled hard, and the brains of both heads boiled, cut the brains in pieces of the size of a nutmeg, make a rich force-meat, and roll it up in a veal caul, and then in a cloth, and boil it an hour cut it in three parts, the middle piece the largest; put the meat into the dish, and lay the head over it, the skin-side uppermost; put the largest piece of force meat between the ears, the other two slices at the narrow end, opposite each other; put the brains, eggs, mushrooms, &c. over and round it, and pour the liquor hot upon it, and send it up as quick as possible, as it soon gets cold.

To make Ice-Cream.

Pare and stone twelve ripe apricots, and scald them, beat them fine in a mortar, add to them six ounces of double-refined sugar, and a pint of scalding cream, and work it through a sieve; put it in a tin with a close cover, and set it in a tub of ice broke small, with four handfuls of salt mixed among the ice. When you see your cream grows thick round the edges of your tin, stir it well, and put it in again till it is quite thick; when the cream is all froze up, take it out of the tin, and put it into the mould you intend to turn it out of; put on the lid and have another tub of salt and ice ready as before; put the mould in the middle, and lay the ice under and over it; let it stand four hours, and never turn it out till the moment you want it, then dip the mould in cold spring water, and turn it into a plate. You may do any sort of fruit the same way.

A Turkey, &c. in Jelly.

Boil a turkey, or fowl, as white as you can, let it stand till cold, and have ready a jelly made thus: take a fowl, skin it, take off all the fat, do not cut it to pieces, nor break the bones; take four pounds of a leg of veal, without any fat or skin, put it into a well-tinned sauce-pan, put to it full three quarts of water, set it on a very clear fire till it begins to simmer; be sure to skim it well, but take great care it does not boil. When it is well skimmed, set it so as it will but just seem to simmer; put two large blades of mace, half a nutmeg, and twenty corns of white-pepper, a little bit of lemon-peel as big as a six-pence. This will take six or seven hours doing. When you think it is a stiff jelly, which you will know by taking a little out to cool, be sure to skim off all the fat, if any, and be sure not to stir the meat in the sauce-pan. A quarter of an hour before it is done, throw in a large tea-spoonful of salt, squeeze in the juice of half a fine Seville orange or lemon; when you think it is enough, strain it off through a clean sieve, but do not pour it off quite to the bottom, for fear of settlings. Lay the turkey or fowl in the dish you intend to send it to the table in, beat up the whites of six eggs to a froth, and put the liquor to it, then boil it five or six minutes, and run it through a jelly-bag till it is very clear, then pour the liquor over it, let it stand till quite cold; colour some of the jelly in different colours, and when it is near cold, with a spoon sprinkle it over in what form or fancy you please, and send it to table. A few nastertium flowers stuck here and there look pretty, if you can get them; but lemon, and all those things are entirely fancy. This is a very pretty dish for a cold collation, or a supper.

All sorts of birds or fowls may be done this way.

To make Citron.

Quarter your melon, and take out all the inside, then put into the syrup as much as will cover the coat; let it boil in the syrup till the coat is as tender as the inward part, then put them in the pot with as much syrup as will cover them. Let them stand for two or three days, that the syrup may penetrate through them, and boil your syrup to a candy height, with as much mountain-wine as will wet your syrup, clarify it, and then boil it to a candy height: then dip in the quarters, and lay them on a sieve to dry, and set them before a slow fire, or put them in a slow oven till dry. Observe that your melon is but half ripe, and when they are dry put them in deal boxes in paper.

To candy Cherries or Green Gages.

Dip the stalks and leaves in white-wine vinegar boiling, then scald them in syrup; take them out and boil the syrup to a candy height; dip in the cherries, and hang them to dry with the cherries downwards. Dry them before the fire, or in the sun. Then take the plums, after boiling them in a thin syrup, peel off the skin and candy them, and so hang them up to dry.

To take Iron-moulds out of Linen.

Take sorrel, bruise it well in a mortar, squeeze it through a cloth, bottle it, and keep it for use. Take a little of the above juice, in a silver or tin sauce-pan, boil it over a lamp, as it boils dip in the iron-mould, do not rub it, but only squeeze it. As soon as the iron-mould is out, throw it into cold water.

To make India Pickle.

To a gallon of vinegar, one pound of garlick, three quarters of a pound of long-pepper, a pint of mustard-seed, one pound of ginger, and two ounces of turmerick; the garlic must be laid in salt three days then wiped clean and dried in the sun; the long-pepper broke, and the mustard-seed bruised: mix all together in the vinegar; then take two large hard cabbages, and two cauliflowers, cut them in quarters, and salt them well; let them lie three days and dry them well in the sun.

N. B. The ginger must lie twenty-four hours in salt and water, then cut small, and laid in salt three days.

NECESSARY DIRECTIONS

Whereby the Reader may easily attain the useful,

ART of CARVING.

To cut up a Turkey.

Raise the leg, open the joint, but be sure not to take off the leg; lace down both sides of the breast, and open the pinion of the breast, but do not take it off; raise the merry-thought between the breast-bone and the top; raise the brawn, and turn it outward on both sides, but be careful not to cut it off, nor break it; divide the wing-pinions from the joint next the body, and stick each pinion where the brawn was turned out; cut off the sharp end of the pinion, and the middle piece will fit the place exactly.

A bustard, capon, or pheasant, is cut up in the same manner.

To rear a Goose.

Cut off both legs in the manner of shoulders of lamb; take off the belly-piece close to the extremity of the breast; lace the goose down both sides of the breast about half an inch from the sharp bone: divide the pinions and the flesh first laced with your knife, which must be raised from the bone, and taken off with the pinion from the body; then cut off the merry-thought, and cut another slice from the breast-bone, quite through; lastly, turn up the carcase, cutting it asunder, the back above the loin bones.

To unbrace a Mallard or Duck.

First, raise the pinions and legs, but cut them not off, then raise the merry-thought from the breast and lace it down both sides with your knife.

To unlace a Coney.

The back must be turned downward, and the apron divided from the belly ; this done, slip in your knife between the kidneys, loosening the flesh on each side ; then turn the belly, cut the back cross-ways between the wings, draw your knife down both sides of the back-bone, dividing the sides and leg from the back. Observe not to pull the leg too violently from the bone, when you open the side, but with great exactness lay open the sides, from the scut to the shoulder ; and then put the legs together.

To wing a Partridge or Quail.

After having raised the legs and wings, use salt and powered ginger for sauce.

To allay a Pheasant or Teal.

This differs in nothing from the foregoing but that you must use salt only for sauce.

To dismember a Heron.

Cut off the legs, lace the breast down each side, and open the breast pinion, without cutting it off; raise the merry-thought between the breast-bone and the top of it ; then raise the brawn, turning it out-ward on both sides : but break it not, nor cut it off ; sever the wing pinion from the joint nearest the body, sticking the pinions in the place where the brawn was ; remember to cut off the sharp end of the pinion, and supply the place with the middle-piece.

In this manner some people cut up a capon or

pheasant, and likewise a bittern, using no sauce but salt.

To thigh a Woodcock.

The legs and wings must be raised in the manner of a fowl, only open the head for the brains. And so you thigh curlews, plover, or snipe, using no sauce but salt.

To display a Crame.

After his legs are unfolded, cut off the wings; take them up, and sauce them with powdered ginger, vinegar, salt, and mustard.

To lift a Swan.

Slit it fairly down the middle of the breast, clean through the back, from the neck to the rump; divide it in two parts, neither breaking or tearing the flesh; then lay the halves in a charger, the slit sides downwards; throw salt upon it, and set it again on the table. The sauce must be chaldron served up in saucers.

Observations on preserving Salt Meat, so as to keep it mellow and fine for three or four months; and to preserve Potted Butter.

Take care when you salt your meat in the summer, that it be quite cool after it comes from the butcher's; the way is, to lay it on cold bricks for a few hours, and when you salt it, lay it upon an inclining board, to drain off the blood; then salt it a fresh, add to every pound of salt half a pound of Lisbon sugar, and turn it in the pickle every day; at the months end it will be fine. The salt which is commonly used hardens and spoils all the meat; the right sort is that called Lowndes's salt; it comes from Nantwich in Cheshire; there is a very fine sort that comes from Malden in Essex, and from Suffolk, which is the reason of that butter being finer than any other; and if every other body would make use of that salt in potting butter, we should not have so much bad come to market; observing all the general rules of a dairy. If you keep your meat long in salt, half the quantity of sugar will do; and then bestow loaf sugar, it will eat much finer. This pickle cannot be called extravagant, because it will keep a great while; at three or four months end, boil it up; if you have no meat in the pickle, skim it, and when cold, only add a little more salt and sugar to the next meat you put in, and it will be good a twelvemonth longer.

Take a leg of mutton piece, veiny or thick flank-piece, without any bone, pickled as above, only add to every pound of salt an ounce of saltpetre; after being a month or two in the pickle, take it out and lay it in soft-water a few hours, then roast it; it eats fine. A leg of mutton or shoulder of veal does the same. It is a very good thing where a market is at a great distance, and a large family obliged to provide a great deal of meat.

As to the pickling of hams and tongues, you have the receipt in the foregoing chapters; but use either of these fine salts, and they will be equal to any Bayonne hams, provided your porkling is fine and well fed.

To make Mock Turtle Soup.

Take a calf's head, and scald the hair off as you would a pig, and wash it very clean; boil it in a large pot of water half an hour; then cut all the skin off by itself, take the tongue out; take the broth made of a knuckle of veal, put in the tongue and skin, with three large onions, half an ounce of cloves and mace and half a nutmeg beat fine, all sorts of sweet herbs chopped fine, and three anchovi es, stew it till tender, then take out the meat, and cut it in pieces about two inches square, and the tongue in slices; mind to skin the tongue; strain the liquor through a sieve; take half a pound of butter, and put in the stew-pan, melt it, and put in a quarter of a pound of flour, keep it stirring till it is smooth, then put in the liquor; keeping it stirring till all is in, if lumpy strain it through a sieve; then put to your meat a bottle of Madeira wine, season, with pepper and salt, and Cayenne pepper pretty high; put in force-meat balls and egg-balls boiled, the juice of two lemons, stew it an hour gently, and then serve it up in tureens.

N. B. If it is two thick, put some more broth in before you stew it the last time.

To dress Haddocks after the Spanish Way.

Take a haddock, washed very clean and dried, and boil it nicely; then take a quarter of a pint of oil in a stew-pan, season it with mace, cloves, and nutmeg, pepper and salt, two cloves of garlick, some love apples, when in season, a little vinegar; put in the fish, cover it close, and let it stew half an hour over a slow fire.

Flounders done the same way are very good.

To dress Haddocks the Jews Way.

Take two large fine haddocks, wash them very clean, cut them in slices about three inches thick, and dry them in a cloth; take a gill either of oil or butter in a stew pan, a middling onion cut small a handful of parsley washed and cut small; let it just boil up in either butter or oil, then put in the fish; season it with beaten mace, pepper and salt, half a pint of soft water: let it stew softly, till it is thoroughly done; then take the yolks of two eggs, beat up with the juice of a lemon, and just as it is done enough, throw it over, and send it to table.

A Spanish Peas-Soup.

Take one pound of Spanish peas, and lay them in water the night before you use them; then take a gallon of water, one quart of fine sweet oil, a head of garlick; cover the pot close, and let it boil till the peas are soft; then season with pepper and salt; then beat the yolk of an egg, and vinegar to your palate; poach some eggs, lay on the dish on sippets, and pour the soup on them. Send it to table.

To make Onion Soup the Spanish Way.

Take two large Spanish onions, peel and slice them; let them boil very softly in half a pint of sweet oil till the onions are very soft; then pour on them three pints of boiling water; season with beaten pepper, salt, a little beaten clove and mace, two spoonfuls of vinegar, a handful of parsley washed clean, and chopped fine; let it boil fast a quarter of an hour; in the mean time, get some sippets to cover the bottom of the dish, fried quick, not hard; lay them in the dish and cover each sippet with a poached egg; beat up the yolks of two eggs, and throw over them; pour in your soup, and send it to table.

Garlick and sorrel done the same way, eats well.

Milk Soup the Dutch Way.

Take a quart of milk, boil it with cinnamon and moist sugar; put sippets in the dish, pour the milk over it, and set it over a charcoal fire to simmer till the bread is soft. Take the yolks of two eggs, beat them up, and mix it with a little of the milk, and throw it in; mix it all together, and send it to table.

Fish Pasties the Italian Way.

Take some flour, and knead it with oil; take a slice of salmon, season it with pepper and salt, and dip it into sweet oil, chop an onion and parsley fine and strew over it; lay it in the paste, and double it up in the shape of a slice of salmon; take a piece of white paper, oil it, and lay under the pasty, and bake it; it is best cold, and will keep a month.

Mackarel done the same way, head and tail together folded in a pasty, eats fine.

Asparagus dressed the same way.

Take the asparagus, break them in pieces, then boil them soft, and then drain the water from them; take a little oil, water, and vinegar, let it boil season it with pepper and salt, throw in the asparagus, and thicken with yolks of eggs.

Endive done this way is good; the Spaniards add sugar, but that spoils them. Green peas done as above are very good, only add a lettuce cut small, and two or three onions, and leave out the eggs.

Red Cabbage dressed after the Dutch Way, good for a cold in the breast.

Take the cabbage, cut it small and boil it soft, then drain it, and put it in a stew-pan, with a sufficient quantity of oil and butter, a little water and vinegar, and an onion cut small; season it with pepper and salt, and let it simmer on a slow fire, till all the liquor is wasted.

Cauliflowers dressed the Spanish Way.

Boil them, but not too much; then drain them, and put them in a stew-pan; to a large cauliflower put a quarter of a pint of sweet oil, two or three cloves of garlick; let them fry till brown; then season them with pepper and salt, two or three spoonfuls of vinegar; cover the pan very close, and let them simmer over a very slow fire an hour.

Carrots and French Beans dressed the Dutch Way.

Slice the carrots very thin, and just cover them with water; season them with pepper and salt, cut a good many onions and parsley small, a piece of butter; let them simmer over a slow fire till done. Do French beans the same way.

Beans dressed the German Way.

Take a large bunch of onions, peel and slice them, a great quantity of parsley washed and cut small, throw them into a stew-pan, with a pound of butter; season them well with pepper and salt, put in two quarts of beans; cover them close, and let them do till the beans are brown, shaking the pan often. Do peas the same way.

Artichoke Suckers dressed the Spanish Way.

Clean and wash them, and cut them in halves; then boil them in water, drain them from the water; and put them into a stew-pan, with a little oil, a little water, and a little vinegar; season them with pepper and salt; stew them a little while, and then thicken them with yolks of eggs.

They make a pretty garnish done thus: clean them and half boil them; then dry them, flour them, and dip them in yolks of eggs, and fry them brown.

To dry Pears without Sugar.

Take the Norwich pears, pare them with a knife, and put them in an earthen pot, and bake them not too soft; put them into a white plate pan, and put dry straw under them, and lay them in an oven after bread is drawn, and every day warm the oven to the degree of heat as when the bread is newly drawn. Within one week they must be dry.

Ginger Tablets.

Melt a pound of loaf-sugar with a little bit of butter over the fire, and put in an ounce of pounded ginger; keep it stirring till it begins to rise into a froth, then pour it into pewter plates and let it stand to cool. The platter must be rubbed with a little oil, and then put them in a china dish, and send them to table. Garnish with flowers of any kind.

Artichokes preserved the Spanish Way.

Take the largest you can get, cut the tops of the leaves off, wash them well and drain them; to every artichoke pour in a large spoonful of oil; season with pepper and salt. Send them to the oven, and bake them. They will keep a year.

N. B. The Italians, French, Portuguese, and Spaniards, have variety of ways of dressing fish, which we have not, viz.

As making fish-soups, ragoos, pies, &c.

For their soups they use no gravy, nor in their sauces, thinking it improper to mix flesh and fish together: but make their fish soups with fish, viz. either of craw-fish, lobsters, &c. taking only the juice of them.

FOR EXAMPLE.

Take your-craw-fish, tie them up in a muslin rag, and boil them; then press out their juice for the above-said use.

For their Pies.

They make some of carp; others of different fish, and some they make like our minced pies, viz. They take a carp, and cut the flesh from the bones, and mince it, adding currants, &c.

Almond Rice.

Blanch the almonds, and pound them in a marble or wooden mortar, and mix them in a little boiling water; press them as long as there is any milk in the almonds; adding fresh water every time; to every quart of almond juice, a quarter of a pound of rice, and two or three spoonfuls of orange-flower water; mix them all together, and simmer it over a very slow charcoal fire, keep stirring it often; when done, sweeten it to your palate; put it into plates, and throw beaten cinnamon over it.

Sham Chocolate.

Take a pint of milk, boil it over a slow fire, with some whole cinnamon, and sweeten it with Lisbon sugar; beat up the yolks of three eggs, throw all together into a chocolate-pot, and mill it one way, or it will turn. Serve it up in chocolate-cups.

Marmalade of Eggs the Jews Way.

Take the yolks of twenty-four eggs, beat them for an hour; clarify one pound of the best moist sugar, four spoonfuls of orange-flower-water, one ounce of blanched and pounded almonds; stir all together over a very slow charcoal fire, keep stirring it all the while one way, till it comes to a consistence; then put it into coffee-cups, and throw a little beaten cinnamon, on the top of the cups.

This marmalade, mixed with pounded almonds, with orange-peel, and citron, are made in cakes of all shapes, such as birds, fish, and fruit.

A Cake the Spanish Way.

Take twelve eggs, three quarters of a pound of the best moist sugar, mill them in a chocolate-mill, till they are all of a lather; then mix in one pound of flour, half a pound of pounded almonds two ounces of candied orange-peel, two ounces of citron, four large spoonfuls of orange-water, half an ounce of cinnamon, and a glass of sack. It is better when baked in a slow oven.

Another Way.

Take one pound of flour, one pound of butter, eight eggs, one pint of boiling milk, two or three spoonfuls of ale yeast, or a glass of French brandy; beat all well together; then set it before the fire in a pan, where there is room for it to rise: cover it close with a cloth and flannel, that no air comes to it; when you think it is raised sufficiently, mix half a pound of the best moist sugar, an ounce of cinnamon beat fine; four spoonfuls of orange-flower-water, one ounce of candied orange peel, one ounce of citron, mix all well together and bake it.

To dry plums.

Take pear-plums, fair and clear coloured, weigh them, and slit them up the sides; put them into a broad-pan, and fill it full of water, set them over a very slow fire; take care that the skin does not come off; when they are tender take them up, and to every pound of plums put a pound of sugar, strew a little on the bottom of a large silver bason; then lay your plums in one, by one and strew the remainder of your sugar over them; set them into your stove all night, with a good warm fire the next day; heat them, and set them into your stove again, and let them stand two days more, turning them every day; then take them out of the syrup, and lay them on glass plates to dry.

To make Sugar of Pearl.

Take damask rose-water half a pint, one pound of fine sugar, half an ounce of prepared pearl beat to powder, eight leaves of beaten gold; boil them together according to art; add the pearl and gold leaves when just done, then cast them on a marble.

To make Fruit-Wafers, of Codlins, Plums, &c.

Take the pulp of any fruit rubbed through a hair-sieve, and to every three ounces of fruit take six ounces of sugar finely sifted. Dry the sugar very well till it be very hot; heat the pulp also till it be very hot; then mix it, and set it over a slow charcoal fire, till it be almost a boiling, then pour it into glasses or trenchers, and set it in the stove till you see it will leave the glasses ; but before it begins to candy, turn them on papers in what form you please. You may colour them red with clove gilly-flowers steeped in the juice of lemon.

To make White Wafers.

Beat the yolk of an egg, and mix it with a quarter of a pint of fair water ; then mix half a pound of best flour, and thin it with damask-rose-water till you think it of a proper thickness to bake. Sweeten it to your palate with fine sugar finely sifted.

To make Brown Wafers.

Take a quart of ordinary cream, then take the yolks of three or four eggs, and as much fine flour as will make it into a thin batter ; sweeten it with three quarters of a pound of fine sugar finely searced, and as much pounded cinnamon as will make it taste. Do not mix them till the cream be cold ; butter your pans and make them very hot before you bak e them.

How to dry Peaches.

Take the fairest and ripest peaches, pare them into fair water ; take their weight in double-refined sugar, of one half make a very thin syrup ; then put in your peaches, boiling them till they look clear then split and stone them. Boil them till they are very tender, lay them a draining take the other half of the sugar, and boil it almost to a candy ; then put in your peaches, and let them lie all night, then lay them on a glass, and set them in a stove till they are dry: If they are sugared too much wipe them with a wet cloth a little ; let the first syrup be very thin, a quart of water to a pound of sugar.

How to make Almond Knots.

Take two pounds of almonds, and blanch them in hot water; beat them in a mortar, to a very fine paste, with rose-water, do what you can to keep them from oiling. Take a pound of double refined sugar, sifted through a fine lawn sieve, leave out some to make up your knots, put the rest into a pan upon the fire, till it is scalding hot, and at the same time have your almonds scalding hot in another pan; then mix them together with the whites of three eggs beaten to froth, and let it stand till it is cold, then roll it with some of the sugar you left out, and lay them in platters of paper. They will not roll into any shape, but lay them as well as you can, and bake them in a cool oven; it must not be hot, neither must they be coloured.

To preserve Apricots.

Take your apricots and pare them, then stone what you can whole; then give them a light boiling in a pint of water, or according to your quantity of fruit; then take the weight of your apricots in sugar, and take the liquor which you boil them in and your sugar, and boil it till it comes to a syrup, and give them a light boiling, taking off the scum as it rises. When the syrup jellies, it is enough; then take up the apricots, and cover them with the jelly, and put cut paper over them, and lay them down when cold.

How to make Almond Milk for a Wash.

Take five ounces of bitter almonds, blanch them and beat them in a marble mortar very fine. You may put in a spoonful of sack when you beat them; then take the whites of three new-laid eggs, three pints of spring water, and one pint of sack. Mix them all very well together; then strain it through a fine cloth, and put it into a bottle, and keep it for use. You may put in lemon, or powder of pearl, when you make use of it.

How to make Gooseberry Wafers.

Take gooseberries before they are ready for preserving, cut off the black heads and boil them with as much water as will cover them all, to mash; then pass the liquor and all, as it will run, through a hair-sieve, and put some pulp through with a spoon, but not too near. It is to be pulped neither too thick nor too thin; measure it, and to a gill of it, take half a pound of double refined sugar; dry it, put to your pulp, and let it scald on a slow fire, not to boil at all. Stir it very well, and then will rise a frothy white scum which take clear off as it rises; you must scald and skim it till no scum rises, and it comes clean from the pan-side, then take it off, and let it cool a little. Have ready sheets of glass very smooth, about the thickness of parchment, which is not very thick. You must spread it on the glasses with a knife, very thin, even, and smooth, then set it on the stove with a slow fire; if you do it in the morning, at night you must cut it into long pieces with a broad case knife, and put your knife clean under it and fold it two or three times over, and lay them in a stove, turning them sometimes till they are pretty dry; but do not keep them too long, for they will loose their colour. If they do not come clear off your glasses at night, keep them till next morning.

How to make the thin Apricot Chips

Take your apricots or peaches, pare them and cut them very thin into chips, and take three quarters of their weight in sugar, it being finely searced: then put the sugar and the apricots into a pewter dish, and set them upon coals; and when the sugar is all dissolved, turn them upon the edge of the dish out of the syrup, and so set them by. Keep them turning till they have drank up the syrup; be sure they never boil. They must be warmed in the syrup once every day, and so laid out upon the edge of the dish till the syrup be drank.

To preserve Golden Pippins

Take the rind of an orange, and boil it very tender, lay it in cold water for three days; take two dozen of golden pippins, pare, core, quarter them, and boil them, and boil them to a strong jelly, and run it through a jelly-bag till it is clear; take the same quantity of pippins, pare them, and take out the cores, put three pounds of loaf sugar in a preserving pan, with three half pints of spring water; when it boils, skim it well, and put in your pippins with the orange rind, cut in long thin slips, let them boil fast till the sugar is thick, and will almost candy, then put in three half-pints of pippin jelly, and boil it fast till the jelly is clear; then squeeze in the juice of a lemon, give it a boil, and put them in pots and glasses, with the orange-peel. You may use lemon peel instead of orange, but then you must only boil it, not soak it.

To preserve Grapes.

Get some fine grapes, not over ripe, either red

or white, but very close, and pick all the specked ones: put them in a jar, with a quarter of a pound of sugar-candy, and fill the jar with common brandy; tie them down close, and keep them in a dry place. You may do morella cherries the same way.

To preserve Green Codlings.

Gather your codlings when they are the size of a walnut, with the stalks, and a leaf or two on; put a handful of vine-leaves into a preserving-pan, then a layer of codlings, then vine-leaves, and then codlings, till it is full, and vine-leaves pretty thick a top, and fill it with spring-water, cover it close to keep in the steam, and set it on a slow fire till they grow soft; then take them out, and take off the skins with a pen-knife, and then put them in the same water again with the vine-leaves, which must be quite cold, or it will make them crack; put in a little rock allum, and set them over a slow fire till they are green; then take them out, and lay them on a sieve to drain. Make a good syrup, and give them a gentle boil for three days, then put them in small jars, with brandy paper over them, and tie them down tight.

How to make Blackberry Wine.

Take your berries when full-ripe, put them into a large vessel of wood or stone, with a spicket in it, and pour upon them as much boiling water as will just appear at the top of them; as soon as you can endure your hand in them, bruise them very well, till all the berries be broke; then let them stand close covered till the berries be well wrought up to the top, which usually is three or four days; then draw off the clear juice into another vessel; and add to every ten quarts of this liquor one pound of sugar, stir it well in, and let it stand to work in another vessel like the first, a week or ten days; then draw it off at the spicket through a jelly-bag, into a large vessel; take four ounces of isinglass, lay it in steep twelve hours in a pint of white wine; the next morning boil it till it be all disolved, upon a slow fire; then take a gallon of your blackberry juice, put in the dissolved isinglass, give it a boil together, and put it in hot.

The best way to make Raisin Wine.

Take a clean wine or brandy hogshead; take great care it is very sweet and clean. put in two hundred of raisins, stalks and all and then fill the vessel with fine clear spring water: let it stand till you think it has done hissing, then throw in two quarts of fine French brandy; put in the bung slightly, and in about three weeks or a month, if you are sure it has done fretting, stop it down close; let it stand six months, peg it near the top, if you find it very fine and good, fit for drinking, bottle it off, or else stop it up again, and let it stand six months longer. It should stand six months in the bottle. This is by much the best way of making it, as I have seen by experience, as the wine will be much stronger, but less of it: the different sorts of raisins make a quite different wine; and after you have drawn off all the wine, throw on ten gallons of spring water; take off the head of the barrel, and stir it well twice a day, pressing the raisins as well as you can; let it stand a fortnight or three weeks, then draw it off into a proper vessel to hold it, and squeeze the raisins well; add two quarts of brandy, and two quarts of syrup of elderberries, stop it close when it has done working, and in about three months it will be fit for drinking. If you do not chuse to make this second wine, fill your hogshead with spring water, and set it in the sun for three months, and it will make excellent vinegar.

How to preserve White Quinces whole.

Take the weight of your quinces in sugar, and put a pint of water to a pound of sugar, make it into a syrup, and clarify it, then core your quinces and pare them put them into your syrup, and let it boil till it be all clear, then put in three spoonfuls of jelly, which must be made thus: over night, lay your quince-kernels in water, then strain them, and put them into your quinces, and let them have but one boil afterwards.

How to make Orange Wafers.

Take the best oranges, and boil them in three or four waters, till they be tender, then take out the kernels and the juice, and beat them to pulp in a clean marble mortar, and rub them through a hair sieve; to a pound of this pulp take a pound and half of double-refined sugar, beaten and searced; take half of your sugar, and put it into your oranges, and boil it till it ropes: then take it from the fire, and when it is cold make it up in paste with the other half of your sugar; make but a little at a time, for it will dry too fast; then with a little rolling-pin roll them as thin as tiffany upon papers; cut them round with a little drinking glass, and let them dry, and they will look very clear.

How to make Orange Cakes.

Take the peels of four oranges, being first pared, and the meat taken out, boil them tender, and beat them small in a marble mortar; then take the meat of them, and two more oranges, your seeds and skins being picked out, and mix it with the peelings that are beaten; set them on the fire with a spoonful or two of orange-flower water, keeping it stirring till that moisture be pretty well dried up; then have ready to every pound of that pulp, four pounds and a quarter of double refined sugar, finely searced: make your sugar very hot, and dry it upon the fire, and then mix it and the pulp together, and set it on the fire again, till the sugar be very well melted, but be sure it does not boil: you may put in a little peel, small, shred, or grated, and when it is cold, draw it up in double papers; dry them before the fire, and when you turn them, put two together; or you, may keep them in deep glasses or pots, and dry them as you have occasion.

How to make White Cakes like China Dishes.

Take the yolks of two eggs, and two spoonfuls of sack, and as much rose-water, some carraway-seeds, and as much flour as will make it a paste stiff enough to roll very thin: if you would have them like dishes, you must bake upon dishes buttered. Cut them cut into what work you please to candy them; take a pound of fine searced sugar perfumed, and the white of an egg, or three or four spoonfuls of rose-water, stir it till it looks white; and when that paste is cold, do it with a feather on one side. This candied, let it dry, and do the other side so, and dry it also.

To make a Lemon Honeycomb.

Take the juice of one lemon, and sweeten it with fine sugar to your palate; then take a pint of cream, and the white of an egg, and put in some sugar, and beat it up; and as the froth rises, take it off, and put it on the juice of the lemon, till you have taken all the cream off upon the lemon; make it the day before you want it, in a dish that is proper.

How to dry Cherries

Take eight pounds of cherries, one pound of the best powdered sugar, stone the cherries over a great deep bason or glass, and lay them one by one in rows, and strew a little sugar: thus do till your bason is full to the top, and let them stand till next day; then pour them out into a great posnet, set them on the fire, let them boil very fast a quarter of an hour, or more; then pour them again into your bason, and let them stand two or three days; then take them out, lay them one by one on hair-sieves, and set them in the sun, or an oven, till they are dry, turning them every day upon dry sieves; if in the oven, it must be as little warm as you can just feel it, when you hold your hand in it.

How to make fine Almond Cakes.

Take a pound of Jordan almonds, blanch them, beat them very fine with a little orange-flower-water to keep them from oiling; then take a pound and a quarter of fine sugar, boil it to a candy height: then put in your almonds; then take two fresh lemons, grate off the rind very thin, and put as much juice as to make it of a quick taste; then put it into your glasses, and set it into your stove, stirring them often, that they do not candy: so when it is a little dry, put it into little cakes upon sheets of glass to dry.

How to make Uxbridge-Cakes.

Take a pound of wheat flour, seven pounds of currants, half a nutmeg, four pounds of butter, rub your butter cold very well amongst the meal; dress your currants very well in the flour, butter, and seasoning, and knead it with so much good new yeast as will make it into a pretty high paste; usually four pence worth of yeast to that quantity; after it is kneaded well together let it stand an hour to rise: you may put half a pound of paste in a cake.

How to make Mead.

Take ten gallons of water, and two gallons of honey, a handful of raced ginger; then take two lemons, cut them in pieces, and put them into it, boil it very well, keep it skimming; let it stand all night in the same vessel you boil it in, the next morning barrel it up, with two or three spoonfuls of good yeast. About three weeks or a month after, you may bottle it.

Marmalade of Cherries.

Take five pounds of cherries, stoned, and two pounds of hard sugar; shred your cherries, wet your sugar with the juice that runneth from them; then put the cherries into the sugar, and boil them pretty fast till it be a marmalade; when it is cold, put it up in glasses for use.

To dry Damosins.

Take four pounds of damosins; take one

pound of fine sugar, make a syrup of it, with about a pint of fair water; then put in your damosins, stir it into your hot syrup, so let them stand on a little fire, to keep them warm for half an hour; then put all into a bason, and cover them, let them stand till the next day; then put the syrup from them, and set it on the fire; and when it is very hot, put it on your damosins; this do twice a day for three days together; then draw the syrup from the damosins, and lay them in an earthen dish, and set them in an oven after bread is drawn; when the oven is cold, take them and turn them, and lay them upon clean dishes; set them in the sun, or in another oven till they are dry.

Marmalade of Quince White.

Take the quinces, pare them and core them, put them into water as you pare them, to be kept from blacking; then boil them so tender that a quarter of a straw will go through them; then take their weight of sugar, and beat them, break the quinces with the back of a spoon; and then put in the sugar, and let them boil fast uncovered, till they slide from the bottom of the pan: you may make paste of the same, only dry it in a stove, drawing it out into what form you please.

To preserve Apricots, or Plums, Green.

Take your plums before they have stones in them, which you may know by putting a pin through them; then coddle them in many waters till they are as green as grass; peel them and coddle them again; you must take the weight of them in sugar, and make a syrup; put to your sugar a jack of water, then put them in, set them on the fire to boil slowly, till they be clear, skimming them often, and they will be very green. Put them up in glasses, and keep them for use.

To preserve Cherries.

Take two pounds of cherries, one pound and an half of sugar, half a pint of fair water, melt your sugar in it; when it is melted, put in your other sugar and your cherries, then boil them softly, till all the sugar be melted; then boil them fast, and skim them; take them off two or three times and shake them, and put them on again, and let them boil fast; and when they are of a good colour, and the syrup will stand, they are enough.

To preserve Barberries.

Take the ripest and best barberries you can find; take the weight of them in sugar; then pick out the seeds and tops, wet your sugar with the juice of them and make a syrup; then put in your barberries, and when they boil take them off and shake them, and set them on again, and let them boil, and repeat the same, till they are clean enough to put into glasses.

Wiggs.

Take three pounds of well-dried flour, one nutmeg, a little mace and salt, and almost half a pound of carraway-comfits; mix these well together, and melt half a pound of butter in a pint of sweet thick cream, six spoonfuls of good sack, four yolks and three whites of eggs, and near a pint of good light yeast; work these well together, and cover it, and set it down to the fire to rise; then let them rest, and lay the remainder, the half pound of carraways on the top of the wigg, and put them upon papers well floured and dried, and let them have as quick an oven as for tarts.

To make Fruit Wafers ; Codlins or Plums do best.

Take the pulp of fruit, rubbed through a hair-sieve, and to three ounces of pulp take six ounces of sugar, finely searced ; do your sugar very well, till it be very hot, heat the pulp also very hot, and put it to your sugar, and heat it on the fire till it be almost at boiling ; then pour it on the glasses or trenchers, and set it on the stove, till you see it will leave the glasses (but before it begins to candy) take them off, and turn them upon papers, in what form you please. You may colour them red with clove-gilli-flowers steeped in the juice of lemon.

To make German Puffs.

Take two spoonfuls of fine flour, two eggs beat well, half a pint of cream or milk, two ounces of melted butter, stir it all well together, and add a little salt or nutmeg, put them in tea-cups or little deep tin moulds, half full, and bake them a quarter of an hour in a quick oven ; but let it be hot enough to colour them at top and bottom : turn them into a dish, and strew powder-sugar over them.

Cracknels.

Take half a pound of the whitest flour, and a pound of sugar beaten small, two ounces of butter cold, one spoonful of carraway-seeds, steeped all night in vinegar ; then put in three yolks of eggs, and a little rose-water, work your paste all together ; and after that beat it with a rolling-pin, till it be light ; then roll it out thin, and cut it with a glass, lay it thin on plates buttered, and prick them with a pin; then take the yolks of two eggs, beaten with rose-water, and rub them over with it; then set them into a pretty quick oven, and when they are brown take them out and lay them in a dry place.

To make Orange Loaves.

Take your orange, and cut a round hole in the top, take out all the meat, and as much of the white as you can, without breaking the skin; then boil them tender, shifting the the water till it is not bitter, than take them up and wipe them dry; then take a pound of fine sugar, a quart of water, or in proportion to the oranges; boil it, and take off the scum as it riseth, then put in your oranges, and let them boil a little, and let them lie a day or two in the syrup; then take the yolks of two eggs, a quarter of a pint of cream (or more), beat them well together, then grate in two Naples biscuits (or white bread), a quarter of a pound of butter, and four spoonfuls of sack; mix it all together till your butter is melted, then fill the oranges with it, and bake them in a slow oven as long as you would a custard, then stick in some cut citron, and fill them up with sack, butter, and sugar grated over.

To make a Lemon Tower or Pudding.

Grate the outward rind of three lemons; take three quarters of a pound of sugar, and the same of butter, the yolks of eight eggs, beat them in a marble mortar at least an hour, then lay a thin rich crust in the bottom of the dish you bake it in, as you may something a so over it: three quarters of an hour will bake it. Make a orange-pudding the same way, but pare the rinds, and boil the them first in several waters till the bitterness is boiled out.

How to make the Clear Lemon Cream.

Take a gill of clear water, infuse it in the rind of a lemon, till it tastes of it; then take the whites of six eggs, the juice of four lemons; beat all well together, and run them through a hair sieve, sweeten them with double-refined sugar, and set them on the fire, not too hot, keeping stirring; and when it is thick enough, take it off.

How to make Chocolate.

Take six pounds of cocoa-nuts, one pound of anise-seeds, four ounces of long pepper, one of cinnamon, a quarter of a pound of almonds one pound of pistachios, as much achiote as will make it the colour of brick, three grains of musk and as much ambergrease, six pounds of loaf sugar, one ounce of nutmegs, dry and beat them, and searce them through a fine sieve; your almonds must be beat to a paste, and mixed with the other ingredients; then dip your sugar in orange-flower or rose-water, and put it on a skillet, on a very gentle charcoal fire; then put in the spice, and stew it well together, then the musk and ambergrease, then put the cocoa-nuts last of all, then achiote, wetting it with the water the sugar was dipt in; stew all these very well together, over a hotter fire than before; then take it up, and put it into boxes, or what form you like, and set it to dry in a warm place. The pistachios and almonds must be a little beat in a mortar, then ground upon a stone.

Another Way to make Chocolate.

Take six pounds of the best Spanish nuts, when

parched, and cleaned from the hulls, take three pounds of sugar, two ounces of the best cinnamon, beaten and sifted very fine ; to every two pounds of nuts put in three good vanelas, or more or less as you please ; to every pound of nuts half a drachm of cardamum-seeds, very finely beaten and searced.

Cheesecakes without Currants.

Take two quarts of new milk, set it as it comes from the cow, with as little runnet as you can ; when it is come, break it as gently as you can, and whey it well ; then pass it through a hair-sieve, and put it into a marble mortar, and beat it into a pound of new butter, washed in rose-water ; when that is well mingled in the curd, take the yolks of six eggs, and the whites of three, beat them very well with a little thick cream and salt ; and after you have made the coffins, just as you put them into crust (which must not be till you are ready to set them into the oven), then put in your eggs and sugar, and a whole nutmeg finely grated ; stir them all well together, and so fill your crusts ; and if you put a little fine sugar searced into the crust, it will roll the thinner and cleaner ; three spoonfuls of thick sweet cream will be enough to beat up your eggs with.

How to preserve White Pear Plums.

Take the finest and clearest from specks you can get ; to a pound of plums take a pound and a quarter of sugar, the finest you can get, a pint and a quarter of water ; slit the plums and stone them, and prick them full of holes, saving some sugar beat fine laid in a bason ; as you do them, lay them in, and strew sugar over them ; when you have thus done, have half a pound of sugar, and your water, ready made into a thin syrup, and a little cold; put in your plums with the slit side downwards, set them on the fire, keep them continually boiling, neither two slow nor too fast; take them often off, shake them round, and skim them well, keep them down into the syrup continually, for fear they lose their colour; when they are thoroughly scalded, stew on the rest of your sugar, and keep doing so till they are enough, which you may know by their glazing; towards the latter end boil them up quickly.

To preserve Currants.

Take the weight of the currants in sugar, pick out the seeds; take to a pound of sugar half a jack of water, let it melt, then put in your berries, and let them do very leisurely, skim them, and take them up, let the syrup boil; then put them on again, and when they are clear, and the syrup thick enough, take them off, and when they are cold put them up in glasses.

To preserve Rasberries.

Take the rasberries that are not too ripe, and take the weight of them in sugar, wet your sugar with a little water, and put in your berries, and let them boil softly, take heed of breaking them; when they are clear, take them up, aud boil the syrup till it be thick enough, then put them in again, and when they are cold put them up in glasses.

To make Biscuit Bread.

Take half a pound of very fine wheat flour, and as much sugar finely searced, and dry them very well before the fire, dry the flour more than the sugar; then take four new-laid eggs, take out the strains, then swing them very well, then put the sugar in, and swing it well with the eggs, then put the four in it, and beat all together half an hour at the least; put to some anise seeds, or carraway-seeds, and rub the places with butter, and set them into the oven.

To candy Angelica.

Take it in April, boil it in water till it be tender; then take it up and drain it from the water very well, then scrape the outside of it, and dry it in a clean cloth, and lay it in the syrup, and let it lie in three or four days, and cover it close, the syrup must be strong of sugar, and keep it hot a good while, and let it not boil, after it is heated a good while, lay it upon a pie-plate, and so let it dry; keep it near the fire lest it dissolve.

To preserve Cherries.

Take their weight in sugar before your stone them; when stoned, make your syrup, then put in your cherries, let them boil slowly at the first, till they be thoroughly warmed, then boil them as fast as you can, when they are boiled clear, put in the jelly, with almost the weight in sugar, strew the sugar on the cherries, for the colouring you must be ruled by your eye; to a pound of sugar put a jack of water, strew the sugar on them before they boil, and put in the juice of currants soon after they boil.

To barrel Morello Cherries.

To one pound of full ripe cherries picked from the stems, and wiped with a cloth, take half a pound of double refined sugar, and boil it to a candy height, but not a high one, put the cherries into a small barrel, then put in the sugar by a spoonful at a time, till it is all in, and roll them about every day till they have done fermenting, then bung it up close, and they will be fit for use in a month. It must be an iron-hooped barrel.

To dry Pear Plums.

Take two pounds of pear-plums to one pound of sugar, stone them, and fill them every one with sugar, lay them in an earthen pot, put to them as much water as will prevent burning them, then set them in an oven after bread is drawn, let them stand till they are tender, then put them into a sieve to drain well from the syrup, then set them in an oven again, untill they be a little dry, then smooth the skins as well as you can, and so fill them, then set them in the oven again to harden, then wash them in water scalding hot, and dry them very well, then put them in the oven again very cool, to blue them; put them between two pewter dishes, and set them in the oven.

The Filling for the aforesaid Plums.

Take the plums, wipe them, prick them in the seams, put them in a pitcher, and set them in a little boiling water, let them boil very tender, then pour most of the liquor from them, then take off the skins and the stones; to a pint of the pulp a pound of sugar well dried in the oven, then let it boil till the scum rises, which take off very clean, and put into earthen plates, and dry it in an oven, and so fill the plums.

To candy Cassia.

Take as much of the powder of brown cassia

as will lie upon two quarters of a dollar with what musk and ambergrease you think proper, the cassia and perfume must be powdered together, then take a quarter of a pound of sugar, and boil it to a candy height; then put in your powder, and mix it well together, and pour it in pewter saucers or plates, which must be buttered very thin, and when it is cold it will slip out, the cassia is sometimes in powder, and sometimes in a hard lump.

To make Carraway Cakes.

Take two pounds of white flour, and two pounds of coarse loaf sugar well dried, and fine sifted; after the flour and sugar are sifted and weighed, then mingle them together, sift the flour and sugar together through a hair sieve, into the bowl you use it in; to them you must have two pounds of good butter, eighteen eggs, leaving out eight of the whites, to these you must have four ounces of candied orange, five or six ounces of carraway comfits; you must first work the butter with rose-water, till you can see none of the water, and your butter must be very soft; then put in flour and sugar, a little at a time, likewise your eggs; but you must beat your eggs very well, with ten spoonfuls of sack, so you must put in each as you think fit, keeping it constantly beating with your hand, till you have put it into the hoop for the oven; do not put in your sweetmeats and seeds, till you are ready to put it into your hoops; you must have three or four doubles of cap paper under the cakes, and butter the paper and hoop: you must sift some fine sugar upon your cake, when it goes into the oven.

To preserve Pippins in Slices

When your pippins are prepared, but not cored, cut them in slices, and take the weight of them in sugar, put to your sugar a pretty quantity of water let it melt, and skim it, let it boil again very high, then put them into the syrup when they are clear, lay them in shallow glasses, in which you mean to serve them up, then put into the syrup, candied orange-peel cut in little slices very thin, and lay about the pippin; cover them with syrup and keep them about the pippin.

Sack Cream like Butter.

Take a quart of cream, boil it with mace, put to it six egg-yolks well beaten, so let it boil up, then take it off the fire, and put in a little sack, and turn it; then put in a cloth, and let the whey run from it; then take it out of the cloth, and season it with rose-water and sugar, being very well broken with a spoon; serve it up in the dish, and pink it as you would do a dish of butter, so send it in with cream and sugar.

Barley Cream.

Take a quart of French barley, boil it in three or four waters, till it be pretty tender; then set a quart of cream on the fire with some mace and nutmeg; when the water begins to boil, drain out the barley from it, put in the cream, and let it boil till it be pretty thick and tender; then season it with sugar and salt. When it is cold, serve it up.

Almond Butter.

Take a pound of cream, put in some mace whole, and a quartered nutmeg, the yolks of eight eggs well beaten, and three quarters of a pound of almonds well blanched, and beaten extremely small, with a little rose-water and sugar; put these all together, set them on the fire, and stir them till they begin to boil: then take it off, and you will find it a little cracked; so lay a strainer in a cullender, and pour it into it, and let it drain a day or two, till you see it is firm like butter; then run it through a cullender, then it will be like little comfits, and so serve it up.

Sugar Cakes.

Take a pound and a half of very fine flour, one pound of cold butter, half a pound of sugar, work all these well together into a paste, then roll it with the palms of your hands into balls, and cut them with a glass into cakes, lay them in a sheet of paper, with some flour under them, to bake them you may make tumblets, only blanch in almonds, and beat them small, and lay them in the midst of a long piece of paste, and roll it round with your fingers, and cast them into knots, in what fashion you please; prick them and bake them.

Sugar Cakes another Way.

Take half a pound of fine sugar searced, and as much flour, two eggs beaten with a little rose-water, a piece of butter about the bigness of an egg, work them well together till they be a smooth paste; then make them into cakes, working every one with the palms of your hands; then lay them in plates; rubbed over with a little butter; so bake them in an oven little more than warm. You may make the knots of the same the cakes are made of; but in the mingling you must put in a few carraway seeds; when they are wrought to paste, roll them with the ends of your fingers into small rolls, and make it into knots lay them upon pie plates rubbed with butter, and bake them.

Clouted Cream.

Take four quarts of new milk from the cow, and put it in a broad earthen pan, and let it stand till the next day, then put it over a very slow fire for half an hour; make it nearly hot to set the cream, then put it away till it is cold, and take the cream off, and beat it smooth with a spoon. It is accounted in the West of England very fine for tea or coffee, or to put over fruit tarts or pies.

Quince Cream.

Take your quinces, and put them in boiling water unpared, boil them apace uncovered, lest they discolour when they are boiled, pare them, beat them very tender with sugar; then take cream, and mix it till it be pretty thick; if you boil your cream, with a little cinnamon, it will be better, but let it be cold before you put it to your quince.

Citron Cream.

Take a quart of cream, and boil it with three pennyworth of good clear isinglass, which must be tied up in a piece of thin tiffany; put in a blade or two of mace strongly boiled in your cream and isinglass, till the cream be pretty thick; sweeten it to your taste, with perfumed hard sugar; when it is taken off the fire, put in a little rose-water to your taste; then take a piece of your green freshest citron, and cut it in little bits, the breadth of point-dales, and about half as long; and the cream being first put into dishes, when it is half cold, put in your citron, so as it may but sink from the top, that it may not be seen, and may lie before it be at the bottom; if you wash your citron before in rose-water, it will make the colour better and fresher; so let it stand till next day, where it may get no water, and where it may not be shaken.

Cream of Apples, Quince, Goosberries, Prunes, or Raspberries.

Take to every quart of cream four eggs, being first well beat and strained, and mix them with a little cold cream, and put it to your cream, being first boiled with whole mace; keep it stirring till you find it begins to thicken at the bottom and sides; your apples, quinces and berries, must be tenderly boiled, so as they will crush in the pulp; then season it with rose-water and sugar to your taste, putting it into dishes; and when they are cold, if there be any rose-water and sugar which lies waterish at the top, let it be drained out with a spoon: this pulp must be made ready before you boil the cream; and when it is boiled, cover over your pulp a pretty thickness with your egg-cream, which must have a little rose-water and sugar put to it.

Sugar Loaf cream.

Take a quarter of a pound of hartshorn, and put it to a pottle of water and set on the fire in a pipkin, covered till it be ready to seeth; then pour off the water, and put a pottle of water more to it, and let it stand simmering on the fire till it be consumed to a pint, and with it two ounces of isinglass washed in rose-water, which must be put in with the second water, then strain it and let it cool, then take three pints of cream, and boil it very well with a bag of nutmeg, cloves, cinnamon and mace; then take a quarter of a pound of Jordan almonds, and lay them one night in cold water to blanch, and when they are blanched, let them lie two hours in cold water, then take them out, and dry them in a clean linen cloth, and beat them in a marble mortar, with fair water or rose-water, beat them to a very fine pulp, then take some of the aforesaid cream well warmed, and put the pulp by degrees into it, straining it through a cloth with the back of a spoon, till all the goodness of the almonds be strained out into the cream, then season the cream with rose-water and sugar; then take the aforesaid jelly, warm it till it dissolves, and season it with rose-water and sugar; and a grain of ambergrease or musk, if you please; then mix your cream and jelly together very well, and put it into glasses well warmed (like sugar loaves) and let it stand all night, then put them out upon a plate or two, or a white china dish, and stick the cream with piony kernels, or serve them in glasses, one on every trencher.

Conserve of Roses boiled.

Take red roses, take off all the whites at the bottom, or elsewhere, take three times the weight of them in sugar, put to a pint of roses a pint of water, skim it well, shred your roses a little before you put them into water, cover them, and boil the leaves tender in the water, and when they are tender put in your sugar, keep them stirring lest they burn when they are tender, and the syrup be consumed. Put them up, and so keep them for use.

How to make Orange Biscuits.

Pare your oranges, not very thick, put them into water, but first weigh your peels, let it stand over the fire, and let it boil till it be very tender; then beat it in a marble mortar, till it be a very fine smooth paste; to every ounce of peels put two ounces and a half of double-refined sugar well searced, mix them well together with a spoon in the mortar, spread it with a knife upon pie-plates, and set it in an oven a little warm, or before the fire; when it feels dry upon the top, cut it into what fashion you please, and turn them into another plate, and set them in a stove till they be dry; where the edges look rough, when it is dry, they must be cut with a pair of scissars.

The following curious Method of rearing Turkeys to advantage, translated from a Swedish Book, entitled Rural Oeconomy.

Many of our housewives, says this ingenious author, have long despaired of succes in rearing turkey's and complained, that the profit rarely indemnifies them for their trouble and loss of time; whereas, continues he, little more is to be done, than to plung the chick into a vessel of cold water, the very hour, if possible, but at least the very day it is hatched, forcing it to swallow one whole pepper corn; after which let it be returned to its mother. From that time it will become hardy, and fear the cold no more than a hen's chick. But it must be remembered, that this useful species of fowls are also subject to one particular disorder when they are young, which often carries them off in a few days. When they begin to droop, examine carefully the feathers on the rump, and you will find two or three, whose quill-part is filled with blood; upon drawing them the chick recovers, and after that requires no other care, than what is commonly bestowed on poultry that range the court yard.

The truth of these assertions is too well known to be denied; and as a convincing proof of the success, it will be sufficient to mention, that three parishes in Sweden have, for many years followed this method, and gained several hundred pounds by rearing and selling turkeys.

How to make Cyder.

After all your apples are bruised, take half of your quantity and squeeze them, and the juice you press from them pour upon the other half bruised but not squeezed, in a tub for the purpose, having a tap at the bottom, let the juice remain upon the apples three or four days, then pull out your tap, and let your juice run into some other vessel set under the tub to receive it, and if it runs thick, as at the first it will, pour it upon the apples again, till you see it runs clear, and as you have a quantity, put it into your vessel, but do not force the cyder, but let it drop as long as it will of its own accord: having done this, after you perceive that the sides begin to work, take a quantity of isinglass, an ounce will serve forty gallons, infuse this in some of the cyder till it be dissolved; put to an ounce of isinglass a quart of cyder, and when it is dissolved, pour it into the vessel, and stop it close for two days, or something more; then draw off the cyder into another vessel, this do so often till you perceive your cyder to be free from all manner of sediment, that may make it ferment and fret itself; after Christmas you may boil it. You may, by pouring water on the apples and pressing them, make a pretty small cyder; if it be thick and muddy, by using isinglass you may make it as clear as the rest, you must dissolve the isinglass over the fire, till it is a jelly.

For fining Cyder.

Take two quarts of skim-milk, four ounces of isinglass, cut the isinglass in pieces, and work it luke-warm in the milk over the fire; and when it is dissolved, then put it cold into the hogshead of cyder, and take a long stick, and stir it well from top to bottom, for half a quarter of an hour.

After it has fined.

Take ten pounds of raisins of the sun, two ounces of turmerick, half an ounce of ginger beaten, then take a quantity of raisins, and grind them as you do mustard-seed in a bowl, with a little cyder, and so the rest of the raisins, then sprinkle the turmerick and ginger amongst it; then put all into a fine canvass bag, and hang it in the middle of the hogshead close, and let it lie. After the cyder has stood thus a fortnight or a month, then you may bottle it at your pleasure.

To make Chouder, a Sea Dish.

Take a belly piece of pickled pork, slice off the fatter parts, and lay them at the bottom of the kettle, strew over it onions, and such sweet herbs as you can procure, take a middling large cod, bone and slice it, as for crimping, pepper, salt, all-spice, and flour it a little; make a layer with part of the slices, upon that a slight layer of pork again, and on that a layer of biscuit and soon, pursuing the like rule, until the kettle is filled to about four inches cover it with nice paste, pour in about a pint of water, lute down the cover of the kettle, and let the top be supplied with live wood embers. Keep it over a slow fire about four hours.

When you take it up, lay it in the dish, pour in a glass of hot Madeira wine, and a very little India pepper, if you have oysters, or truffles or morels, it is still better, thicken it with butter. Observe before you put this sauce in, to skim the stew, and then lay on the crust, and send it to table reverse as in the kettle, cover it close with the paste, which should be brown.

To make Spanish Fritters.

Take the inside of a roll, and slice it in three: then soak it in milk, then pass it through a batter of eggs, fry them in oil, when almost done, repass them in another batter, then let them fry till they are done, draw them off the oil, and lay them in a dish, over every pair of fritters you must throw cinnamon, small coloured sugar plums, and clarified sugar.

To fricasey Pigeons the Italian Way.

Quarter them, aud fry them in oil, take some green peas, and let them fry in the oil till they are almost ready to burst; then put some boiling water to them, season it with salt, pepper, onions, garlick, parsley, and vinegar. Veal and lamb do the same way, and thicken with yolks of eggs.

Pickled Beef for present Use.

Take the rib of beef, stick it with garlick and cloves, season it with salt, Jamaica pepper, mace, and some garlick pounded, cover the meat with white-wine vinegar and Spanish thyme, you must take care to turn the meat every day, and add more vinegar, if required, for a fortnight, then put it in a stew-pan, and cover it close, and let it simmer on a slow fire for six hours, adding vinegar and white wine, if you chuse, you may stew a good quantity of onions, it will be more palatable.

Beef Steaks after the French Way.

Take some beef steaks, broil them till they are half done, while the steaks are doing, have ready in a stew-pan some red-wine, a spoonful or two of gravy, season it with salt, pepper, some shalots, then take the steaks, and cut in squares, and put in the sauce; you must put some vinegar, cover it close, and let it simmer on a slow fire half an hour.

To make Hamburgh Sausages.

Take a pound of beef, mince it very small, with half a pound of the best suet, then mix three quarters of a pound of suet, cut in large pieces, then season it with pepper, cloves, nutmeg, a great quantity of garlick cut small, some white-wine vinegar, some bay-salt, and common salt, a glass of red-wine, and one of rum; mix all these very well together; then take the largest gut you can find, and stuff it very tight; then hang it up in a chimney, and smoke it with saw-dust for a week or ten days; hang them in the air till they are dry, and they will keep a year. They are very good boiled in peas-pottage, and roasted with toasted bread under it, or in an amlet.

Sausages after the German Way.

Take the crumb of a threepenny loaf, one pound of suet, half a lamb's lights, a handful of parsley, some thyme, marjory, and onion; mince all very small, then season it with salt and pepper. These must be stuffed in a sheep's gut; they are fried in oil or melted suet, and are only fit for immediate use.

A Turkey stuffed after the Hamburgh Way.

Take one pound of beef, three quarters of a pound of suet, mince it very small, season it with salt, pepper, cloves, mace, and sweet marjoram; then mix two or three eggs with it, loosen the skin all round the turkey, and stuff it. It must be roasted.

Chickens dressed the French Way.

Take them and quarter them, then broil, crumble over them a little bread and parsley; when they are half done, put them in a stew-pan with three or four spoonfuls of gravy, and double the quantity of white-wine, salt and pepper, some fried veal-balls, and some suckers, onions, shalots, and some green gooseberries or grapes when in season; cover the pan close, and let it stew on a charcoal fire for an hour; thicken the liquor with the yolks of eggs, and the juice of lemon; garnish the dish with fried suckers, sliced lemon, and the livers.

A Calf's Head dressed after the Dutch Way.

Take half a pound of Spanish peas, lay them in water a night; then one pound of whole rice, mix the peas and rice together, and lay it round the head in a deep dish; then take two quarts of water, seasoned with pepper and salt, and coloured with saffron; then send it to bake.

Chickens and Turkies, dressed after the Dutch Way.

Boil them, season them with salt, pepper, and cloves; then to every quart of broth, put a quarter of a pound of rice or vermicelli: it is eat with sugar and cinnamon. The two last may be left out.

To make a Fricasee of Calves Feet and Chaldron, after the Italian Way.

Take the crumb of a three-penny loaf, one pound of suet, a large onion, two or three handfuls of parsley, mince it very small, season it with salt and pepper, three or four cloves of garlic, mix with eight or ten eggs; then stuff the chaldron; take the feet and put them in a deep stew-pan; it must stew upon a slow fire till the bones are loose; then take two quarts of green peas, and put in the liquor; and when done, you must thicken it with the yolks of two eggs, and the juice of a lemon. It must be seasoned with pepper, salt, mace, and onion, some parsley and garlick. You must serve it up with the abovesaid pudding in the middle of the dish, and garnish the dish with fried suckers and sliced onions.

To pickle the fine Purple Cabbage, so much admired at the great Tables.

Take two cauliflowers, two red cabbages, half a peck of kidney beans, six sticks, with six cloves of garlick on each stick; wash all well, give them one boil up, then drain them on a sieve, and lay them leaf by leaf upon a large table, and salt them with bay-salt, then lay them a drying in the sun, or in a slow oven, until as dry as cork.

To make the Pickle.

Take a gallon of the best vinegar, with one quart of water, and a handful of salt, and an ounce of pepper; boil them, let it stand till it is cold, then take a quarter of a pound of ginger, cut in pieces, salt it, let it stand a week; take half a pound of mustard-seed, wash it, and lay it to dry; when very dry, bruise half of it, when half is ready for the jar, lay a row of cabbage, a row of cauliflowers and beans, and throw betwixt every row your mustard-seed, some black pepper, some Jamaica pepper, some ginger, mix an ounce of the root of turmerick powdered; put in the pickle, which must go over all. It is best when it hath been made two years, though it may be used the first year.

To raise Mushrooms.

Cover an old hot-bed three or four inches thick with fine garden mould, and cover that three or four inches thick with mouldy long muck, of a horse muck-kill, or old rotten stubble; when the bed has lain some time thus prepared, boil any mushrooms that are not fit for use, in water, and throw the water on your prepared bed; in a day or two after, you will have the best small button mushrooms.

The Stag's Heart Water.

Take balm four handfuls, sweet marjoram one handful, rosemary flowers, clove-gilliflowers dried, dried rose-buds, borrage-flowers of each an ounce; marigold flowers half an ounce, lemon-peel two ounces, mace and cardamum, of each thirty grains; of cinnamon sixty grains, or yellow and white sanders, of each a quarter of an ounce, shavings of hartshorn an ounce: take nine oranges, and put in the peel, then cut them in small pieces; pour upon these two quarts of the best Rhenish, or the best white-wine; let it infuse three or four days, being very close stopped in a cellar or cool place: If it infuse nine or ten days, it is the better.

Take a stag's heart, and cut off all the fat, and cut it very small, and pour in so much Rhenish or white-wine as will cover it; let it stand all night close covered in a cool place; the next day add the aforesaid things to it, mixing it very well together; adding to it a pint of the best rose-water, and a pint of the juice of celandine: If you please you may put in ten grains of saffron, and so put it in a glass still, distilling in water, raising it well to keep in the steam, both of the still and receiver.

To make Angelica Water.

Take eight handfuls of the leaves, wash them and cut them, and lay them on a table to dry; when they are dry put them into an earthen pot, and put to them four quarts of strong wine lees; let it stay for twenty-four hours, but stir it twice in the time; then put it into a warm still or an alembic, and draw it off; cover your bottles with a paper, and prick holes in it; so let it stand two or three days; then mingle it all together, and sweeten it; and when it is settled, bottle it up, and stop it close.

To make Milk Water.

Take the herbs agrimony, endive, fumitory, baum, elder-flower, white-nettles, water-cresses, bank cresses, sage, each three handfuls; eye-bright, brooklime, and celandine, each two handfuls; the roses of yellow-dock, red-madder, fennel, horse radish, and liquorice, each three ounces; raisins stoned one pound, nutmegs sliced, Winter's bark, turmerick, galangal, each two drachms; carraway and fennel seed three ounces, one gallon of milk. Distil all with a gentle fire in one day. You may add a handful of May wormwood.

To make Slip-coat Cheese.

Take six quarts of new milk hot from the cow, the stroakings, and put to it two spoonfuls of rennet; and when it is hard coming, lay it into the fat with a spoon, not breaking it at all; then press it with a four pound weight, turning of it with a dry cloth once an hour, and every day shifting it into fresh grass. It will be ready to cut, if the weather be hot, in fourteen days.

To make a Brick-Bat Cheese. It must be made in September.

Take two gallons of new milk, and a quart of good cream, heat the cream, put in two spoonfuls of rennet, and when it is come, break it a little, then put it into a wooden mould, in the shape of a brick. It must be half a year old before you eat it: you must press it a little, and so dry.

To make Cordial Poppy Water.

Take two gallons of very good brandy, and a peck of poppies, and put them together in a wide-mouthed glass, and let them stand forty-eight hours, and then strain the poppies out; take a pound of raisins of the sun, stone them, and an ounce of coriander-seed, an ounce of sweet-fennel seeds, and an ounce of liquorice sliced, bruise them all together, and put them into the brandy, with a pound of good powder sugar, and let them stand four or eight weeks, shaking it every day; and then strain it off, and bottle it close up for use.

To make White Mead.

Take five gallons of water, add to that one gallon of the best honey; then set it on the fire, boil it together well, and skim it very clean; then take it off the fire, and set it by; then take two or three races of ginger, the like quantity of cinnamon and nutmegs, bruise all these grossly, and put them in a little Holland bag in the hot liquor, and so let it stand close covered till it be cold; then put as much ale-yeast to it as will make it work. Keep it in a warm place, as they do ale; and when it has wrought well, tun it up; at two months you may drink it, having been bottled a month. If you keep it four months, it will be the better.

To make a Scotch Haggass.

Take the lights, heart, and chiterlings of a calf, chop them very fine, and a pound of suet chopped fine: season with pepper and salt to your palate; mix in a pound of flour, or oatmeal, roll it up, and put it into a calf's bag, and boil it; an hour and a half will do it. Some add a pint of good thick cream, and put in a little beaten mace, cloves, or nutmeg; all-spice is very good in it.

To make it sweet with Fruit.

Take the meat and suet as above, and flour,

with beaten mace, cloves, and nutmeg, to your palate, a pound of currants washed very clean, a pound of raisins stoned and chopped fine, half a pint of sack; mix all well together, and boil it in the calf's bag two hours. You must carry it to table in the bag it was boiled in.

To make Sour Crout.

Take your fine hard white cabbage, cut them very small, have a tub on purpose with the head out, according to the quantity you intend to make; put them in the tub; to every four or five cabbages throw in a handful of salt; when you have done as many as you intend, lay a very heavy weight on them, to press them down as flat as possible, throw a cloth on them and lay on the cover; let them stand a month, then you may begin to use it. It will keep twelve months; but be sure to keep it always close covered, and the weight on it; if you throw a few carraway-seeds pounded fine amongst it, they give it a fine flavour. The way to dress it is with a fine fat piece of beef stewed together. It is a dish much made use of amongst the Germans, and in the Northern countries where the frost kills all the cabbages; therefore they preserve them in this manner before the frost takes them.

Cabbage-stalks, cauliflower-stalks, and artichoke-stalks, peeled, and cut fine down in the same manner, are very good.

To keep Green Peas, Beans, &c. and Fruit, fresh and good till Christmas.

Observe to gather all your things on a fine clear day, in the increase or full moon; take well-glazed earthen or stone pots quite new, that have not been laid in water, wipe them clean, lay in your fruit very carefully, and take great care none is bruised or damaged in the least, nor too ripe, but just in their prime; stop down the jars close, pitch it, and tie a leather over. Do kidney beans the same; bury two feet deep in the earth, and keep them there till you have occasion for them. Do peas and beans the same way, only keep them in the pods, and do not let your peas be either too young or too old: the one will run to water, and the other the worms will eat; as to the two latter, lay a layer of fine writing-sand, and a layer of pods, and so on till full; the rest as above. Flowers you may keep the same way.

To make Paco lilla, or Indian Pickles, the same the Mangoes comes over in.

Take a pound of race ginger, and lay it in water one night; then scrape it, and cut it in thin slices and put to it some salt, and let it stand in the sun to dry; take long-pepper two ounces, and do it as the ginger. Take a pound of garlick, and cut it in thin slices, and salt it, and let it stand three days; then wash it well, and let it be salted again, and stand three days more; then wash it well, and drain it, and put it in the sun to dry: take a quarter of a pound of mustard-seeds bruised, and half a quarter of an ounce of turmerick, put these ingredients, when prepared, into a large stone or glass jar, with a gallon of very good white-wine vinegar, and stir it up very often for a fortnight, and tie it up close.

In this pickle you may put white cabbage, cut in quarters, and put in a brine of salt and water for three days, and then boil fresh salt and water and just put in the cabbage to scald, and press out the water, and put it in the sun to dry, in the same manner as you do cauliflowers, cucumbers, melons, apples, French-beans, plums, or any sort of fruit. Take care they are well dried before you put them into the pickle; you need never empty the jar, but as the things come in season, put them in, and supply it with vinegar as often as there is occasion.

If you would have your pickle look green, leave out the turmerick, and green them as usual, and put them into this pickle cold.

In the above you may do walnuts in a jar by themselves: put the walnuts in without any preparation, tied close down, and kept for some time.

To preserve Cucumbers equal with any Italian Sweetmeats.

Take fine young gerkins, of two or three different sizes; put them into a stone jar, cover them well with vine-leaves, fill the jar with spring water, cover it close; let it stand near the fire so as to be quite warm, for ten days or a fortnight; then take them out, and throw them into spring water; they will look quite yellow, and stink, but you must not mind that. Have ready your preserving pan; take them out of that water, and put them into the pan, cover them well with vine-leaves, fill it with spring-water, set it over a charcoal fire, cover them close, and let them simmer very slow; look at them often, and when you see them turned quite of a fine green, take off the leaves, and throw them into a large sieve; then into a coarse cloth, four or five times doubled when they are cold, put them into the jar, and have ready your syrup, made of double-refined sugar, in which boil a great deal of lemon peel, and whole ginger; pour it hot over them, and cover them down close: do it three times: pare your lemon-peel very thin, and cut them in long thin bits about two inches long: the ginger must be well boiled in water before it is put in the syrup. Take inside; do them cut them in halves, scoop out the long cucumbers, the same way: they eat very fine in minced pies or puddings; or boil the syrup to a candy, and dry them on sieves.

The Jews way of preserving Salmon, and all Sorts of Fish.

Take either salmon, cod, or any large fish, cut off the head, wash it clean and cut it in slices as crimped cod is, dry it very well in a cloth; then flour it, and dip it in yolks of eggs, and fry it in a great deal of oil, till it is of a fine brown, and well done; take it out, and lay it to drain, till it is very dry and cold. Whitings, mackarel, and flat fish, are done whole. When they are quite dry and cold, lay them in your pan or vessel, throw in between them a good deal of mace, cloves, and sliced nutmeg a few bay-leaves: have your pickle ready made of the best white-wine vinegar, in which you must boil a great many cloves of garlick and shalot, black and white pepper, Jamaica and long pepper, juniper-berries and salt; when the garlick begins to be tender, the pickle is enough; when it is quite cold, pour it on your fish, and a little oil on the top. They will keep good a twelve-month, and are to be eat cold with oil and vinegar they will go good to the East Indies. All sorts of fish fried well in oil, eat very fine cold with shalot, or oil and vinegar. Observe in the pickling of your fish to have the pickling ready; first put a little pickle in, then a layer of fish, then pickle, then a little fish, and so lay them down very close, to be very well covered, put a little saffron in the pickle. Frying fish in common oil is not so expensive with care; for present use a little does, and if the cook is careful not to burn the oil, or black it, it will fry them two or three times.

To preserve Tripe to go to the East Indies

Get a fine belly of tripe, quite fresh, take a four gallon cask well hooped, lay in your tripe and have your pickle ready, made thus: take seven quarts of spring-water, and put as much salt into into it as will make an egg swim, that the little end of the egg may be about an inch over the water (you must take care to have the fine clear salt, for the common salt will spoil it); add a quart of the best white-wine vinegar, two sprigs of rosemary, an ounce of all-spice, pour it on your tripe, let the cooper fasten the cask down directly; when it comes to the Indies, it must not be opened till it is just going to be dressed, for it will not keep after the cask is opened. The way to dress it is, lay it in water half an hour, then fry it or broil it as we do here.

The Manner of dressing various Sorts of dried Fish, as Stock-fish, Cod, Salmon, Whitings, &c.

The general Rule for steeping of dried Fish, the Stock-fish excepted.

All the kinds, except stock-fish, are salted, or either dried in the sun, as the most common way, or in prepared kilns, or by the smoke of wood fires in chimney- corners, and, in either case, require the being softened and freshened in proportion to their bulk, their nature or dryness; the very dry sort, as bacalao, cod fish, or whiting, and such like should be steeped in luke-warm milk and water; the steeping kept as near as possible to an equal degree of heat. The largest fish should be steeped twelve; the small, as whiting, &c. about two hours; the cod are therefore laid to steep in the evening, the whitings, &c, in the morning before they are to be dressed; after the time of steeping, they are to be taken out, and hung up by the tails until they are dressed; the reason of hanging them up is, that they soften equally as in the steeping, without extracting too much of the relish, which would make them insipid; when thus prepared, the small fish, as whiting, tusk, and such like, are floured and laid on the gridiron, and when a little hardened on the one side, must be turned and basted with oil upon a feather; and when basted on both sides, and well hot through, taken up, always observing, that as sweet-oil supples and supplies fish with a kind of artificial juices, so the fire draws out those juices, and hardens them; therefore be careful not to let them broil too long; no time can be prescribed, because of the difference of fires, and various bigness of the fish. A clear charcoal fire is much the best, and the fish kept a good distance to broil gradually: the best way they know when they are enough is, they will swell a little in the basting, and you must not let them fall again.

The sauces are the same as usual to salt-fish, and garnish with oysters fried in batter.

But for a supper, for those that like sweet-oil,

the best sauce is oil, vinegar and mustard, beat up to a consistence, and served up in saucers.

If boiled, as the great fish usually are, it should be in milk and water, but not so properly boiled, as kept just simmering over an equal fire; in which way, half an hour will do the largest fish, and five minutes the smallest. Some people broil both sorts after simmering, and some pick them to pieces, and then toss them up in a pan with fried onions and apples.

They are either way very good, and the choice depends on the weak or strong stomachs of the eaters.

Dried Salmon must be differently managed.

For though a large fish, they do not require more steeping than a whiting; and when laid on the gridiron, should be moderately peppered.

The dried Herring,

Instead of milk and water, should be steeped the like time as the whiting, in small-beer; and to which, as to all kinds of broiled salt-fish, sweet-oil will always be found the best basting, and no ways affect even the delicacy of those who do not love oil.

Stock Fish

Are very different from those before mentioned; they being dried in the frost without salt, are in their kind very insipid, and are only eatable by the ingredients that make them so, and the art of cookery: they should be first beat with a sledge hammer on an iron anvil, or on a very solid smooth oaken block; and when reduced almost to atoms, the skin and the bones taken away and the remainder of the fish steeped in milk and water until very soft; then strained out, and put into a soup dish with new milk, powdered cinnamon, mace, and nutmeg, the chief part cinnamon; a paste round the edge of the dish, and put in a temperate oven to simmer for about an hour, and then served up in place of pudding.

N. B. The Italians eat the skin boiled, either hot or cold, and most usually with oil and vinegar, preferring the skin to the body of the fish.

To dress cured Mackarel.

Either fry them in boiling oil, and lay them to drain, or broil them before, or on a very clear fire, in the last case, baste them with oil and a feather, sauce will be very little wanting, as they will be very moist and mellow, if good in kind; otherwise you may use melted butter and crimped parsley.

Calves Feet Stewed.

Cut a calf's foot into four pieces, put it into a sauce-pan, with half a pint of soft-water, and a middling potatoe, scrape the outside skin clear off, slice it thin, and a middling onion peeled and sliced thin, some beaten pepper and salt, cover it close, and let it stew very softly for about two hours after it boils, be sure to let it simmer as softly as you can, eat it without any other sauce: it is an excellent dish.

To make Fricandillas.

Take two pounds of lean veal, and half a pound of kidney suet chopped small, the crumb of a four-penny French roll, soaked in hot milk, and squeeze the milk out, put it to the veal, season it pretty high with pepper and salt, and grated nutmeg, make it into balls as big as a tea cup, with the yolks of eggs over it, and fry them in butter till they are of a fine light brown, have a quart of veal broth in a stew-pan, stew them gently three quarters of an hour, thicken it with butter rolled in flour and add the juice of half a lemon, put it in a dish with the sauce over, and garnish with notched lemon and beet-root.

To make a fine Bitter.

Take an ounce of the finest Jesuit powder, half a quarter of an ounce of snake-root powder, half a quarter of an ounce of salt of wormwood, half a quarter of saffron, half a quarter of cochineal, put it into a quart of the best brandy, and let it stand twenty-four hours; every now and then shaking the bottle.

An approved Method practised by Mrs. Dukely, the Queen's Tyre-Woman, to preserve Hair, and make it grow thick.

Take one quart of white-wine, put in one handful of rosemary flowers half a pound of honey, distil them together, then add a quarter of a pint of oil of sweet almonds, shake it very well together, put a little of it into a cup, warm it blood warm, rub it well on your head, and comb it dry.

To make Carolina Snow-Balls.

Take half a pound of rice, wash it clean, divide it into six parts, take six apples, pare them, and scoop out the core, in which place put a little lemon peel shred very fine; then have ready some thin cloths to tie the balls in, put the rice in the cloth, and lay the apple on it, tie them up close, put them into cold water, and when the water boils, they will take an hour and a quarter boiling: be very careful how you turn them into the dish that you do not break the rice, and they will look as white as snow, and make a very pretty dish. The sauce is, to this quantity, a quarter of a pound of fresh butter, melted thick, a glass of white-wine, a little nutmeg and beaten cinnamon made very sweet with sugar, boil all up together, and pour it into a bason, and send it to table.

A Carolina Rice Pudding.

Take half a pound of rice, wash it clean, put it into a sauce pan, with a quart of milk, keep stirring it till it is very thick, take great care it does not burn, then turn it into a pan, and grate some nutmeg into it, and two tea spoonfuls of beaten cinnamon, a little lemon-peel shred fine, six apples pared and chopped small, mix all together with the yolks of three eggs, and sweeten to your palate, then tie it up close in a cloth, put it into boiling water, and be sure to keep it boiling all the time; an hour and a quarter will boil it. Melt butter and pour over it, and throw some fine sugar all over it, a little wine in the sauce will be a great addition to it.

To distil Treacle Water Lady Monmouth's Way.

Take three ounces of hartshorn, shaved and boiled in borrage water, or succory, wood sorrel or respice water, or three pints of any of these waters boiled to a jelly, and put the jelly and hartshorn both into the still, and add a pint more of these waters when you put it into the still; take the roots of elecampane, gentian, cypress, tuninsil, of each an ounce ;. blessed thistle called carduus, and angelica, of each an ounce ; sorrel root two ounces, balm, sweet marjoram, and burnet, of each half a handful ; lily-comvally flowers, borrage, bugloss, rosemary, and marigold flowers, of each two ounces ; citron-rinds, carduus seeds, and citron-seeds, alkermes berries, and cochineal, each of these an ounce.

Prepare all these Simples thus :

Gather the flowers as they come in season, and put them in glasses with a large mouth, and put with them as much good sack as will cover them, and tie up the glasses close with bladders wet in the sack, with a cork and leather tie it up close, adding more flowers and sack as occasion is, and when one glass is full, take another, till you have your quantity of flowers to distill, put cochineal into a pint bottle, with half a pint of sack, and tie it up close with a bladder under the cork, and another on the top, wet with sack, tied up close with brown thread, and then cover it up close with leather, and bury it standing upright in a bed of hot horse-dung for nine or ten days, look at it, and if dissolved, take it out of the dung, but do not open it till you distil, slice all the roses, beat the seeds and the alkermes berries, and put them into another glass ; amongst all, put no more sack than it needs ; and when you intend to distil, take a pound of the best Venice treacle, and dissolve it in six pints of the best white wine, and three of red rose-water, and put all the ingredients into a bason, and stir them all together, and distill them in a glass still, balneam Mariæ, open not the ingredients till the same day you distil.

THE ORDER OF A
MODERN BILL OF FARE,
FOR EACH MONTH,
In the Manner the Dishes are to be placed upon the Table.

FOR

JANUARY.

FIRST COURSE.

Soup.

Leg of Lamb. Petit Patties. Boiled Chickens.

Chicken and Veal Pie. Cod's Head. Roasted Beef.

Tongue. Patties. Scotch Collops.

Vermicelli Soup.

SECOND COURSE.

Roasted Turkey.

Marinated Smelts. Tartles. Mince Pies.

Roast Sweetbreads. Stands of Jellies. Larks.

Almond Tort. Maids of Honour. Lobsters.

Woodcocks.

THIRD COURSE.

Morels.

Artichoke Bottoms. Dutch Beef scraped. Macaroni.

Custards. Cut Pastry. Black Caps.

Scolloped Oysters. Potted Chars. Stewed Celery.

Rabbit Fricaseed.

N. B. In your first course always observe to send up all Kinds of Garden Stuff suitable to your Meat, &c. in different dishes, on a Water-dish filled with hot Water on the side Table; and all your Sauce in Boats or Basons, to answer one another at the corners.

The ORDER of a MODERN BILL of FARE,

FOR

FEBRUARY.

FIRST COURSE.

	Peas Soup.	
Chickens.	Chicken Patty.	Mutton Collops.
Harrico of Mutton.	Salmon and Smelts.	Rump of Beef
Pork Cutlets. Sauce.	Oyster. Patties.	Small Ham.
	Soup.	

SECOND COURSE.

	Wild Fowl.	
Cardoons,	Dish of Jelly.	Stewed Pippins.
Scolloped Oysters.	Epergne.	Ragout.
Pears.		Artichoke Bottoms.
	Hare.	

THIRD COURSE.

	Two Woodcooks.	
Crawfish.	Asparagus.	Preserved Cherries.
Pig's Ears.	Fruit.	Lamb Chops larded.
Blanched Almonds and Raisins.	Mushrooms.	Prawns.
	Larks.	

The ORDER of a MODERN BILL of FARE,

FOR

MARCH.

FIRST COURSE.

	Soup.	
Sheeps Rumps.	Almond Pudding.	Fillet of Pork.
Chine of Mutton and Stewed Celery.	Stewed Carp or Tench.	Lamb's Head.
Veal Collops.	Beef Steak Pie.	Calves Ears.
	Onion Soup.	

SECOND COURSE.

	A Poulard larded and roasted.	
Asparagus.	Blancmange.	Prawns.
Ragooed Sweet-breads.	A Trifle.	Fricasee of Rabbits.
Crawfish.	Cheesecakes.	Fricasee of Mushrooms.
	Tame Pigeons roasted.	

THIRD COURSE.

	Ox Palates shivered.	
Tartlets.	Potted Larks.	Stewed Pigeons.
Cardoons.	Jellies.	Spanish Peas.
Black Caps.	Potted Partridge.	Almond Cheese-cakes.
	Cock's Combs.	

The ORDER of a MODERN BILL of FARE,

FOR

APRIL.

FIRST COURSE.

Crimp Cod and Smelts.
Chickens. Marrow Pudding. Maintenon.
Breast of Veal in Rolio. Spring Soup. Beef Tremblonque
Lamb's Tails à la Bashemel. Pigeon Pie. Tongue.
Whitings boiled and broiled.

SECOND COURSE.

Ducklings.
Asparagus. Tartlets. Black Caps.
Roast Sweet-breads. Jellies and Syllabubs. Oysters Loaves.
Stewed Pears. Tansey. Mushrooms.
Ribs of Lamb.

THIRD COURSE.

Petit Pigeons.
Mushrooms. French Plums. Pistachio Nuts.
Marinated Smelts. Sweetmeats. Oyster Loaves.
Blanched Almonds. Raisins. Artichoke Bottoms.
Calves Ears à la Braise.

The ORDER of a MODERN BILL of FARE

FOR

MAY.

FIRST COURSE.

	Calvert's Salmon broiled.	
Rabbits with Onions.	Veal Olives.	Collared Mutton.
Pigeon Pie raised.	Vermicelli Soup.	Maccaroni Tort.
Ox Palates	Chine of Lamb.	Matelot of Tame Duck.
	Mackerel.	

SECOND COURSE.

	Green Goose.	
Asparagus.	Custards.	Cocks Combs.
Green Gooseberry Tarts.	Epergne.	Green Apricot Tarts.
Lamb Cutlets.	Blancmange.	Stewed Celery.
	Roast Chickens.	

THIRD COURSE.

	Lamb's Sweetbreads.	
Stewed Lettuce.	Rhenish Cream.	Rasberry Puffs.
Lobsters ragooed.	Compost of Green Apricots.	Buttered Crab
Lemon Cakes.	Orange Jelly.	French Beans.
	Ragout of Fat Livers.	

The ORDER of a MODERN BILL of FARE,

FOR

JUNE.

FIRST COURSE.

	Green Peas Soup.	
Chickens.	Haunch of Venison.	Harrico.
Lamb Pie.	Turbot.	Ham.
Veal Cutlets	Neck of Venison.	Orange Pudding.
	Lobster Soup.	

SECOND COURSE.

	Turkey Poults.	
Peas.	Apricot Puffs,	Lobsters.
Fricasee of Lamb.	Half Moon.	Roasted Sweetbreads.
Smelt	Cherry Tart.	Artichokes.
	Roasted Rabbits.	

THIRD COURSE.

	Sweetbreads à la Blanche.	
Fillets of Soals.	Potted Wheat Ears.	Ratafia Cream
Peas.	Green Gooseberry Tart.	Forced Artichokes.
Preserved Oranges.	Potted Ruff.	Matelot of Eels
	Lambs Tails à la Braise.	

The ORDER of a MODERN BILL of FARE

FOR

JULY.

FIRST COURSE.

Mackerel, &c.
Breast of Veal. Tongue and Turnips. Pulpeton.
Venison Pasty. Herb Soup. Neck of Venison.
Chickens. Boiled Goose and Stewed Red Cabbage Mutton Cutletts.
Trout boiled.

SECOND COURSE.

Roast Turkey.
Stewed Peas. Apricot Tart. Blancmange.
Sweetbread. Jellies. Fricasee of Rabbits.
Custards. Green Codlin Tarts. Blaized Pippins.
Roast Pigeons.

THIRD COURSE.

Fricasee of Rabbits.

Apricots. Pains à la Duchesse. Forced Cucumbers
Crawfish Ragooed. Morella Cherry Tart. Lobsters à la Braise.
Jerusalem Artichokes. Apricot Puffs. Green Gage Plums.
Lamb Stones.

The ORDER of a MODERN BILL of FARE,

FOR

AUGUST

FIRST COURSE.

Stewed Soals.

Fillets of Pigeons.	Ham.	Turkey
French Patty.	Crawfish Soup.	Petit Patties.
Chickens.	Fillet of Veal	Loin of Beef. Palates.

Whitings.

SECOND COURSE.

Roast Ducks.

Macaroni.	Tartlet.	Fillet of Soals.
Cheesecakes.	Jellies.	Apple Pie.
Matelot of Eels.	Orange Puffs.	Fricasee of Sweetbreads.

Leveret.

THIRD COURSE.

Partridges.

Stewed Peas.	Potted Wheat Ears.	Crawfish.
Apricot Tart.	Fruit.	Cut Parsley.
Prawns.	Scraped Beef	Blanched Celery.

Ruffs and Reifs.

The ORDER of a MODERN BILL of FARE,

FOR

SEPTEMBER.

FIRST COURSE.

Dish of Fish.
Chickens. Chin of Lamb. Veal Collops.
Pigeon Pie. Gravy Soup. Almond Tort.
Harrico of Mutton. Roast Beef. Ham.
Dish of Fish.

SECOND COURSE.

Wild Fowls.
Peas. Damson Tarts. Ragooed Lobsters.
Sweetbreads. Crocant. Fried Piths.
Crawfish. Maids of Honour. Fried Artichokes.

THIRD COURSE.

Ragooed Palates.
Comport of Biscuits. Tartlets. Fruit in Jelly.
Green Truffles. Epergne. Cardoons.
Blancmange. Cheesecakes. Ratafia Drops.
Calves Ears.

The ORDER of a MODERN BILL of FARE,

FOR

OCTOBER.

FIRST COURSE.

Cod and Oyster Sauce.

Jugged Hare. Neck of Veal. Small Puddings.

French Patty. Almond Soup. Fillet of Beef larded and roasted.

Chickens. Tongue and Udder. Torrent de Veau.

Broiled Salmon.

SECOND COURSE.

Pheasants.

Stewed Pears. Apple Tarts. Mushrooms.

Roast Lobsters. Jellies. Oyster Loaves.

White Fricasee. Custards. Pippins.

Turkey.

THIRD COURSE.

Sweetbreads

Fried Artichokes. Potted Eels. Pig's Ears.

Almond Cheesecakes. Fruit. Apricot Puffs.

Amulet. Potted Lobsters. Forced Celery.

Larks.

The Order of a MODERN BILL of FARE

FOR

NOVEMBER.

FIRST COURSE.

	Dish of Fish.	
Veal Cutlets.	Roasted Turkey.	Ox Palates.
Two Chickens and Brocoli.	Vermicelli Soup.	Leg of Lamb and Spinach.
Beef Collops.	Chine of Pork.	Harrico.
	Dish of Fish.	

SECOND COURSE.

	Woodcocks.	
Sheep's Rumps.	Apple Puffs.	Dish of Jelly.
Oyster Loaves.	Crocant.	Ragooed Lobsters.
Blancmange.	Lemon Tort.	Lamb's Ears.
	Hare.	

THIRD COURSE.

	Petit Patties.	
Stewed Pears	Potted Chars.	Fried Oysters.
Gallantine.	Ice Cream.	Collared Eel.
Fillets of Whitings.	Potted Crawfish.	Pippins.
	Lamb's Ears.	

The ORDER of a MODERN BILL of FARE

FOR

DECEMBER.

FIRST COURSE.

Cod's Head.

Chickens. Stewed Beef. Fricandau of Veal.

Almond Pudding. Soug Santea. Calves Feet Pie.

Fillet of Pork with sharp Sauce. Chine of Lamb. Tongue.

Soals fried and broiled.

SECOND COURSE.

Wild Fowls.

Lamb's Fry. Orange Puffs. Sturgeon.

Gallantine. Jellies. Savoury Cake.

Prawns. Tartlets. Mushrooms.

Partidges.

THIRD COURSE.

Ragooed Palates.

Savoy Cakes. Dutch Beef scraped. China Oranges.

Lamb's Tails. Half Moon. Calve's Burs.

Jargonel Pears. Potted Larks. Lemon Biscuits.

Fricasee of Crawfish.

C 6 2

RECEIPTS
FOR
PERFUMERY &c.

To make Red, Light, or Purple Wash-Balls.

Get some white-soap, beat it in a mortar; then put it into a pan, and cover it down close; let the same be put into a copper, so that the water does not come to the top of the pan; then cover your copper as close as you can, to stop the steam; make the water boil some time: take the pan out, and beat it well with a wooden stirrer, till it is all melted with the heat of the water; then pour it out into drops, and cut them into square pieces as small as a walnut; let it lie three days on an oven in a band-box, afterwards put them into a pan, and damp them with rose-water, mash it well with your hands, and mould them according to your fancy, viz. squeeze them as hard and as close as you possibly can; make them very round, and put them into a band-box or a sieve two or three days; then scrape them a little with a wash-ball scraper (which are made for that purpose,) and let them lie eight or nine days; afterwards scrape them very smooth and to your mind.

N. B. If you would have them red, when you first mash them, put in a little vermillion; if light, some hair-powder; and if purple, some rose-pink.

To make Blue, Red, or Purple Wash-balls, or to marble Ditto.

Get some white-soap, and cut it into square pieces about the bigness of dice; let it lie in a band-box or a sieve on the top of an oven to dry; beat it in a mortar to a powder, and put it into a pan; damp it with rose-water, mix it well with your hands, put in some hair-powder to make it stiff; then scent it with oil of thyme, and oil of carraways.

If you would have them blue, put in some powder-blue; if red, some vermillion; if purple; some rose-pink; mix them well together with your hands, and squeeze them as close as possible; make them very round; of a size agreeable to your mind; put them into a sieve two or three days; then scrape them a little with a wash ball scraper, and let them lie in the sieve eight or nine days. Afterwards scrape them very smooth, and agreeable to your mind.

If you would have them marbled, after being scented with oil of thyme and oil of carraways (as in the first process), cut them into pieces, about as much as will make a ball each, make it into a flat square piece, then take a very thin knife, and dip it into the powder-blue, vermillion, or rose pink (according to the colour you would fancy), and chop it in according to your mind; double it up, and make it into a hard and round ball, and use the same process as before mentioned.

White Almond Wash-Ball.

Take some white-soap and slice it thin, put it into a band-box on the top of an oven to dry three weeks or more; when it is dry beat it in a mortar till it is a powder: to every four ounces of soap, add one ounce of hair-powder, half an ounce of white-lead put them into a pan, and damp them with rose-water, to make it of a proper consistency; make them into balls as hard and close as possible, scrape them with a ball-scrape, and use the same process as before mentioned, letting them lie three weeks in a sieve to dry; then finish them with a ball-scraper to your mind.

Brown Almond Wash-Balls.

Take some common brown hard soap, slice it thin and put it into band-box on the top of an oven to dry, for the space of three weeks, or more; when quite dry, beat it in a mortar to a powder; to every three ounces of soap add one ounce of brown almond-powder; put it in a mortar, and damp it with rose-water, to make it of a proper consistency; beat it very well, then make them into balls according to a process before mentioned, letting them lie three weeks in a sieve to dry: then finish them with a ball-scraper, agreeable to your mind.

To make Lip Salve.

Take half a pound of hog's lard, put it into a pan, with one ounce and a half of virgin-wax; let it stand on a slow fire till it is melted; then take a small tin-pot, and fill it with water, and put therein some alkanet-root; let it boil till it is of a fine red colour; then strain some of it, and mix it with the ingredients according to your fancy, and scent it with the essence of lemon; pour it into small boxes, and smooth the top with your finger.

FINIS.

INDEX.

INDEX.

INDEX.

INDEX.

L.

M.

INDEX.

INDEX.

INDEX.

☞ Pages 294, 295, 296, 297, 298, 299, 300, 301, 302, 303, 304, and 305, contain *The Order of a Modern Bill of Fare for every Month in the Year.*

ERRATA.

Page 144, Dele six lines at bottom.

Abbreviated Glossary

Candlemas. February 2.
Codlins, codlings. From Middle English *querdlyng*, meaning young immature apples, or cooking apples.
Damosins. Damson plums, so called because they came, or were thought to have come, from Syria.
Gill. Pronounced *jill*. In common use, considered to be the equivalent of 4 fluid ounces, that is, one-half cup.
Gilliflowers. Pronounced *jillyflowers*. Carnations, or clove-scented pinks (*Dianthus caryophyllus*), long used in English preserving.
Hamburgh. The term was early applied in English cookery to preparations involving chopped beef (pages 176-77).
Hartshorn. In this case, shavings of deer horn, used in making gelatin.
Love apples. Tomatoes.
Michaelmas. September 29.
Petty-toes. The term is a charming corruption of French *petit oie*, effectively giblets, pinions, etc., of the goose, but in English cookery early came to refer to animal pluck, including and especially the feet, most often of pig.
Ruff. A special domesticated pigeon, *reiss* being presumably the female.
Sack. Sherry.
Salmagundy. The dish, effectively a composed salad, appears in French by 1546 as *salmigondin*; it became very popular in English cookery and, for that matter, in early American cookery, with Mary Randolph giving a recipe in 1824, for instance.
Simples. A term used for herbs specifically gathered for medicinal purposes.